The Pursuit of the Divine Snowman

The Pursuit of the Divine Snowman

Peter Macky

Word Books, Publisher

Waco, Texas

THE PURSUIT OF THE DIVINE SNOWMAN

Copyright © 1977 by Word, Incorporated, Waco, Texas.

All rights reserved.
No part of this book may be reproduced in any form,
except for brief quotations in reviews,
without written permission from the publisher.

Scripture quotations are from the Revised Standard Version
of the Bible, copyrighted 1946 (renewed 1973), 1956,
and © 1971 by the Division of Christian Education
of the National Council of the Churches of Christ in the U.S.A.
and are used by permission.

ISBN: 0–87680–484–9
Library of Congress catalog card number: 76–19540
Printed in the United States of America

To my father

Contents

Introduction

In mountain villages stories abound of the Abominable Snowman, a giant figure resembling a man whose footprints are occasionally found in the snow. One day three men decided to follow up the latest sighting, to seek out the mountain where it was supposedly seen, in order to pursue him and solve the mystery once and for all. So they made a base camp at 10,000 feet and early in the morning set out for the peak they were investigating. When they came within 1,000 feet of the top they decided to separate in order to go up different sides of the mountain, hoping in this way to see anything that moved. They agreed to wait for each other at the top, but none of the three ever reached it. Each turned back. When they met again hours later back at the camp, they had strange stories to tell.

The first to tell his story had a glazed look in his eyes, as if he had been riding a cloud engulfed by the beauties of the arctic lights. He told of heading up on the north side, looking into the sun reflecting off the snow that covered the peak. As he drew near the top he saw something that seemed like a figure clothed in sunlight, sprinkled with snow, so awesome as to be beyond description. He stood transfixed, just gazing upward, feeling an overwhelming wonder flow through him, making him feel as if he had been given a glimpse into the greatest glories of the universe. In just a few seconds, though it seemed like hours, the sight drove him to his knees for relief from the blinding beauty. When he rose he turned and stumbled back down the mountain in a daze, unable to think of anything but the exhilarating sight that was still shimmering in his memory.

The second climber told how he approached from the south side, looking beyond the peak to a thunderstorm off to the north, its black clouds covering the whole northern sky, and seeming to reach right down to the stark, rocky cliffs of the peak's south side. As he approached the top he too saw something moving: it seemed to be a black ghost walking on the rocks, outlined in the thunder clouds, yet not miles away but right on the mountain. As lightning flashed in the sky beyond, and the craggy rocks of the mountain peak seemed about to fall on him, he was struck with a deep, overwhelming fear of the powers arrayed against him. If there really was something up there he could not now bear to face it, for he felt he had seen the threat of the mountain and that drove him to turn and escape.

The third pursuer had come up from the west, up a valley that had harbored a touch of morning fog. He followed the valley until within a few hundred feet of the top he found that the fog was too thick for him to see back, he could see only forward. He could not find the way back down and knew that if he started back he could easily stumble over a precipice. Just as that fearful image came into his mind he saw movement ahead, something gliding in the sunbeams, playing on snowflakes in a small whirlwind blowing the fog around. He immediately thought it was the snowman, and when it began to move slowly toward him he was sure it was something meaning harm. He yelled for his friends but heard nothing except an echo and the wind whistling between the rocks.

So in his fright he began to back up to keep the thing away from him. He had forgotten that he was lost in the fog, that he did not know how to get down. All he could think was that he the pursuer had become the pursued. But then an amazing thing happened: as he moved backwards to try to keep his distance, he seemed to be guided by an unseen hand for his feet moved right back to the trail he had lost, enabling him to find his way back down again even though still engulfed by fog. Just as he found his trail he looked back to see if his pursuer was still after him. But all he saw was fog, snowflakes, and sunlight.

As the third climber finished his tale, all three knew that they had found much more than they had sought. They instinctively knew that their three experiences complemented each other, filling out for them the depths of reality. They had come seeking an abominable snowman and had been found by the Divine Snowman.

Witness by Symbols

The Bible is filled with stories like the one just told, stories in human language that express something utterly beyond normal earthly realities. Moses told of seeing a burning bush that was unconsumed; Jacob saw a ladder with angelic climbers; Isaiah saw an enthroned king dressed in blinding light; Ezekiel saw a figure on a chariot that he could barely describe; Peter, James, and John saw Jesus transformed into a figure of light talking to Moses and Elijah. Each of these visionary stories was an expression of something far beyond vision, an encounter with the Creator of all.

Visions are just one form of symbolic language in the Bible. Everywhere the reader turns he finds the biblical writers using parts of their human experience as symbols to point toward God who is immensely unlike his world. We simply have no other language than that designed for picturing our world, so that is the language we must use to speak of God. He is called father, king, judge, warrior, shepherd, creator, friend, liberator, sun, wind, lion, panther, dew, and hundreds more. Just as if he were a man he is described as walking, talking, acting, thinking, changing his mind; as having hands, ears, eyes, arms, legs, fingers, a heart, a mind, a spirit, and many other parts of human make-up. None of these is to be taken literally for the biblical writers also make it clear that God is completely beyond description. But each is to be taken seriously, for it suggests something about God by comparing him to something on earth. He is never exactly like the earthly counterpart, so we must always seek to see where the analogy breaks down.

Biblical readers usually recognize that when reading biblical parables they must seek the central point and not take all the details literally. But they often fail to recognize that they must do the same thing with every biblical reference to God. This is equally true of historical stories that speak of God acting in the world: these too are symbolic in that they intend to help us see *through* the event that took place to the One whose ways are hidden within it. For example, the story of God rescuing his people from Egypt is not told primarily for the facts of what happened: much more important is the message hidden within, that God loves his people, acts to do good to them, and so is to be understood as the Liberator of slaves. The historical story is also a parable, for it points beyond this one occasion to the way God eternally acts.

One central characteristic of symbols, whether they are visions, images, parables, or historical events is that they have emotional and not just intellectual impact on those who are familiar with the symbol. Calling God *Father* may lead us to bring into our imagination many experiences of our human fathers, and these feelings are then available to help us imagine what God is like. The same is true of all the other symbols with which we have had experience, such as light, sun, wind, dew, friend, ruler, servant. Thus, when we come across biblical symbols for God we will not get the full impact the authors intended unless we allow our own personal experience to come into play, to let our own imagination draw out the emotional content.

Changing Cultures

As soon as we speak of personal experience as the opening through which these symbols reach us, we can see that there are many biblical symbols that are powerless for us because they are no longer part of our experience. Our culture is so vastly different from ancient Israelite and Hellenistic cultures that many common experiences of their day are no longer found in ours. For example, all ancient people—in all religions—practiced animal sacrifice as part of their religious rites. Therefore when Jesus' death was spoken of as a "sacrifice for sin" every reader had a deep reservoir of temple sacrificial rites to draw on to help him experience the meaning. In the Western world today such sacrifices are gone, so the full emotional meaning of this image is no longer available to us—no matter how well we dig up its intellectual meaning.

Therefore when we come to interpret the biblical (or any other culture's) symbolism we must recognize various groups of symbols. We start with universal symbols, those that are part of human experience throughout time and space: sun, wind, dew, father, husband, ruler, judge, the parables of the Prodigal Son, the Lost Coin. Then we must point out the symbols that are tied to the particular cultural context of the biblical writer and are largely absent from ours: angels and demons, sacrifices and slaves, Exodus as our history, Jerusalem as God's seat, temple and priests, shepherd and wild animal fights, the parable of the Good Samaritan. Then third, we might note those that fall in-between these two groups, symbols that have some connection with our culture so that we do have a beginning insight even though there is considerable difference between our meaning and theirs. A good example is *king:* we still have kings in the world so we can get some meaning from the word; but we in this country have no king and certainly no experience of the type of absolute monarch the biblical writers are alluding to when they spoke of God as King.

When we try to express the meaning the biblical writers are trying to convey by their symbols, we must treat these groups differently. The first group we can continue to use because we still experience much of their impact. The third group (the borderline cases) we can continue to use with caution, if we make a point of saying how the symbols' impact differs in our culture from the original intention of the authors. The second group—those symbols that we have no direct contact with today—is the most difficult. We cannot simply continue to use them because we can no longer experience their full impact. Therefore we must "transculturate" these symbols by finding what symbols in our culture can evoke and express the personal impact the ancient symbols had on their readers. We must find what images and experiences we are familiar with today can convey something of the power of the originals. We must find new parables, tell new stories, point to historical events of our times that we are influenced by. We can use these—in conjunction with the universal symbols found in the Bible—to express the biblical witness of God in a form that is able to reach the personal, intuitive depths of modern readers the way the culturally conditioned biblical symbols did in their own times.

This book is intended to be a beginning search for such modern symbols. It takes up the central characteristics of the biblical witness to God and tries to express them in modern language. In most cases biblical symbols that have universal impact are the starting point, the foundation used to try to ensure that it is indeed the biblical message which is kept in view. But in every chapter new stories, new images, new experiences and events are brought in to help the modern reader see how his own experience is tied into the biblical picture of God.

A number of the stories which follow are biblical parables that I have transposed from Palestine to Pennsylvania in order to help my children make contact with them. Some other stories simply grew out of biblical images or brief metaphors that could easily be elaborated into a parable to bring home their point. My hope in presenting these parables is that they may stimulate readers to tell their own stories as a way of conveying the good news of God's love and care in our world today.

In the chapters which follow, reference will be made to the way symbols *mediate* the reality that lies behind them. Some readers may not be familiar with this transitive use of the verb, for the more common usage is intransitive, "to mediate between" two hostile parties. In the way the verb is used here a symbol is seen as a *medium* between an indescribable reality and an observer. For example, a painting mediates the artist's vision to us. Other verbs that are close but not quite adequate are *communicate* and *make present. Communicate* is too intellectual in its connotations. *Make present* overstates the case, for a painting does not actually make the artist's vision present. A symbol is intimately related to the reality it mediates but it should not be confused with the reality by being taken literally. It is the medium that makes contact possible between the indescribable reality and our minds and our hearts.

Chapter One: Imaging God

Introduction

Our Invisible Sun

HEIGHT
LIGHT
FIRE
POWER
CONCLUSION

The Visible Son

SEEKING THE LOST
"THE LOST SCHOOLBOY"
OPPOSING THE PROUD
"THE MINISTER AND THE MOBSTER"
SUFFERING THE CONSEQUENCES
"THE UNEXPECTED RESCUER"
CONCLUSION

Power of Love

LOVE AND LOVE
COMMUNAL SPIRIT
CONCLUSION

CHAPTER ONE

Imaging God

Introduction

In the twentieth century the word *God* has come to be used in such vastly differing ways that some writers have urged that it be retired for a while. Some people use it to name a person sitting on a throne above the sky whereas others use it to refer to Being itself, that which is basic to everything that exists, that has being. If a word denoting a common object on earth were used this variously (e.g., if *table* could refer to anything from a box to a planet) then its uselessness would force it out of the language. But God is not an object to be found in the universe, for he is utterly beyond the universe, being unimaginably different from it, so we cannot precisely describe him. In fact the biblical writers use something approaching a thousand different symbols to indicate something of what he is like. Therefore the variety in modern uses of the word *God* is solidly founded on the biblical witness.

This is no ground for complacency, however, for modern users of the term often think that the primary image that comes to their mind when they hear *God* is a definition, rather than one of a thousand useful symbols. Therefore our need at the moment seems to be to bring modern people, Christians and non-Christians alike, to see that God can be rightly imagined only when we hold together in tension a number of the central symbols for him. We cannot (and need not) keep a thousand different images in our memories, but we can and must keep a few central ones. The central symbols are those that are most basic to the biblical picture of God, that include many other symbols within them, and that are meaningful to us today.

In this chapter we shall consider three symbols for God that perhaps will provide the modern reader with a beginning grasp of the biblical witness to God. The first is *Our Invisible Sun.* While the sun was rarely used by the biblical writers as a symbol for God it is significant because it summarizes, includes within itself (as we shall see), four other basic symbols. In addition the sun is universally experienced, and so is as much a part of our present experience as it was of the biblical writers.' Sun used as a symbol for God points to God's otherness, to the unimaginable difference between God and us.

The second central symbol is *Jesus* who is seen by the New Testament as "the image [symbol] of the invisible God." The second symbol is utterly different from the first, but it (he) summarizes all that is said of God as personal, as historical, as one with particular attitudes and character.

The third symbol we will point to is *love,* the suggestion that the bond of personal caring and involvement found among human beings is the presence and power of God, as well as a natural phenomenon. This third symbol is one that is tied immediately to our deepest personal experiences and thus suggests to us where in our daily lives God is continuously known.

These three symbols of God are not exhaustive of the biblical witness, they are just a beginning. These three together can provide something of an experience of the three most significant aspects of the biblical God: his beyondness, his historical action, his presence in the depths of our lives. These three aspects may well be seen as another way of bringing out what the early church sought to point to when it spoke of one God who was known as Father, Son, and Spirit.

Our Invisible Sun

The biblical writers rarely use the symbol *sun* to speak of God, apparently for a simple reason: in the ancient world many people worshiped the sun as a god, if not *the* god, and so the use of the sun as a symbol for Israel's God could easily be misunderstood. Instead of sun both Old and New Testament writers refer to God as the "light" of his people, the one who will eventually take the place of the sun (cf. Isa. 60:19 f. and Rev. 21:23). We today, however, need not fear that anyone will misunderstand "God is our Sun" in an idolatrous way as "the sun is our god." Therefore we can take up this particular symbol that is used sparingly by the biblical writers and make it central, if it does indeed convey to most people what it conveys to me.

The great value of the symbol *God our Sun* is that it includes within it a number of other very widespread biblical symbols and so concentrates them into a single image. First, the sun is on high, in the heavens, far above us, beyond our reach, and so it represents the vast array of biblical allusions to height as a basic symbol for God. Second, the sun is our source of light, the one thing we eventually think of when we think of light, and so it brings together the great variety of biblical uses of the symbols, light and glory (which means overwhelming light). In the third place the sun is a fire, and God is often symbolized by fire in the Bible, for it suggests purity, mystery, and awesomeness, something to stand away from lest we get burned. Finally, the sun is our source of power, of energy, and thus of life; it is a source that transmits itself to us, that is trustworthy and unchanging, and so is the absolutely necessary foundation for our continuing life. A few thoughts on each of these aspects of the sun will show how much this symbol opens up to us the Otherness of God.

Height

Many modern writers have suggested that the symbolism of God on high, on the mountaintop, on the clouds, on the top of the world, in heaven, is a primitive superstition that we can no longer use. There can be no doubt that literally describing God as an object residing somewhere above us is superstition. But the biblical writers show us that this height imagery is not to be taken literally, for they also say God is everywhere. As long as we hold firmly to this second symbol, we will not take God on high literally and so we can consider its possible value even for us today, in our world of rockets to Mars and Venus and beyond.

Every culture has used height as a symbol of that which is more valuable, more powerful, more worthy of praise than ordinary things are. We speak of higher values, of low life, of ascending the heights of achievement. We cannot escape the symbol *height*, for it is impressed upon our experience ineradicably.

Have you ever lain on the grass or the sandy seashore on a warm clear night and looked up at the stars? Have you felt just a little of the immensity of space, of the number of other worlds there must be revolving around the countless suns that are visible and invisible? Have you seen yourself as a microscopic fleck of dust standing beneath those awesome heights, a drop of water in an infinite ocean, a blade of grass on a meadow covering the universe? If you have experienced that, then you have a beginning feeling of the awesomeness of God, of the way height may suggest to you the infinite difference between you and Him.

I can remember clearly the first time I climbed a mountain—Mt. Adams in New Hampshire. As we stood at the bottom and looked up to the 6,000-foot peak it seemed as if this huge block of stone stood over us like a giant, daring us to climb, to try to reach the heights. Struggling up its side gave me the feeling of how we must work and strive and drive ourselves on if we are to get above, for that which is higher is also harder, that which is valuable calls for dedication and commitment and sacrifice. But most of all I remember the view from the top: I sat on a stone at the very peak and could see for thirty miles in every direction. Being on high means having vision, seeing how things are, being able to direct those below who cannot see far. Thus my experience with the heights has given me beginning feelings of God's "height," his power standing over me, the struggle to which he calls me, the vision that he has which guides me on that upward way.

One final memory may round this out, for the heights are not only attractive, but also awesome and dangerous. We must not come unprepared into the presence of the One on High. The last time I climbed Mt. Adams two of my companions found another student dead near its top. He had ventured up the mountain in street shoes, without adequate clothing, in late afternoon and had been caught at the top in the freezing darkness of a 6,000-foot night. In trying to walk down he stumbled, hit his head, and froze to death. The heights are attractive, but they are also awesome. They provide joy, but also inspire fear. The God of the biblical writers is that kind of God. He looms far above us, overpowering, guiding, calling us on; but he is also to be feared, to be taken seriously, to be worshiped in awe, for the heights are dangerous as well as fulfilling.

Light

The overwhelming, dangerous yet attractive God we know can be seen in the sun's light as well as in its height. The central meaning of light as a symbol is found throughout all civilizations, for there are two experiences we all (except the blind) have of light that makes it a significant symbol for God. First, light is our companion whenever we have work to do, whenever we wish to play, whenever we wish to live. If we cannot see the world around us, we are in chains forged by a darkness that holds us as tightly as a strait jacket. Light frees us to live, guides us in our living, makes us alive. But second, light is seen as a symbol of good, of virtue, because people do in the light the things they are proud of, whereas they leave for the darkness the evil of which they are ashamed or afraid.

Think of the last time a storm blew down the power lines in your neighborhood. Do you remember the stumbling around, bumping into chairs, feeling in bottom drawers for candles or flashlights, trying to dig up matches, and generally being disoriented? Do you remember the feeling of relief when finally a candle was lit and light seemed to flood the room, making it once again your room and not a black pit with traps awaiting your slightest misstep? If you remember such an experience, then you have something of the feeling of what light is, of how it gives us our world, our life, our friends.

Our two sons have always wanted a night light on—Cameron's is a round one he calls his "sun"—for the dark is threatening, fearful, destructive, filled with anything our imagination can conjure up. Light seems to us to be good, to be benevolent, letting us be ourselves without fear. Have you ever tossed and turned through a sleepless night with troubles on your mind and found that the first rays of sunlight seemed soothing, liberating, welcoming? I have. That is the way God is.

Even beyond its gift of sight and its goodness the sun's light is absolutely dazzling and overwhelming, just as God is. We cannot look at the sun directly because it would blind us. Its majesty and brilliance are completely beyond the capacity of our eyes to absorb without damage. We must not dare to come into God's presence audaciously, the way some people try to look at eclipses with their naked eyes. We must always recognize that the Light which illumines our lives, inspires us with the good and the true and the beautiful, must be held in awe, not cuddled like a pet dog.

It is the nature of light that it does not force itself upon us, for we may hide from it if we wish, living underground, or sleeping during the day, or just closing our eyes. If we are to receive it, we must be open to it. A boy went down into a cave he had been warned away from many times, thinking he would just go a little way and then come back. But his curiosity got the better of him and he went on and on until he got lost and his flashlight went out. He was only ten, so very quickly the absolute darkness and the sharp rocks he banged against made him more afraid than he had ever been in his life. He shouted and stumbled and ran and cried and finally fell down exhausted. But soon he stumbled on again and suddenly found a small trap door which he pushed open, allowing the midday sun to shatter his darkness. The light was his salvation, his life, but it was absolutely blinding to his cave-dimmed eyes. He was alive again and would never abandon the light in that way again.

The sun on high is our light, our source of sight, the backdrop for good, the banisher of evil. Therefore light points us toward God, who gives us eyes to see ourselves and him, is the source of all good, the conqueror of evil, dazzling us with the wonder of himself.

Fire

A third characteristic of the sun that serves to draw together biblical symbols of God is the fact that it is a magnificent fire. Many times the biblical writers use this symbol for God, from Moses' vision of the burning bush, to the pillar of fire that led the Israelites in the wilderness, to the destructive fire God is among his people (Isa. 10:17), to the symbolism of the Spirit in the New Testament as tongues of fire (Acts 2:3). Fire has many qualities that make it admirable as a symbol for God, a few of which we can note.

First, fire provides warmth, protection, and more food. When fire was first harnessed by man it was one of the most decisive breakthroughs in his advancement beyond the other animals of the world. Fire is a friend, as anyone who has ever sat around a campfire cooking supper, staying warm, and driving away the darkness knows. In the cold we huddle around a fire, for it keeps us alive, protects us from the destructive forces of cold and wild animals. So too, God is a fire, protecting, warming, giving life.

But fire is also destructive, for it can rage unchecked through a house, a city or a forest. Even a small campfire is destructive to everything that gets put in it. We cannot put our hands too close or they will burn. The warmth that is protective at three feet becomes heat that is devastating at three inches. Therefore our God who is a consuming fire must not be taken lightly as if we can treat him as we please. In some circumstances he is warming and benevolent, but if we misuse him he may become a forest fire that ravages our land and consumes our life.

Yet fire is notable also for its purity, for its ability to burn away the impurities in something precious, leaving what is good. Iron ore put into a fire comes out purified, the impurities having been separated out, and the iron is ready for use. God's ravaging fire in our lives is often that kind, for it destroys our false foundations, our useless baggage, our proud achievements, our self-centered values, and leaves us naked before him so that once again he can be warming, protecting, light- and life-giving.

Most of all fire is mysterious. The burning unburnt bush before Moses and the tongue of fire over the apostles at Pentecost both point to the unfathomable mystery that God is to us. When I sit before a fire I become mesmerized by the flames, drawn to stare at their infinite, ever-changing variety, unable to look at other things. As I stare into the fire my mind becomes open to the mysteries surrounding me, my own life and subconscious, my companions' similar absorption, the wonder of dancing figures coming and going in the wood. God is not only a mystery like that, but is present to us in all such mysteries, for when we bow or stare in wonder before something we cannot grasp, we open ourselves to the presence of the Ultimate Mystery.

The sun is fire, and fire is an experience all men know, so it may be a vehicle to carry our imaginations beyond to the Beyond. The God of All is one who warms and protects those who are open to him, but becomes a consuming threat to those who do not. Yet in consuming he is often refining, burning away impurities to produce fine gold in his mysterious involvement with mankind.

Power

The fourth aspect of the sun that draws together a number of other biblical symbols is the fact that it is the source of our heat, energy, power and thus life. Without the sun's light we would have a very degraded existence, but without the sun's power we would have no existence at all. We may generally ignore the facts of life that come to us in the light but without the sun's energy there would be no vegetation growing and so no animal life at all. We are so absolutely dependent on the sun's power that the only way we could escape it would be to bottle some of it (in a spaceship) and find another sun, another star, to replenish our supply once it is exhausted. We can imagine escaping dependence on our present sun, but not escaping dependence on a sun. Our absolute dependence on this constant source of what we need for sustaining life makes the sun's power an excellent symbol for God on whom we are absolutely dependent for personal and spiritual life.

The sun's power comes to us first of all as an almost invisible part of the background so that most of the time we do not notice it. We think of our biological life as dependent upon vegetation and meat, but rarely think beyond them to the sun as the source that makes them grow. Most of us recognize our need for fuels such as coal and oil and natural gas, but we generally ignore the fact that the energy stored in them is the sun's energy that made the vegetation grow that has now decayed into fossils that will burn. Even further from our minds is the fact that the gravitational pull of the sun holds us near enough to receive these benefits, for without it we would fly off into the dark, cold emptiness beyond. In all these ways the sun is a symbol for God who undergirds all our existence, even when we ignore him.

But we do not always ignore the sun. When I used to go home from college in New England to summer vacation in Bermuda, the first day home I would spend every minute out in the sun. When we have missed it we celebrate its return, we rejoice in it, we bask in it, we cannot seem to get enough of it. In a similar way our awareness of God's nearness is periodic, leading to times of rejoicing and celebration following days or months of cold. In our relationship to God the problem is that *we* go away from him unlike the sun's recession from us in the winter; but the feeling of coming home, jumping for joy, stretching ourselves in the warmth, is quite similar.

We find that this power on which we depend does not fail us, for it has proven itself to be completely trustworthy. It comes and it goes by day and night, summer and winter, but it never fails to provide us with the energy we need for life. We can find ways to spurn the gift, by denuding our soil, so that nothing grows in our dust-bowls, or fouling our air so that the sun cannot fully shine through, but its gift is always poured out on us, ready to be absorbed when we are willing. In doing so it symbolizes the utter trustworthiness of God, who makes continually available to us all we need for life, yet does not force it on us, allowing us to go our own corrupt way if we please. Yet always the powerful warmth is there, attracting us, calling us out from behind our protective masks, offering real life.

Conclusion

The sun is a magnificent symbol for God because of its height, light, fire and power, all of which are used by the biblical writers as symbols pointing out something of the majesty, greatness, and mystery of God. The sun combines all these characteristics and so when we contemplate God our Sun many of the thoughts, and especially the feelings, suggested in the previous pages may flood in upon us. There is no way really to describe the feelings we have as we stand beneath a high mountain, or surrounded by dazzling light, or gaze into the impenetrable depths of a fire, or absorb the powerful warmth of the sun's heat. Those are the kind of feelings that are appropriate for us to have before God and so pointing to God our Sun may help bring us to a significant experience, awareness and understanding of the awesome, overwhelming, pure and trustworthy God of All.

Like all symbols sun has its limitations. There are a number of characteristics of the sun that do not apply to God. For example, the sun is physical and visible, contributing to our physical well-being and our physical seeing. But God is not physical or visible and his involvement in our lives is centrally in our personal, spiritual dimension. Second, the sun is impersonal and amoral, having none of the character or attitudes or will that are central aspects of the biblical God. Therefore we find God our Sun only introduces us to one aspect of God—his otherness, his Awesomeness. Now we need to take another symbol that speaks to us of a quite different aspect of God, overcoming the limitations of the sun symbolism. For this second aspect we turn to Jesus.

The Visible Son

The sun symbolizes the otherness of God, but the Son symbolizes his nearness. The core of biblical thought on God is found in the use of man as a symbol for God and the center of that core is the conviction that Jesus of Nazareth was "the image of the invisible God" (Col. 1:15, KJV), that is, the ultimate symbol we have of God. Like all symbols this one too has a central part that is applicable to God and peripheral details that are not. We can never be exactly sure where to draw the line between these two but it seems that the early Christians might have agreed with the following distinction: the heart of the symbol *Jesus* is to be found in his personal and spiritual attitudes, character, relationships and action which all mediate or manifest what God is really like; the peripheral details include Jesus' physical make-up, his temporal limitations, his finite characteristics.

That this one man is the ultimate symbol of God is an amazing claim to make considering all that has just been suggested of the mystery, grandeur and awesomeness of God. Yet men and women who came into contact with Jesus had a peculiar experience: they met a man like other men, yet in and through him they met God. It was not that he said, "Thus says the Lord," for he never did. Instead he spoke for himself, "I say to you," overturning Mosaic ordinances that had supposedly come from the mouth of God himself. The odd thing was that some people heard Jesus and believed they heard God, not a blasphemer. When he said, "Your sins are forgiven," they experienced a forgiveness that can come only from God himself. It was uncanny the way his presence overcame evil, both the evil of diseased minds and the evil of guilty pasts. To those who knew him he made God present, just as the return of many a mother makes peace and love and fairness present to a house of squabbling children.

It is not quite true to say that Jesus' comrades already knew precisely what God was like and saw in their companion the same characteristics, and so could logically conclude, "Therefore he must be God." God was a mystery to Israel: he was their rescuer, who also judged them, yet his name was the mysterious "I will be what I will be." They saw him as a shadow flitting across their history—a cloud at the Red Sea, a thunderstorm at Sinai, a plague on the besieging army at Jerusalem's gates, a dazzling light in the Temple. They worshiped him in awe, prayed to him in times of trouble, feared his destruction in times of rebellion. They usually imagined him as a King sitting on a high throne far away, sending messengers in his intercourse with men.

God was to Israel something like King George V of England was to his subjects in Uganda, a people who had heard his proclamations but never seen him. Then one great day the king's son appeared in the land, bringing more than just a message for he was the incarnation of royalty so the Ugandans could see and experience what their king was really like. The Prince of Wales arrived with pomp and pageantry, but the Prince of Peace arrived in a mule train, known only to those who would take the trouble to come close and look inside.

These arrivals were characteristic. The pageantry of the visit of an English heir to the throne to the outposts of the British Empire conveyed the majesty and power and dignity of the king himself. The arrival of the heir to the throne of the universe in a stable conveyed a new understanding of his Father: God does not come into our lives as One who stands on his rights, forcing a bended knee, demanding obedience whether we want to conform or not. Instead he comes quietly, humbly, as a servant, reaching out to us personally, seeking our personal, responsible love in return. The image of the Roman emperor who demands sacrifice and payment of taxes is the opposite of the image of God as servant that the disciples experienced in Jesus.

This is an amazing result. The Face that in the fullness of time stood out from the shadows was a human face. This radically changed the basis of all theology: the Jews had for centuries been tending to imagine God as such an exalted, majestic, fearsome figure that man could have no direct contact with him; the Greek theologians, going back to Plato, had defined God as the opposite of man—infinite opposed to finite; omnipotent, not weak; omniscient instead of ignorant; immovable rather than in process. But in Jesus, the early Christians claimed, the Word became *flesh* and has lingered on as a scandal ever since: God has a human face. Far from God and man being opposites for whom no mingling is possible, God has ultimately made himself known as a man.

Naturally not everything true about God is revealed in this man, any more than King George V could be fully revealed in his son the Prince of Wales. Even the ultimate symbol for God, which Jesus is, has its inapplicable details. But all that God wants mankind to know is revealed in this man, not in anything nonhuman about him but in his very humanity. God created man to be an image, reflection, representation of his own character and life (as chapter two will show), but all men failed to live up to that possibility. All except one. He was the true representative of God, his ultimate image, so when we want to know what God is like, Christians say, "Look at Jesus."

When we look at Jesus and try to summarize his personal, spiritual characteristics, we are naturally strongly influenced by the way we have learned to read the Gospels. Every reader concentrates on the things that are most significant to him, and this reader is no exception. The following brief summary of what I see as Jesus' main characteristics is thus in no way thought to be definitive. It is simply how I look at the story of Jesus and see through that story to the God who is revealed in it. Jesus' whole life is the basic Christian symbol for God, so we need to look as closely as we can at that life if we are to have our eyes opened to what God is really like in our lives today.

Three points summarize for me much of what Jesus was and did. First, he spent his time seeking out, serving and trying to save the lost, the suffering and the oppressed; second, as he did that he stood up and opposed the proud, the self-righteous, the oppressors, working to overcome the forces of evil he uncovered; third, he accepted the consequences of his action, suffering the pain of rejection and ignominy, reaching out in forgiveness even through the pain of the Cross. A great deal more will be said about Jesus in a later chapter, but this will be enough for this initial symbol: God is "the One who was present in Jesus of Nazareth."

Seeking the Lost

A constant refrain in the Gospels is that Jesus refused to spend his time with the successful, powerful, proper people but instead searched out those who were failures. He looked for the sick, the oppressed, the outcast, the defeated, the possessed, the poor—everyone who recognized his need—and poured himself out for them. It was obvious to those who knew him that he saw this kind of people as ripe for the harvest he was gathering whereas the proper people were too ensconced in their propriety to be open to him. Jesus interpreted this attitude in many sayings and stories, one of which can be thought of today as "The Lost Schoolboy."

"The Lost Schoolboy"

One spring day the first grade class in the New Wilmington Elementary School went down to the lake to learn about willows and fish and seaweed and other things that grow around and in water. They numbered themselves when they left and had twenty-one, but after coming back they had only twenty—a boy named Johnny had gotten lost on the way back. So the teacher asked the children to draw or read and not leave the room until she got back. She looked in the buildings on the way to the lake, called his name down near the lake, went to his house to see if he had gone home, but could not find him. Then just as she was about to give up she saw a small figure sitting forlornly on a swing in the park. She rushed to him and threw her arms around him—so happy to have found him she forgot to ask what happened. Back to the school they went, but found when they arrived that some mothers had come to take their children home and were upset at finding no teacher. When she returned they said: "You should have let Johnny take care of himself!" Her reply was, "He was lost; I had to go and find him."

The people Jesus sought out, however, were not just those who had lost themselves, but even more those who had suffered at the hands of forces beyond their control. The religious and political systems undermined the personal lives of many, declaring them to be failures, outcasts, and sinners because they did not fit in. Jesus stood on the side of the sinners, those who knew their need. In doing so he rejected law and custom and tradition when it threatened to destroy. No story is more revealing of this attitude in Jesus than the account of a woman taken in adultery (John 8:3–11). Self-appointed executioners (male) were about to unleash the Mosaic law's storm of stones on her, when the leaders brought her to Jesus as a trap. His response was that no sinner has any right to stand in judgment on another—thus setting the law aside. To the woman in her despair turned to joy he offered forgiveness and the call to start life anew. Here as elsewhere the law was an instrument in the hands of oppressors and Jesus stood with the oppressed and gave them new life and new hope, thereby showing God's own attitude and action.

Opposing the Proud

An essential part of reaching out to the lost and oppressed is always standing up in opposition to the proud, to oppressors, and that was characteristic of Jesus also. Some people are lost because the system they find themselves in labels them as failures for not conforming, and Jesus found the Pharisees to be the masters of the Jewish system of his day. They built themselves up by emphasizing the minutiae of their religion, downgrading everyone who did not accept and apply the interpretation of God's desires that their tradition had developed. They were the pillars of the church, the socially prominent citizens, the members of the intellectual and social elite, and Jesus denounced them for their pride, self-righteousness, intolerance and lack of love. His attitude toward them (and so God's attitude also) is summarized in one of his stories that we can translate as "The Minister and the Mobster."

"The Minister and the Mobster"

One Sunday in church as the time for silent prayer drew near the minister saw in the back row a man he had heard was a local mobster, a man who sold bootleg liquor and ran a numbers racket. As he called his congregation to silent prayer the minister's thoughts took this series of odd turns: "What's he doing here? Does he think he's fooling anybody? Lord, don't listen to him, listen to the rest of us who do what is right. Who does he think he is, coming in here and demeaning my respectable congregation? Lord, throw him out. Or I will. Amen." But back in the corner the mobster was saying, "God, if you listen to a punk like me—and I won't blame you if you don't—help me. I'm lost. I don't mean to hurt people, just to sell them what they want. I didn't know that whiskey was poisonous . . . help me, help me." Which one of these men found himself entering a new life that day?

Standing up openly and telling stories like this when the proud, the self-righteous, the oppressors, are listening is a dangerous game. But it is also liberating. The people who had thought they had to conform or be condemned by God came to hear that God loves them as they are if they are willing to turn to him. The forces of evil in that society, seen in demons, diseases, ritual demands and political oppression began to seem less overwhelming when Jesus stood up and opposed them. The funny thing was that while outwardly the forces retained their power, within many people freedom had begun to ring. But at a price.

Suffering the Consequences

No one can ever stand for the oppressed and against their oppressors with impunity. No one can seek to change the values and structures of a traditional—especially religious—society without paying for it. No one can tell the proper people, the powerful people, that God is known only by those who recognize their need for his forgiveness, without finding that proper power descending upon him. Jesus knew it, faced it, accepted it and suffered the inevitable consequences of his rescuing, challenging, reconciling activity. His recognition of the cost is hinted at in the story we could call "The Unexpected Rescuer."

"The Unexpected Rescuer"

A traveler was walking along the back road from New Wilmington to New Castle when suddenly he was attacked by two muggers who beat him over the head, robbed him and left him lying by the road. Soon afterward a city councilman drove up on his way to a meeting, but only slowed down to look at the body before speeding on his way. A little later an insurance salesman happened by, on his way to an appointment with a prospective client, and his business drew him on with a gruff, "They ought to lock these drunks up permanently." Finally, a ten-year-old boy, riding a bicycle on the way to the movies, saw the man and stopped. He found some water and washed his face and helped him revive. Then he hailed down a taxi that came by and said, "Would you please take this man to the hospital. Here is a dollar to pay for it. It's all I have. If it costs any more I will pay you the next time I see you." So the robbery victim got to the hospital, and the boy rode his bicycle home again, the time for the movie having passed and all his money now gone.

That is the way things are in this world, Jesus shows us. The rescuer pays the price. The forgiver bears the pain. The savior dies on a cross. In saving others we must lose ourselves. Our world is in such a condition and human life has developed in such a way that there is no alternative. Naturally those who are lost, oppressed, trapped by sin, endure suffering also for there is no escaping the inevitable consequences of our deeds. But rescue comes to us when someone is willing to come down into our hell with us, to shoulder the load with us, and so enable us to escape.

If Jesus' life is really a symbol of God's, then the profoundest insight offered us into the attitude and action of God is seen in Jesus' death. God does not overcome his human opponents by bolts of lightning or legions of angels. He overcomes them by bearing the worst they have to give—their rejection, rebellion, distortion, enmity, crucifixion—and then arising from it more alive and present and powerful than ever before. The God to whom the Bible points is thus one whose goal is to overcome evil by rescuing all who know their need and driving the self-righteous to the wall until the light dawns on them. His method is not overwhelming force but the silent revolution of a cross.

Conclusion

The symbol of the sun offers us very significant intuitions of the awesomeness, the otherness, the majesty of God, but it was impersonal and so limited in that respect. The symbol *Jesus* is just the opposite, for it is intensely personal, mediating (making present) to us God's love, judgment, rescuing and suffering. But it comes out of a past that is gone by two thousand years and so says nothing directly about today, about our suffering and rejoicing, loving and hoping today. The stories Jesus told were stories interpreting himself, suggesting that he embodied the approaching victory of God over evil, the time when the goodness of God would be the dominant reality in every person's experience. But what do we experience today? For those who have eyes to see, the same God who is represented, manifested, mediated, symbolized by his blazing sun and his crucified Son is known still in the spirit of love that almost all have tasted.

Power of Love

The sun as a symbol represents, and so in some way makes present, the beyond that is the foundation of reality. Jesus of Nazareth symbolizes God's character and action in history, summarizing in his life and teaching the whole thousand-year relationship of

God and his people Israel. Jesus, the man who once lived, breathed, died and rose, represents God behind us, in our history that is now gone. But out of that past story there arose a present power—the Power of Love—which still today mediates to us the present God, the one who is within.

As with the first two symbols, this one too is explicitly used in the Bible, most clearly in the words of 1 John: "The ability to love comes from God, so anyone who loves has been enabled to do so by God whose presence he has experienced. Anyone who does not love has not even begun to experience God's presence within him; for God is love" (4:7 f.). This is not to be taken as a definition of God (i.e., "love is God") any more than "God is light" in the same book (1 John 1:5) is to be thought of as a definition. Both are symbols. Both take a profound human experience, one that has deep feelings and intuitions involved with it, and use it as a symbol to point beyond to God. Both light and love mediate the power of God, make present the care of God, represent a significant aspect of God, and so they are significant symbols that enable us to experience and understand something of the divine reality.

In English *love* is a broad concept covering a much larger chunk of reality than the biblical writer intended to refer to when he suggested love (in Greek *agape*) as a symbol for God. Therefore we need to narrow it down, and then try to see in what way human love may mediate, symbolize, represent God. An important part of understanding love is a grasp of deep personal involvement, the way we become persons by communicating ourselves to another. Finally, we need to show how this significant biblical symbol is an expression of the Church which finds at its heart a Spirit, a power producing love, a personal reality that was first found in Jesus.

Love and Love

The most common use of the word *love* in English is probably found in the context of the attraction between the sexes. This type of love was designated *eros* in New Testament times, and can be well described today as erotic love. It is based upon physiological impulses of sexual attraction and has a large measure of possessiveness in it, as the cry "I want you to be *mine*" suggests. There is nothing wrong with this type of love, it is good, but it is not what the biblical writers had in mind when they spoke of love as the presence of God.

The love that manifests God is *agape,* which perhaps can be translated "self-giving love." It may well happen that a relationship between a man and a woman may exhibit both erotic love and self-giving love, but we can see what the latter means much more clearly in other relationships. When a soldier falls upon a live grenade and gives his life to save his buddies, that is self-giving love. When a father takes a second job because his child wants to go to college, that may well be self-giving love. When a boy stands up for his younger brother, protecting him from attack by shielding him, there is a sign of self-giving love.

Unlike erotic love, which is instinctual, self-giving love must be learned by being experienced. We certainly have a natural potential for loving in this way but all the evidence seems to suggest that we only activate that potential when we experience being loved in that way. That means that self-giving love is a gracious gift that comes to us from beyond us. We cannot earn it. We cannot force another to love us in this way. All that we can do is gratefully accept it when it comes and allow it to make us into its own carriers.

Many children experience this from their parents. They discover that life in their home is based upon the premise that "big people help little people," not on the premise that "big people are masters and little people are slaves." If parents convey the attitude "I belong to you," then their children will grow up with self-giving love as the atmosphere they breathe in, and that is the kind of people they will become—self-giving. But if that has not happened, for whatever reason, then the child can learn to love only if somehow someone breaks through to him so that his potential to love becomes actual.

A psychiatrist who runs a school for autistic children tells the story of a little girl, Pam, who was completely unsocialized. Her only way of relating to others was by screaming, crying, kicking and fighting when anyone came near her. She was virtually a little animal. One day when she was throwing a tantrum, the doctor picked her up and held her in his arms while she tried to kick and bite him, screaming at him and crying at the same time. After ten minutes of this embrace, she quieted down, threw her arms around his neck, holding on to him instead of pushing him away, for she realized that he was not hurting her but showing her he cared for her and wanted to make contact with her. That experience was the beginning of Pam's road to normal life. Love had broken through to her and so she began to be able to love other people instead of fearing them.

The Christian understanding of reality is that the love that broke through to Pam is an indication of the deepest reality of the universe, the presence of the power that undergirds everything, a hint of the ultimate truth about life. While on the surface the handing on of self-giving love from one person to another can be described in psychological terms, the deeper understanding offered by a theological perspective is that more than just man's psyche is involved. There is of course no way of proving this, any more than we can prove that the experience of love itself is something more than a chemical reaction in our brains. But most people believe self-giving love is more than chemistry; we believe it is a deep, personal, mysterious reality. The Christian goes further, pointing to love as something transcending the merely human and earthly, being in addition a shaft of light and warmth from our invisible sun.

"God is love" is a way of telling us something of who God is, where he is to be found, how he is experienced, thus what life is really like. If love is a significant symbol for God, then love is the undergirding reality of life, binding God and man together. If God is love, then our love of God and our love of others are both inevitable signs of God's presence in us. Querry, the apostate Catholic in Graham Greene's *A Burnt-Out Case,* saw in a tentative way this presence of God in human love: "Perhaps it's true that you can't believe in a god without loving a human being, or love a human being without believing in a god. They use the phrase 'make love,' don't they? But which of us are creative enough to 'make' love? We can only be loved, if we are lucky."

Communal Spirit

The source of the Christian pointing to love in deep personal relationships as a symbol for God is the experience of the church, first with Jesus and then with his unseen presence. The odd thing about Jesus was that he seemed to be completely animated by a spiritual power that reached out personally to all who were in need and stood recklessly against all who oppressed others in any way. Those who knew him saw his life as the ultimate expression of self-giving love, and believed in knowing him that they had come in contact with the deepest, most powerful, most valuable reality in the universe. In this experience of knowing him in his life lived for others, they came to believe that this was God expressing himself to them, that the Spirit that animated Jesus was God himself. That was the beginning of the confession "God is love."

The confirmation of the confession, its spread outward throughout the world, took place after Jesus died. The strangest thing happened: the Spirit that was Jesus' deepest characteristic came into their lives; he was experienced as alive, and now alive in a universal way, as a Spirit that could be shared with others and thus increased in themselves also. This "spirit" that bound together the first Christians (and many in the church today) went far beyond the team spirit or community spirit or group pride that is found in every group. This spirit seemed personal, for it changed men's lives, enabling them to grow in love and involvement as they never had before. Within the Christian community there was a personal bond which meant that when one person wept all wept, and when one rejoiced all were filled with joy. They were united into one family, one economic unit, for all their money was held in common as it is in most of our families today. They found that the Spirit of Jesus, the self-giving love they experienced, was a greater reality than the bonds of genes and ancestry. Unfortunately for much of the church in the centuries that followed the natural ties of blood and flesh—the way of the world—came to supersede the bond of the self-giving spirit.

The problem most people in the world today have in accepting the claim that God is self-giving love exemplified in Jesus and universalized in the spirit in the church is that they do not see anything like that in the church. The difference between this community and others, such as the Masons, the bridge club, the country club, or the Republican Party, is only that the church talks a great deal about God and love. Talk without experience is hypocritical. If we claim that the church is the place where God is worshiped, Jesus is followed and their spirit of self-giving love experienced, how does it happen that church people in this country are among the richest, most prejudiced, most self-righteous and snobbish of all groups? Is it that we are simply "religious," as the Pharisees were, and have not experienced the overwhelming, transforming power of self-giving love that those who came into contact with Jesus experienced?

David, the eight-year-old big brother, was so possessive of his prize train, even though it was small and old, that when his brother Andy, age four, came anywhere near it a pushing, shoving "Yes I can—No you can't" struggle broke out. Outside the house David had come to know an old man down the street who liked to tinker with broken things in his basement, and whenever David came by they would work together fixing an old motor or a lawn mower or a radio. One day David found him working on a boy's bicycle and couldn't help showing how much he longed for one because his family couldn't afford one. So when the bicycle was fixed the old man said, "I always wanted a grandson to do things with and make things for but I never had one. You've been like a grandson to me, so here, it's yours." David thanked him exuberantly and rushed home to tell Andy, whom he found standing beside the train. David was just about to tell him to get away when he thought of his bicycle and all the new fun he would have now, so he said, "I was just given a bicycle, so you can have my train."

Conclusion

The Bible is filled with symbols and images taken from earthly experiences that point beyond themselves to their Source, and thus reveal him. We must choose a few of these symbols to hold more firmly in our minds than the rest, because: we cannot remember them all; some are more basic, more encompassing, more revealing than others; some are more universal, and so tied to our present experience, than are those that are more culture-bound. So we need to pick a few central symbols, ways of looking at God from different perspectives, and hold them together so that they correct each other, pointing out each other's limitations.

In this chapter I have suggested three quite different symbols as a beginning for thinking about God—Sun, Jesus, Love. The sun as a symbol for God conveys to those who have eyes to see and imaginations working the exaltation, magnificence, awesomeness, dazzling overwhelmingness that is one aspect of God. But the sun is distant, physical, and impersonal and thus limited in these ways as a symbol, so second, we point to Jesus. He is the symbol that summarizes God's attitudes, character, relationships and action so that seeing him we know how God feels toward us. But Jesus was temporally and physically limited, a figure of the past, and thus is limited in those respects as a symbol for God. Therefore we turned finally to that which was deepest in Jesus—Love—and see that as our final basic symbol. Self-giving love is a mysterious gift given to many throughout the world, a power to change lives and make them self-giving also, a reality that recalls Jesus' way with people and is found sometimes as the Spirit that permeates and integrates the church.

Together these three symbols point us to the transcendent Creator-Father, the historical Savior-Son, the immanent loving Spirit of traditional trinitarian approaches. The difference between this presentation and a traditional one is that here the reality of biblical symbolism is emphasized instead of trying to transform biblical symbols into precise, rational, philosophical concepts that can be argued about logically. The symbols offered here are meant to appeal through our mind to our intuition, imagination, emotions and will so that they begin to work *on us*, instead of our minds controlling and working on graspable concepts. Ultimately God is a mystery completely beyond our comprehension, but we have had experiences—seeing the sun, hearing of Jesus, feeling loved—that are ways into that mystery if we allow them to carry us on.

Suggested Reading

Baillie, John. *Our Knowledge of God.* New York: Scribner's, 1959.

Berger, Peter. *A Rumor of Angels.* Garden City, New York: Doubleday, 1969.

Capon, R. F. *Hunting the Divine Fox: Images and Mystery in Christian Faith.* New York: Seabury, 1974.

Dewart, L. *The Future of Belief: Theism in a World Come of Age.* New York: Herder, 1966.

Gilkey, Langdon. *Maker of Heaven and Faith.* New York: Doubleday, 1959.

King, R. H. *The Meaning of God.* Philadelphia: Fortress, 1973.

Macquarrie, John. *God and Secularity: New Directions in Theology Today,* vol. 3. Philadelphia: Westminster Press, 1967.

Schilling, S. Paul. *God Incognito.* Nashville: Abingdon, 1974.

Chapter Two: Created Image

Introduction

Dominion

Man's Ordered World
Divine Dominion
Imitating God
Conclusion

Community

Man and Woman
The Husband of His People
God's Covenant and Ours
Conclusion

Spirit

The Heights of Humanity
Unified Person
God's Spirit and Body
Conclusion

Chapter Two

Created Image

Introduction

The first chapter has begun our attempt to think about God as the biblical writers did—in terms of great symbols and parables that not only reach man's mind but go down to the depths of his intuition, imagination and emotions. The three central symbols presented there were an attempt to give a general survey as a starting-point, suggesting an essential three-sidedness: God's otherness, his historical manifestation and his immediate presence within. Now an elaboration of some of the details of that biblical witness to God will be offered, pointing here to man, who was created by God in his own image.

While there has been great debate in the history of the Church over just what the phrase "image of God" means, it can hardly be doubted that its root meaning is that man in some way reflects God, symbolizes him, represents him and mediates him. Some writers point to man's dominion over the animal world as the chief mark of this reflection, while others point to man plus woman as the image, for both of these ideas are mentioned along with the "image" in Genesis 1:26 f. A more traditional standpoint has been to see the New Testament emphasis upon the moral and spiritual renewal of man in God's image (Col. 3:10; Eph. 4:24) as central, thus defining the image as an original moral nature which is lost when man sins. Finally, many interpreters note that the image distinguishes man from animals and so they point to man's reason, his spirit, his self-consciousness, his moral capacity or something similar and call it the image. To a large extent the dispute is semantic, for the biblical passages explicitly referring to God's image are small and no great theological conclusion really depends on how the word is used.

The view presented here is that all of these interpretations are correct, but too limiting. The fact that significant evidence for each of them can be found is a suggestion that some way to combine them needs to be sought. The combination offered is this: the biblical writers use man in his relationship with the world as the chief source of symbols for God. Thus to say man is made in the image of God is to say first of all that it is not only justifiable but necessary to find the controlling symbols for God in human life rather than in animals (as the Egyptians did) or in the forces of nature (as the Canaanites and primitive people generally did).

This means that all of the biblical stories in which God is spoken of as if he were a man are not primitive anthropomorphisms but significant symbols. God is described walking in the Garden of Eden, sitting on a throne, wrestling with Jacob, speaking to prophets, seeing, hearing, touching, loving, angry, jealous, forgiving, as a shepherd, father, husband, judge and many more. All of these are seen to be justifiable by biblical writers because man more than any other creature is a reflection of God.

This, however, does not mean that everything man is and does reflects God. Each man may more or less adequately image God, and this is the second point of the phrase "God's image." It is not only a statement about mankind in general but a task given to every individual in particular. In some ways no man can escape reflecting God, but no one is ever as full a reflection as he could be. What we cannot help is that we must use symbols taken from human life to point beyond to the Creator. What we can do something about is to see how well our individual lives are imitations of God, how true a reflection we are of his character, attitudes and actions.

The conclusion toward which we are driven is thus that knowledge of God and knowledge of ourselves are intimately intertwined. Only as we are aware of some of the essential aspects of human life can we see through them to God who is reflected in them. But as we begin to see what God is like then that reveals more truly what man is called to be, what he potentially is. Thus we must go back and forth between God and man seeing deeply into the mystery of both if we are to understand either.

In this chapter, three central aspects of human life that reflect the truth about God will be discussed. The first is man's dominion over the natural world. The second is the community man needs, seen in God making man and woman together. The third is man's en-spiritedness, the spirit-body unity that he is. Each of these aspects of human life has been used by someone to define the image of God, so gathering them all together should provide a broader insight than any could offer alone.

Dominion

When God is depicted as saying to man, "Have dominion over every living thing on earth," a central aspect of human life is pointed out—the fact that there is order, mutual dependence and service in man's organization of the world. A few comments on that order will prepare us to see that it reflects the divine order, the way God is related to man. That will then in the third place lead us to see how man's ordering of the world needs to be changed in order to reflect God more truly.

Man's Ordered World

We cannot escape order. We would not be human without it. No one needs to tell us that we ought to create some order in the world as a framework for life because we seem congenitally driven to bring order. The three most prominent types of order in our experience are man over nature, parent over child, and ruler over subject. That these orders exist is inevitable, but how they are exercised is an open question. In the inevitability of these orders there is a constant imaging of God's way with the world. In the openness of practice there is the possibility of imitating God in his way of relating to his creation.

From the earliest days of human existence on this planet man has ruled over nature to one extent or another. Simply being man led him to create ways to control or modify the other parts of creation. He first controlled animals and fire; then later he learned to control vegetation, and civilization was born. When he developed the ability to use the buried resources stored up over billions of years he got into his hands the ability to restructure the face of the earth, for better or for worse. So far he has learned to control the animals and even bacteria and viruses to a certain extent. Control of weather and earthquakes is now beginning. Man is master of the earth and becoming more so all the time. There is only one form of life that he cannot control—man.

Of course a certain amount of self-control is found, for mankind has developed an ordered system of life, beginning with the biologically necessary control of parents over infants. Unlike insects which need no parenting, and birds and animals that need only small doses of it, man needs many years of parental protection and guidance. A human infant is helpless, so a parent decides what he will eat, dress in, live in and experience. The child finds himself completely naturally as one under the control of parents, if only to the extent of not getting what he needs if he does not obey adequately. Eventually, of course, most children grow up and escape this particular order, but then most will develop a new one of their own in which they are the parents, so the dominion continues.

The third great area of dominion in human life is society, a hierarchy that has developed as the way to help make human life as full as possible. Every human being is somewhere in a political order and in an economic order, with almost everyone being both a receiver and a giver of orders. Human life is unimaginable without the leadership of some over others, for the solitary pioneer out in the wilderness continues to be part of both orders even though he may be able to ignore it for months at a time. Human life is ordered life and we all recognize how absolutely essential this is: we need people above us who can see farther than we can and so can direct the operation of our business or nation. Everyone needs people lower in the order, to do things we cannot do, or do not wish to do. Order means cooperation, and without it man would not have survived his first brush with the tiger and the wolf.

The orderedness of human life is so all-pervasive that we are usually able to ignore it most of the time, accepting its benefits without noticing its presence. But the striking part of this human situation is that we all are under orders, yet all also at some times are the giver of orders. The child grows to be a parent. The employee hires others to build his house. Even an absolute monarch is at times under his doctor's orders. Thus our life is paradoxical, shifting back and forth from one in control to one who is controlled. In that order we see the beginning of the way man's situation is a symbol, a reflection, even a representation of God's ordering.

Divine Dominion

The reason for bringing out this obscure aspect of human life—orderedness—is that it points beyond itself to an ultimate order, and must be made to conform to that divine order if human life is to be lived to its fullest. Three great symbols of God's relationship to man correspond to the three areas of man's dominion just outlined: as man is master of the creatures of the earth, God is the Creator standing over the whole creation; as man is parent to his children, so God is called Father of his sons and daughters; as men rule over others, so God is King, Lord, the Ruler of All.

Man's rule over nature is the inevitable result of man's transcending nature by his self-consciousness, ability to see past and future, imagination and creativity, and superior rationality. In a quite analogous way God's rule over his whole creation, including man, is the result of his infinite transcendence of the whole creation. We may try to imagine the difference between God and the world by thinking of something we have made—a sand castle, a cake, a soap-box car, a sculpture—and recognize the infinite difference between ourselves and our creation. Two central characteristics of these relationships stand out: the creation is designed for the creator and finds its well-being in being what the creator wants; when the creator is pleased with his creation, calling it good, then he cherishes it as a part of his own life. Both these points will be important for our discussion below on the way man is to exercise lordship over nature.

Just as man's rule over nature is inevitable, so the parent's rule over a child is inevitable, for the infant is at first a helpless part of nature unable to rule itself. The difference between parent and newborn is a reflection of the difference between God and man. The way a parent treats a helpless infant is a significant reflection of the way God treats man. A further significant aspect of God as Father is the fact that a son not only resembles his father in some ways, but he may also represent him, that is, in some way may make the father present by representing his desires, his power, his attitudes, his person. A son *may* do that, but he also may be a rebellious son who does quite the contrary. But even in that case the possibility remains, if man ever wishes to turn back to it: man still remains capable of reflecting God's fatherly care for the helpless, guidance of the unwary, and chastening of the rebellious. What this means for a parent in relating to his child will be suggested below.

Finally, man's political and economic lordship over others is an image of God as King, or Lord, or Ruler of All. The mutual dependence and mutual service of people in these orders offer an interesting suggestion of what God's rule may mean. Even in the most totalitarian government the people on top have to provide for the needs of those on the bottom or there will be no continued order. Even in the worst tyranny, the ruler keeps the people fed and clothed and distracted for he cannot stay in power if they are not rewarded for their work for him. Thus we perhaps should see in God's rule a certain mutuality also, and so not imagine that God supplies only orders and man supplies only obedience. God's demands are part of his gifts, and man's response is due to gratitude more than fear. In fact the rule of God is seen in the biblical writings as itself a great gift to man. The one thing man cannot control is himself, so if and when man is willing to accept God's ordering of the world then man's destructive lack of self-control will be ended.

In these three symbols—Creator, Father and Ruler—human experiences have been used by the biblical writers as symbols that point beyond man to God. Man's dominion images God's dominion. Thus we come to see more of what God is like by looking at the ordering of human life. Unfortunately, the human order we see is corrupted by selfishness, by man seeing himself as the measure of all things. Therefore these three realms only dimly reflect what God is like: man's rape of the earth offers no insight into God; parental abuse and even murder of helpless infants in no way image God; the tyranny of the strong over the weak says much more about man than it does about God. Thus, we need to take what we know of God from the whole biblical picture of him, and see what kind of dominion over nature, children and subjects will most adequately reflect him.

Imitating God

Eight-year-old Jonathan had earned his bruised knee, but not his hurt feelings. Coming home through the woods he had heard a baby bird chirping and found it on the ground under a nest from which it seemed to have fallen. He picked it up and climbed the tree to put it back. As he reached out and set it in, his foot slipped and he fell down through the branches bruising his knee and ripping his pants as he fell. When he got home his mother exploded at the sight of another ruined pair of pants and asked whatever made him try to do such a foolish thing as putting the baby bird back. His answer was simple and effective: "Daddy did the same thing last summer in our own tree."

In a similar way God's relationship to his "creation," his "children," his "subjects" provides for us deeper insights into the way we are called to live. In the first place in all three of these areas we can see that God cares, that his dominion is not exploitation but enhancement, bringing out the potential that is innate. This means that man as master of nature is not its owner but God's steward given the task of using it and caring for it at the same time. Man is the manager of God's farm, not a frontiersman farming for himself and moving on when the land is worn out. While it is not at all clear precisely how man can bring this earth-farm to its fullest potential, the starting-point is in renouncing our false claims to ownership and submitting to God as the owner.

God as father can be seen as one who does not look upon his children as his possessions, his slaves, his inferiors, who can be used for his convenience and ignored when it is inconvenient. God's fatherhood is exercised in loving, guiding, chastening and relating to his sons with their growth to manhood as the goal. There is no other "urgent matter" for him, no working on weekends, no going out with the boys for relaxation and so leaving his children to fend for themselves. This father is always available, for his fulfillment is in the growing relationship with his children. This father does not say no to things that are merely inconvenient. This father does not stand by his "rights," but reaches out in suffering forgiveness to any returning prodigal. This father is the model of what human fathers are called to be, and the more they attain to these heights the more truly they image, represent, indeed make present the Father of All.

Finally, we can see similar principles at work in the way God as Ruler is the model by which human rulers may see the heights and depths of their calling. First, a human ruler has the calling to exemplify the highest in moral, spiritual and personal behavior. "God is King" means (among other things) that he represents the best, the highest of values, and so human rulers are called to the same thing. Second, this King has his eyes on the least of all, seeking to right the wrongs that are a constant part of human disorder. This King is known and seen best in kings like Josiah of whom Jeremiah said: "He judged the cause of the poor and the needy; then it was well. Is not this to know me? says the Lord" (Jer. 22:16). Human history has seen and continues to experience many more rulers who rather judged (i.e., supported, maintained) the causes of their friends the wealthy and surfeited, but the Ruler of All is not seen in such action. He is the One whose own desires and goals are completely wrapped up in what is ultimately the full life for his people. There is no conflict between his will and their real needs, for their real needs are to know him, support him, obey him, imitate him.

Conclusion

The dominion of man over other men, over children, and over nature is at the foundation of human life. Without this order there would be no human life, indeed barely any animal life because most animals lead ordered existences also. The order of creation is a central symbol pointing beyond itself to the One who created the order, and so is the Head of the order. But the symbol does not stop there, for God's order, as we begin to see it in the biblical witness, is a call to man, a task given. Man's present order is often corrupt, selfish, intransigent and oppressive, and so in need of being renewed in the image of its Creator. Man stands paradoxically as the lord who is a servant, the dominator who is dominated, the father who is a child, and so he must learn to keep his footing as he aims in the direction of becoming what he is—the image of God.

A farmer had three sons who were his lieutenants in running their large farm. The oldest son was in charge of marketing the farm's products, but he was rebellious, jealous of his father's position as owner and boss. The youngest son ran crop production, and while he was completely obedient to his father, he was so obsequious and dependent that he could only impose past decisions, not being able to adapt to new situations, to decide anything himself. The middle son was the manager of the animal crew, and was a man who trusted and depended on his father but was also creative and imaginative himself, constantly working on ways to improve his branch of the farm's operation.

One day the farmer was hospitalized and left the farm in control of all three sons together. The oldest took this as a golden opportunity to pad his own pockets and to get control of the whole farm. So he made crooked deals with some buyers, fired some workers in his division in order to keep their pay, and conspired with workers in his brothers' areas to try to undermine them. The youngest son tried to continue as his father would want, but when two tractors broke down he could not decide what to do immediately, and when some of his workers began refusing to obey he began to be eaten by anxiety. Meanwhile the middle brother found himself able to handle the trouble brewing among his subordinates because he treated them as his father treated him, listening to them, becoming involved with them, working with them to solve the problem.

When the farmer returned to the farm, which one of this three did he see as his heir, the next farmer?

Community

A second central aspect of man's possibility and calling to reflect God is seen in his sexuality, the division of the race into man and woman both of whom are incomplete alone. The necessity for man and woman to live a married life is the sign of their essential communal nature, for however much each person is an individual, his life is always rooted in various communities. This second central aspect of human life reflects God's way with man because God is spoken of as the Husband of his people (one who makes a covenant with their community) and the New Testament speaks of the Church as the bride of Christ in a marriage created as a new covenant. Here again we find that human phenomena of marriage, covenant and communal life are used as symbols to point toward God. But then the reverse also happens: our understanding of God as covenant partner leads us to see what our communal and covenantal relationships may be.

Man and Woman

The author of Genesis 1 presents the creation of mankind in these words: "So God created man in his own image, in the image of God he created him; male and female he created them." (1:27). While it is not certain that the author meant that the division of mankind into male and female was a definition of God's image, it is clear that the unity of the two is used throughout the Bible as a way to point beyond to God. Here again the biblical writers see down to one of the deepest, most basic experiences of human life and recognize that in a fundamental way God himself is reflected, even represented, in this profound mystery of man and woman becoming one. Three points need to be stressed here: the covenant between man and woman; their fruitfulness in bearing children as a continuation of God's creation of man in his image; their need for each other so that life in community is a necessary source of true individual life.

The covenant of husband and wife is a commitment of two people to each other that can be seen as simply a contract but is intended to be much more. At its basic level a covenant is an agreement that each will do certain things for the other in return for certain benefits. It demands willingness to depend on another, to trust the other to fulfill the covenant, an openness to each other so that difficulties can be settled. But in a marriage covenant the possibility is much greater, for the complementarity of man and woman means that something new can grow out of their union: the two may become one new reality, "one flesh." This means that the other does not simply do things, as in a contract, but that she becomes the one who fills in what is lacking in me, as I do in her. Our physical oneness in our sexual relationship is then the symbol of, and means of, deepening a personal and spiritual oneness that is made possible by our differences.

In no part of life is the necessity for man and woman to be together as obvious as in the conceiving of children. Further still, the children born to them become themselves living representations of the oneness of husband and wife. Just as man is the image and likeness of God so a child is the image and likeness of his parents (Gen 5:3). God's command to "be fruitful and multiply" is the first word spoken by God after making man and woman in his image (Gen. 1:28), the first way they behave in his image. Here man and woman together take on the role of God in the continued creation of new sons and daughters born in God's image so that human parentage continues to reflect the Divine. Bearing children is something man and woman naturally do, they find it fulfilling to reduplicate their union by bringing children of that covenant to life, perhaps thereby pointing beyond themselves to God as One whose nature is to create children in his image to relate to. How far we can take that suggestion will be discussed shortly.

One final comment on the nature of marriage is to see it as the solution to man's basic problem: "It is not good that man should be alone" (Gen. 2:18). There is no doubt that man is an individual, for no one else can live inside his skin; but there is likewise no doubt that no man is solely an individual, for all need the presence of others if they are not to go crazy. Marriage, and man's constant seeking for someone to whom he can relate closely, is the sign of this dual nature—both individual and social. We need to be ourselves, to find our own value and identity, but the odd thing is that only in community do we find our individuality. We thus have a difficult task, holding on to both of these sides of life, keeping ourselves from slipping to one extreme or the other.

The individual extreme is seen in the traditional lone gunman of the American frontier. He wandered from place to place, running from the consequences of his past acts, seeking mainly to stay alive. The collective extreme is seen in a fanatic for a cause who lets his own personality become absorbed in his movement, as some communists in many countries have done for the last fifty years. The temptations most of us face today are not to go to those extremes but to tend more in one direction than the other and not to hold on to both. Conservatives often tend toward a collectivism, an acceptance of the group's past or present stance. Liberals sometimes tend toward overindividualism being contemptuous of past and present group ideas and so failing to find the community they need.

Probably most people tend toward the safety of the crowd, whereas most great literature is the product of strong individualists and so goes too far in that direction.

The Husband of His People

Throughout the Bible God's relationship to his people is symbolized as a covenantal one. Often this refers to political covenants made between an emperor and a vassal king, but at other times the marriage bond is the covenant used to symbolize God's way with them. Hosea is the writer who makes the most of this image, but Jeremiah follows him and the New Testament representation of Christ as the Bridegroom and the Church as his bride reemphasizes it. For some reason this particular type of symbolization has rarely been used in the modern Church, but it says a great deal we need to hear.

In the first place seeing a marriage covenant as a central symbol for God's relationship to his people illumines the oneness he has with them. The dominion imagery (Creator, Father, Ruler) stresses his distinction from man, his power over them. While a Hebrew marriage had similar connotations since the husband was master, the symbol of God as husband emphasized even more his love, his desire for his wife's fulfillment, his service and his oneness with her. Just as husband and wife become one and fulfill each other, so also God becomes one with his people, his Spirit being in them. Just as this oneness is symbolized by the wife bearing her husband's name, so also God's people bear his name, identifying themselves with him. As a wife who is one with her husband can represent him, indeed be his presence and act in his name, so also God's people are his presence on earth, reflecting him, representing him, making him present, being his body.

In the second place a marriage covenant fulfills the needs of both partners, for they are incomplete by themselves. To some extent this can be said of God too. Since God has chosen to create a world and to bind himself to his people in a loving, trusting covenant, this must be an expression of something essential in him. Thus we can rejoice in the fact that by loving him we give him something he needs and desires, for this will greatly enhance our love for him.

Yet here the symbol has reached the limits of its usefulness, so at the same time we must hold firmly to a contrary truth: he is complete in himself and has no need of us. His love is not the grasping, possessive love of a human being who is empty and needs to be filled. Far from it. He is overflowing love, fulfillment, perfection itself. He needs nothing. So his love for us is pure bounty. Not because we deserve it, or give him something he needs in return does he love us. He loves simply because he is love.

God's Covenant and Ours

Since God can be spoken of only in symbols taken from his creation, our full knowledge of God can reflect back upon the human situation and provide insight into what our lives might be at their best. If God is the Husband of his people, then his way of treating them is a model of the way Christian husbands are to treat their wives. Paul explicitly speaks this way when he says, "Husbands, love your wives, as Christ loved the Church and gave himself up for her" (Eph. 5:25).

God's suffering and redeeming love seen in Jesus' death offers a striking way to understand the love of husbands and wives for each other. Both need and bounty are involved: God needs his people to be his hands and heart and voice to reach out to the whole world, so the need of man and woman for each other is a good thing too. But ultimately God's love is pure bounty, unadulterated graciousness, giving with no taking involved, for his reaching to the whole world is simply the overflowing of his nature of self-giving love. In marriage on earth, therefore, that side too needs to blossom. Husbands and wives need to find themselves filled with God's love so that giving is their primary action, not taking. Somehow the need husbands and wives have for each other must be wrapped up in the divine way of pouring oneself out for the other with no need to think about taking in. Clearly the more each learns to fulfill the other's needs the less they will need to worry about themselves.

The amazing result of this growing self-giving is that it does not deplete the individuality of each, but rather enhances it. Christ does not cease being himself by pouring himself out for his bride; in fact it was precisely that act of self-giving that makes him stand out in history as he does. Likewise as husband and wife lose themselves in each other they find the fertile ground of loving acceptance in which their own individual potential can sprout and blossom.

The paradox of man's individuality depending on community, of man and woman becoming themselves only when united to another, is due to the mystery of love. Love is absolutely essential to a true human life, but comes only to those who are involved closely with another. Strangely the closer the bond, the deeper the individuality, for the more boundless then is the love that is the presence and power of the Source of All. Juliet's words echo this mystery:

> My bounty is as boundless as the sea
> My love as deep; the more I give to thee
> The more I have, for both are infinite.
>
> *Romeo and Juliet,* Act II.

Those who know that in their own experience are polished mirrors reflecting the love that holds the universe together.

Conclusion

Down in the dust of the earth the Chinese ant couple fitted tightly into the scheme of their colony. Every problem was solved by conforming to the expectations of parents, community and tradition. Whenever a disagreement arose they repressed it so their individuality was gradually squeezed out and they became merely efficient machines in the assembly line. Far above them in the sky circled a pair of American eagles—though it would be difficult to tell they were a pair since each went his own way most of the time. They flew off in search of their own treasures, wanting only what they could get, not concerned with giving. So their lives were composed of conflicts punctuating loneliness. Between the ants and the eagles was a pride of British lions, a family in which unity contributed to individuality. The king and queen each had their own essential roles, so they knew their need for each other. Thus the pride was a community which provided what each needed and so enabled the family to grow to heights of communal individuality.

Spirit

The first two sections of this chapter have suggested that the human experiences of dominion and community are central aspects of human life and significant symbols of the way God relates himself to man. Now we are going to move on to the very heart of human life as we speak of man's spirit in this section and his responsibility in the next chapter. Dominion and community are found to some extent among all animals; but spirit and responsibility are found only in the human animal.

Although the word *spirit* as a way of speaking about the deepest aspect of human life is not as common as some other words (*soul, person, self*), it is important to use it if we are to understand what is meant by the biblical use of *Spirit* as an aspect of God. Only when we recognize that here again the biblical writers have taken one of the deep human experiences and see through it to the divine reality can we grasp the biblical witness. *Spirit* when used of God is thus not a precise concept that can be defined, analyzed and learned; it is a symbol taken from human life and used to express something of the life of God. If we understand God as Spirit it can only be because we experience ourselves as spirit.

In this section the first goal will be to suggest some of the heights of humanity that are included when his spirit is mentioned. Second, we will stress the body-spirit unity that is equally emphasized by ancient Hebrews and modern biologists. Then finally a few of the implications of this view of man for understanding God's people as the Body (of Christ) expressing his Spirit will be mentioned.

The Heights of Humanity

Man's spirit is not used by the biblical writers as a term denoting one part of man that can be separated from other parts of him. Instead it refers to one aspect of the whole, unified man, one way of speaking of him. Just as life is not a part of man, but is a way of being, an aspect of the whole, so also spirit is. In particular, of course, spirit refers to the hidden aspect of man, that which cannot adequately be observed from the outside but is experienced only from within. Among the most significant characteristics of this inner aspect are man's self-awareness, his imagination, personal relatedness, and his mysterious depths.

Man transcends the animal world, as far as we can tell, by his self-consciousness, his self-awareness, which allows him to stand outside of himself and consider himself as an object of knowledge. This central human possibility is expressed in the fact that he can be related to himself; he can feel comfortable with himself, or he can respond as a teen-age girl did after watching herself on television for ten minutes: "I hate her." No matter how hard we try to ignore who we are and what we do to ourselves and others, some of the truth will always break through and force us to take a stand.

An essential aspect of man's self-awareness is his amazing imagination. This is man's substitute for the instincts that are found in other animals. To be more precise, we should think of a continuum: at the lowest end the animals are completely bound by instinct; in the middle there is mostly instinct but the rudiments of imagination; in man instinct plays only a very small part and so his capacity to act creatively by using his imagination is immense. To imagine means to abandon the constraints of the past, of the way things have always seemed before, and to soar into the unknown as astronauts rocketed to the moon. They did not know what they would find there (though imagination had gone ahead and paved the way) just as the inventor, the scientific genius, the poet and creative people in all walks of life are not sure where they will land when they fly into the outer space of creativity. Children are especially imaginative, until they get into most schools, for then conformity is demanded and rewarded and creativity is ignored or even discouraged.

The third major characteristic of man as spirit is personal relatedness. Although I am I and you are you, we can meet if we are willing to go beyond our own narrow boundaries and allow our spirits to be intertwined in a new reality—a friendship. In fact it seems to be precisely this kind of personal involvement that is necessary for the development of the depths of the person, if we are right in thinking that love, trust and patience are basic to full personhood. It is not as if I could develop myself as a person first and then try becoming involved, for involvement is the only way for the person to develop. As a bird's wings develop only by flying, and atrophied muscles can be renewed only by exercise, so also imaginative, empathetic, personal involvement with others is the only way we can develop within.

Finally we need to realize that the "within" of human life is ultimately mysterious. The questions "what is man?" and "who am I?" are finally unanswerable because they are really not as much requests for information as they are expressions of wonder. When man looks within himself, his relationships and his experiences he discovers depths and heights that cannot be fathomed or climbed, mysteries before which he can only stand in wonder even as he tries further to understand. The questions man asks about himself are the signs of his intuition of the mystery that expresses itself within him, surrounds him as his home and is his ultimate source and destination. Thus to say that man is spirit is to say that he is touched by, related to, involved with, dependent on, the deepest Mystery of the universe, that which is beyond all yet within all, holding it all together. *Spirit* at its depths thus is a suggestion that man as person is the deepest reality of created life, the capstone to the whole creation.

In so believing the biblical writers stand over against the rationalist tradition inherited from the Greeks. Aristotle called man the rational animal. Hamlet expressed that intellectualist view when he said:

What a piece of work is man!
How noble in reason!
How infinite in faculties!
In form and moving, how express and admirable!
In action how like an angel!
In apprehension, how like a god!

The Hebrew view was that man's greatness lies elsewhere: "What is man that Thou art mindful of him?" Being known by God, with the possibility of knowing him in return, that is what makes man man.

Unified Person

The biblical stress upon man as spirit has often been misinterpreted to mean that man has a soul or spirit that is an inner part of him, separable from his body. That image of man is Platonic, not Hebraic, for the biblical viewpoint parallels the modern scientific one in which man is seen as a psychosomatic unity. The modern evidence of this unity is found in all the physical ailments such as ulcers and hysterical paralysis that are caused by psychological problems. The biblical evidence for this view is that the *whole* man can be spoken of as flesh, or as spirit, and the hope of eternal life is not for a separate immortality of the soul but for a resurrected embodied person.

For many people this paradox of man as the animal-angel is difficult to accept. They have heard for so long of man's immortal soul that needs to be saved that the thought of the whole man being an indivisible unity is traumatic. It calls for the kind of thought revolution that a child brought up by racist parents must go through when he finds a child of another race who is just like him. But the revolution is necessary if we are to hear what the Bible has to say: it sees man as rooted in the earth but with his head in the heavens.

The unity of man can perhaps be imagined if we see man's body as the necessary expression of his spirit and his spirit as the unifying aspect of his body. Without our bodies we could not be persons, for our language and communication take place only by means of our bodies. Not only our voices but our faces and hands and whole bodies are the expression of our deep humanity, the way we reach out and make contact with others. Without that contact we could not have personal involvement, could not know what it is to be a person, could not love. Our bodies are the visible aspect of our spirit, and without them we would no more exist than the length of an object could exist if its width and depth disappeared.

Not only is the body necessary for the spirit but the spirit is necessary for the body. The biblical writers speak of the passions of man's flesh, probably referring to the impulses that man shares with other animals—food drive, sexual instinct and the impulse of self-preservation. These are all necessary and valuable, but man has no adequate instinctual, biological limits placed upon them so he needs other limits to be developed. These impulses need to be integrated into the whole human organism so that the other needs —for growth, for community, for friendship, for self-control—can be satisfied also. Man's spirit is the unifying, integrating factor that allows these needs all to be satisfied appropriately. Naturally the weaker the integration the more the physical impulses can come to rule, a problem that will be depicted in a later chapter.

Man's spirit-body unity is the foundation for the importance of sexuality that was discussed earlier in this chapter. Only because man is such a unity can the physical oneness of the sexual relationship be a symbol of, and thus the means of enhancing, the personal and spiritual oneness that is the heart of marriage. Thus whenever people reject sexuality, as do many Buddhists and Christian monks and other ascetics down through the ages, we find a denial of the spirit-body oneness that is a characteristic view of the biblical writers. In a similar way man's psychosomatic unity is the basis for communal life, for we share with others a physical aspect that unites us with them and makes it possible for us to become involved with them. Here again it is usually mystics and individualists stressing that man is an immortal spirit who find life in community to be degrading and physical. In truth man is enspirited body or embodied spirit so that holding hands, patting backs, hugging, eating together, walking together and a whole array of other physical acts deepen our spiritual, personal bonds with each other. Spirit and body form a unity like a man and his horse.

On the edge of Death Valley one spring day two men borrowed horses to ride down into the desert and see its wonders. As they rode away, one of the riders showed quickly that he had little use for horses: "Why do we have to be dependent on these ignorant mountains of muscle and instinct? I'm a man, I'm independent. It's demeaning to be stuck up here, having to fit in with it." He therefore treated his horse quite brutally trying to express his superiority to it. The other rider thought differently, for he said: "I find it delightful, without him I cannot go far enough or fast enough to get to the oasis; without me he doesn't know where to go. Together we are much more than we either could be alone. By ourselves in the desert we would both be dead." So he and his horse got along very well.

The brutal rider found his horse difficult in return. Finally, because he had hit it once too often the animal bolted, racing over sand dunes, around rocks, down valleys, finally tossing the rider off in the rocks in the left-field corner of nowhere. A week later the bodies of both horse and rider were found by a search team, too late to do any good.

God's Spirit and Body

In the Old Testament the word we translate "spirit" meant three different things: wind, breath and inner life. When the symbol *spirit* was used to speak of God's presence all three of these meanings seem to have been included, for God's Spirit is powerful and mysterious like the wind, is the source of man's life (breath), and is understood as a manifestation of God's self. It is important to realize that the word was first used of created phenomena, then later taken up as a symbol to express something of the unfathomable mystery of God. In the later writings of the New Testament the breath and wind meanings move into the background and so the basic meaning is "inner life" with man's spirit being a way to begin to imagine something of what God is like.

To speak of God as spirit is to call to mind many of the characteristics that were outlined above under human spirit. First of all it points to the transcendence of God: just as man is able to stand over against himself, to be aware of his createdness and so to transcend it, so God stands over against the whole creation, completely aware of all that it is. This over-againstness then leads to creativity, for just as man by his imagination is able to dream of what is new, so also God is not bound by what has been but is the Source of all creativity. Third, we can see in man's personhood a symbol of the divine personhood, for man's possibility of being a person in loving relationship with others is a dim suggestion of the infinite love and personhood of God.

All three of these central characteristics of man's spirit thus point beyond themselves to something in God that is like them but goes far beyond them in ways unimaginable to us. Thus, finally it is probably the mystery of the human spirit that is the ultimate symbol of God's Spirit. We simply cannot grasp the depths of our own lives and possibilities, let alone another person's, so we can only stand in wonder before the infinite possibilities God has placed within us. And if they are his creations, we simply cannot even begin to fathom the depth of the mystery and wonder of God himself. We cannot pin him down, analyze him, constrain him, for like the wind that blows where it will he is here, there and everywhere continually confounding our calculations.

One central result of this divine mystery is that we dare not take any of our images of him literally, for that is an attempt to put him in a box, to control his blowing. For example, many people take literally the image of God as a "person" who "hears" our prayers and "speaks" to us in return. That is certainly a central image, but another one is that God's Spirit dwells with ours, so that he becomes a part of us, not an Other standing apart from us. We need both symbols, but neither is to be taken literally. God is appropriately imagined as both a person apart from us and a spirit infused within us, inseparable from our very selves so that because of this inner unity with him we can be his body.

Man's body-spirit unity does not provide a symbol of God in himself, for he is only Spirit. One of the ways we mark his unimaginable difference from us is to realize that we are rooted in the dust of the earth—we *are* dust—whereas he is the Spirit Creator of that dust. Yet, even though God is complete in himself, he has chosen his people to be his body, to be the outward and visible expression of his Spirit. This is precisely what Paul means when he speaks of the Church as the Body of Christ, with God's Spirit as the integrating, humanizing reality at its center. Thus man's spirit-body unity is used as a central symbol of the way God is related to the world.

We can imagine God's Spirit becoming the renewing, wooing power in man's spirit, so that love and joy and patience and the other great human possibilities begin to rule in each person's life. When God's Spirit and man's have become one, then indeed it is God's Spirit that is expressed in man's body, in his language, in his action, in his communal life. When this has happened then God's people can be the expression of his deepest self. They may become a light offered to the nations, a covenant bond extended to the alienated people (Isa. 49:6, 8). Then God's gift of reconciliation will become a present carried in the hearts, hands and mouths of his agents of reconciliation (2 Cor. 5:18 ff.) who are enabled to be loving and accepting as Jesus himself was. Jesus himself was the foundation laid, the beginning of God's renewed body, but now the work is in the hands of other builders, other sowers and cultivators, all of whom are God's co-workers (1 Cor. 3:7 ff.).

Conclusion

The major thesis of this chapter is the classic Christian view that knowledge of man and knowledge of God go hand in hand. Our beginning knowledge of man provides us with symbols to use in speaking of God who is known directly in inner experience. But then our growing knowledge of God enables us to come back to man's dominion, community, and spirit and to go deeper into the possibilities that God's way provides for us. Our language must be founded on human phenomena. But our deep knowledge of both God and man is developed only through our relationship with God which leads us deeper and deeper into the mysteries of what it means to be human.

One of the greatest of those mysteries is the paradox of man's freedom and responsibility in an environment that determines him. It is precisely this combination that makes man a historical being, one who acts in and is acted upon by history. A beginning insight into this human experience may thus provide the way for us to grasp the central biblical imagery of God as the Author of History.

Suggested Reading

Berkouwer, G. C. *Man: The Image of God.* Translated by D. W. Jellema. Grand Rapids: Eerdmans, 1962.

Come, A. B. *Human Spirit and Holy Spirit.* Philadelphia: Westminster, 1959.

Gelin, A. *The Concept of Man in the Bible.* Translated by D. M. Murphy. London: Chapman, 1968.

Heschel, Abraham J. *Who Is Man?* Stanford: Stanford University Press, 1965.

Jenkins, D. *What Is Man?* Valley Forge: Judson, 1971.

Le Fevre, P. *Understandings of Man.* Philadelphia: Westminster, 1966.

Niebuhr, Reinhold. *The Nature and Destiny of Man.* Vol. 1. New York: Scribner's, 1943.

Pannenberg, Wolfhart. *What Is Man?* Translated by D. A. Priebe, Philadelphia: Fortress, 1970.

Pittenger, W. Norman. *The Christian Understanding of Human Nature.* Digswell Place, England: Nisbet, 1964.

Shinn, R. L. *Man: The New Humanism.* Vol. VI. *New Directions in*

Theology Today. Edited by W. Hordern. Philadelphia: Westminster, 1968.

Verduin, L. *Somewhat Less Than God*. Grand Rapids: Eerdmans, 1970.

Chapter Three: The Author of History

Introduction

The Agent of History

LIBERTY, FREEDOM, AND CHOICE

Physical Liberty

Spiritual Freedom

A Matter of Choice

CONCLUSION

IMAGINATION AND HISTORY

Imaginative Future

Shaping History

The Art of Drama

CONCLUSION

God in History

USEFUL SYMBOLS

Puppeteer

Repairman

Person

Wisdom

CONCLUSION

AUTHOR

Characters and Actors

Autobiography and Trinity

Plus and Minus

CONCLUSION

CHAPTER THREE

The Author of History

Introduction

The central idea that we are pursuing in these chapters is that the biblical writers point to God by using symbols taken from the experiences of man. It may well be that this imaging of God in the deepest human experiences is the meaning of man as the image of God. Our discussion of dominion, community and spirit in the last chapter has laid the groundwork for looking into the great biblical theme of God as the Author of History. The symbol *author* is clearly taken from human experience, and is used here to suggest how the two common symbols for God as Creator, and as Ruler (Lord, King) of History can be combined into one.

The approach we will take to understanding God's relationship to history is the same as we have taken earlier: to try to grasp the human experience the biblical writers use as a symbol, and then to move from that to the understanding of God that it mediates. In particular we shall see that the biblical writers use man's power to make history, his decisions on how he is to live his own life, as a constant symbol for God's involvement in history. Thus if we grasp something of man's freedom, his power of choice, and its relationship to the determining structures of the world, we will have a beginning insight into God's choosing and acting.

The Agent of History

Man is the only animal that has a history, and so man is the only creature who is a maker of history. How much history makes man in return is a much debated issue, for there have always been thinkers who believed that man is wholly determined by past events and present forces, leaving him no power of choice. In this section we will present a version of this debate that tries to express the biblical writers' dual emphasis, both on man's responsibility to decide and upon the shaping power of forces beyond his immediate control. First, we will see what can reasonably be said about freedom in biblical perspective. Second, we will pursue the role of imagination and artistry in human creativity, not only in the arts and sciences but also in living. Building on those two pillars we will suggest how man's role in molding history can best be understood.

Liberty, Freedom, and Choice

A great deal of confusion has surrounded the debate over freedom and determinism because of confusing use of language. Therefore we shall begin our discussion by distinguishing (though not separating) liberty, freedom and choice (free will). *Liberty* as used here will refer to the absence of *external* restraints that prevent a person from living to the fullest. *Freedom* will be used as the biblical writers generally use it to speak of *inner* life when it is free from inner forces of habit—sin. Finally, we will talk of man's choosing, whatever can be said about the way his will operates, in particular how his decisions are related to whatever amount of liberty and freedom he enjoys.

Physical Liberty

Every man, woman and child experiences a certain amount of liberty, and everyone has drastic limitations placed upon him. Some have a great deal more than others but everyone has some and no one has unlimited liberty. By liberty I mean the limitation of external, physical restraints. All of us live within some such restraints, first from our bodies; second, from our physical environment; and third, from our social environment.

Our bodies put great limitations on our actions. We must eat, drink, breathe and sleep or we shall not live. Whether or not we have other restraints depends on how healthy we are. To a certain extent how much liberty we have in this realm is up to us—for we can care for our bodies. But to an extent it is out of our hands, for we cannot control many diseases. Thus in addition to the natural, inherent constraints of our bodies we must add the constraints of our physical environment.

In nature as a whole, as in our individual bodies, there is a balancing of forces we can control with those we cannot, so that we have liberty within limits. We cannot control the fact our bodies are designed for the earth's surface and can move elsewhere only with loads of equipment weighing us down. Likewise we cannot escape hurricanes, earthquakes, viruses, bacteria and the ecosystem's intricacies. We are constrained by them, but we are gradually gaining more and more liberty in dealing with them. Unfortunately this liberty often produces greater constraints in our social environment.

Here, in social life, is the area of our greatest concern for liberty. We use the term most of all for absence of political restraints, in particular those noxious and dehumanizing restraints found in tyrannical political systems. But there is no complete liberty possible here either. Government *means* restraint, but good restraint because the alternative is the chaos of anarchy and the rule of the strong and brutal. The open question is what combination of liberty and restraint maximizes the good life, the truly human life. Western nations think a somewhat free press helps, but communist nations disagree. Some businessmen think that almost no government regulation of business is helpful, but others have come to believe that significant restraints on business provide greater liberty for consumers and workers. The crucial point is this: in our social environment constraint of some provides liberty for others. Therefore there is no absolute liberty, just a choice of how to balance it with restraints.

In both the physical and social realms therefore we find that there is always some restraint mixed with some liberty. Man is never alone, he is part of an environment, and thus liberty and constraint are inseparable. There is no way to escape the facts of life—both physical and social—and so man's life must be lived within boundaries if he is to have liberty.

Spiritual Freedom

Most modern discussion of freedom is mainly concerned with the external forces just discussed, so in our terms it is the problem of liberty. The biblical writers, however, were less concerned with external liberty than they were with internal freedom. At its heart the Christian meaning of freedom is deliverance from the inner forces that prevent us from living our lives to the fullest. Jesus was the epitome of the free man because nothing could lead him or force him to deviate from his life's goal of expressing God's love and judgment. Everyone else is a sinner, that is, they are under the power of inner forces that prevent them from living the truly human life Jesus did.

These inner forces have a variety of causes. Our past constrains us, because we have formed bad habits we find it difficult if not impossible to break. Our internalized law enslaves us: first, because we believe demands that are bad for us ("make money," "be prejudiced against . . . ," "our kind of people never . . ."); but also because any failure to obey that law makes us feel guilty, for which we try to compensate in destructive ways. Our physical impulses often get the better of us, for if we do not have a truly human value and belief system then our hunger, sex and self-protection impulses may hold inordinate power over us.

Freedom from the rule of these destructive inner forces does not mean an absence of all inner constraints; we must serve someone, either God or something else. For the Christian, freedom *means* freedom from the something else, and that happens only by serving God, allowing his Spirit of love to dominate us. There is no way human beings can escape orienting their lives around something, so every person must serve and worship something—either God or something less (Rom. 6), a cause, a country, a person or oneself. Whichever one of these is chosen it involves entanglement in an inhuman way of life (as we shall point out in a later chapter). Allegiance to God, on the other hand, leads to true freedom: the enhancement of all that is truly human in us, love, wonder, responsibility, thought, personal involvement, control and integration of our passions.

A Matter of Choice

The biblical standpoint is that liberty is good for people and that the growth of liberty by means of a restraining social structure ought to be encouraged by God's people. Second, but more centrally, the view is stressed that inner freedom is what man lacks and needs restored to him by God. Naturally liberty and freedom are intertwined, neither being found absolutely alone. But neither can be seen as the direct cause of the other either, for liberty is the fulfillment of man's animal and rational needs whereas freedom is found on the spiritual-personal plane. The question so far left untouched is how these two gifts of liberty and freedom relate to man's ability to choose—to man's free will. There is significant reference to liberty and freedom in the biblical writings but as to free will there is only the constant call to man to choose, and the assertion that he is responsible for his choices.

The biblical message seems to express just what man's ordinary experience suggests: he is molded by forces beyond his control so that causes for everything he does can be found; and yet, he experiences being responsible for his choices. These two insights cannot be rationally integrated for the first comes from viewing man from without, as an object, while the second comes from viewing ourselves from within, as subjects. Any attempt to deny one side or the other is blindness in one eye. We must see ourselves through both eyes if we are to overcome the inadequacies of each.

Clearly there is some truth in a determinist view of human behavior. Deliberate actions are based on decisions which flow from settled attitudes, our basic motivations to decrease pain and increase pleasure, and our perception of what lies before us. All of these—decisions, attitudes, motivation and perception—are to a certain extent variable in differing circumstances but behind them lies our more settled inner life, our goals, values and beliefs, the core of our personality. Thus when a stimulus comes to us from outside, what action we take is essentially determined for us in the moment by our previously determined goals, character, habits, knowledge, perception, motivation and attitudes. All of these inner attributes are used here in fairly loose everyday language. Even though it is by no means an exact or exhaustive description it does seem to suggest that there is no room for free will, if by that is meant an arbitrary choice at the point of decision. Our decision is our own, and not coerced: but it can be described as being caused by all these inner realities.

Yet, we feel responsible and experience freedom in choosing. Viktor Frankl stresses this experience when he describes his life in *Man's Search for Meaning:* "We who lived in concentration camps can remember the men who walked through the huts comforting others, giving away their last piece of bread. They may have been few in number, but they offer sufficient proof that everything can be taken from a man but one thing: the last of the human freedoms —to choose one's attitude in any given set of circumstances, to choose one's own way." Frankl's view is that our inner world is under our own control. But, an attitude of humble service cannot be decided on out of the blue; it can be only an outcome of our basic goals, our value orientation, our choice of whom we will follow.

From the biblical emphasis on it, it seems that there is only one basic choice man must make—whom he will serve. All other choices flow from this basic life decision, and it is to this that our feeling of responsibility points. Even though in the crisis of this moment I can do nothing other than what my inner structure determines, in the long run that inner structure can be changed by a new allegiance.

Our decision on whom we will serve is part of the deep mystery of personality. It is indeed influenced by the views of people who are important to us, the results we have perceived in the lives of different people, the way we have been treated. There is no way that we can fully understand the influences that go into our choosing at this basic level but our feeling of responsibility for our lives demands that we see our choice as our own. The practical significance of this is that we will continually see the possibility of change lying before us. That is the essence of the power of choice visualized by the biblical writers—the choice to change our allegiance from the demonic to the divine.

Conclusion

One day in 1970 Edward Trench, an American millionaire playboy on a trip to Greece, met old Alex Nikos, a political prisoner who taught him that liberty and freedom are not the same thing. The American had all the liberty any man can use: he was young, healthy and attractive so his physical make-up provided far fewer limitations than many people experience; he was rich, and so any barrier that money could break down was no obstacle to him; and he was American, the beneficiary of all the liberties of his homeland, as well as those offered in foreign countries to anyone backed by American power. Alex Nikos was old, in broken health, poor, a native of Greece where liberty was then largely a dream, in prison for life for openly objecting to governmental brutality.

Yet Alex was a free man, as his conversation hinted. Having learned his story the American asked:

"Why didn't you escape from Greece, rather than protest?"

"Perhaps you value not being in prison too much. I value being true to myself, to my people."

"How can you hope to be yourself unless you conform to whatever powers control things?"

"Conforming to such power is slavery. Look at you, your money and flitting around the world mean so much to you that you're nobody."

"I am who I choose to be. I enjoy my liberties, my pleasures. Your pain is a price I refuse to pay."

"You couldn't pay it anyway! You've been so brainwashed to

treasure physical liberty that you have not seen that real freedom is within—the result of choosing a truly human life."

If you had to choose the situation of one or the other of these men, which would you choose?

Imagination and History

One central aspect of man's spirituality mentioned in the previous chapter is imagination. It is one of the mysterious ways the inner man works, seeming to create something out of nothing continually. In fact man's imagination can be understood as the root of his power of choice, for it provides him with an openness to the future that transcends the determining power of the past. If this is the case then it is man's imagination that is the basis for his role as the maker of history, suggesting that man's influence on the course of events is to be seen as the result of his visions of what might be. Nowhere do these visions become more expressive than in the work of the creative artist and so the final subject pursued in this section will be the mind of an author, the foundation of the symbol for God as the Author of History.

Imaginative Future

Imagination is man's share in God's creativity. From out of the depths of the subconscious, images, stories and ideas well up and burst out for those who have kept the channels open. We may become prosaic if we refuse to use our imaginations, for they can atrophy just as any other potential can. But when we encourage imagination, allow it to work, use its gifts and seek to be more and more imaginative we find that the creativity of the universe may be channeled through us.

Undoubtedly the elements of our imaginings are to a certain extent the things we have seen, heard, and experienced, but the significant factor is that the elements do not determine the result. All the great advances of science were originally imaginative hypotheses that "this" may be like "that." For some reason Newton imagined that the motion of the planets was like the falling of an apple and so the Laws of Motion began to be developed. A new insight is not a recognition of something obvious just waiting to be observed. It is a new creation. Just as life was something inexplicable on the basis of nonlife, and mind is inexplicable by what is irrational, so every new creation is more than just the product of what went before.

For most people the most significant type of imagining is concerned with the future. Above all personal questions is this one: "What shall I become?" Whether we ask this question explicitly or not it lies at the root of our lives, for it is the way the goals we have chosen express themselves. It does not matter how conformist and conventional we are, we must use our imaginations to see ourselves in the conventional role we have laid down for ourselves. Only when we can come to imagine ourselves as being a doctor or a teacher or an explorer or a mother or an artist or whatever we envision does that vision come to be our guiding light. Thus imagination seems to be an essential source of our human life.

It seems likely that man's imagination can meaningfully be understood as the outworking of God's presence on earth. This is not to identify human creativity with divine, but to say that at this point man joins in the creativity God has implanted in creation. Man's imagination images God's creativity, for God too (we may imagine) has dreamed of worlds he could have created but did not and of alternate futures among which he has chosen. Here, in the choice of what we would like the future to be, we find man's power of shaping history.

Shaping History

The goal in front of us in this chapter is to discern and express something of the biblical witness to God's involvement in history. Therefore it seems appropriate to ask if we can see in dim outline at least something of how man is involved in shaping history. We have already suggested that the biblical writers see man as both a shaper and one shaped. His choices do make a difference but he must also recognize that there are forces beyond his control which impinge upon him, limit his options, sometimes even pin him down to virtually one choice. We cannot here offer any great detail on the forces shaping history, but a few suggestions may prepare the way for seeing God's involvement.

When we think of shaping history, our thoughts often turn to influential political figures, Alexander the Great, Julius Caesar, Charlemagne, Henry VIII, George Washington, Lenin and others. How did they influence events? To a great extent it was due to their personal influence over the people who surrounded them. No one man can wield much direct power for governing, for even nuclear bombs can only destroy, they cannot govern. Only as a political leader can get a number of associates to accept his vision and become extensions of him, can he influence the course of events. But central to that influence is a vision of what might be: if a leader is staying put, defending the status quo, ruling without a vision, he cannot shape history but is a pawn in others' hands. It was not the Czar who moved history, but Lenin.

But second, we must think of the unseen forces, particularly ideas and techniques, that are equally apparent in the shaping of history. In the world of the twentieth century the equality of races is an idea shaping men and nations. The long-held belief in superior and inferior races has given way and with it the colonialism it engendered. From the seventeenth century onward there has been a growing belief in the rights of the people as superior to the privileges of rulers, and however hypocritically rulers may agree, it is a force shaping history. In addition to ideas, techniques shape history: agriculture seems to have been the foundation for civilization; the printing press may have been the beginning of democracy; the industrial revolution made modern war possible and has made the destruction of life on earth—by either a bang or a whimper—conceivable. None of these social forces is under anyone's control. They are man-made and man-carried but not man-controlled.

Finally, and perhaps most important of all, we must look at the genius, the man or woman of creative imagination and life, as the source of both the shaping powers just described. The ideas were some one person's ideas before they came to be social forces. The inventions were in one person's mind before they were made concrete and usable. The visions of the possible held by political leaders are usually not their own but borrowed from someone else. Who were the really influential men in history? Men of ideas, the philosophers, writers and spiritual innovators, who told stories and lived mostly as outcasts in their own days: Confucius and Buddha, Homer and Plato, Jeremiah and Jesus, Erasmus and Luther, Galileo and Darwin, Schweitzer and St. Francis, Shakespeare and Dostoevsky, Marx and Freud. These were all men who not only could see what was happening before their eyes but were granted inspired imaginations to see what others could not see without their guidance. Few if any of these men had any political, economic or social control over others. Yet they were the most influential men who ever lived. By their dreams, visions, stories, ideas and lives they seemed to many to have shown the way into the future. By showing the way, they made the way.

The object of this brief excursion into man's role in making history is to call attention to significant aspects of that shaping: no one man has much physical control over others, it is only by personal influence and vision communicated that he can control his nation; beyond individuals there are great forces at work, ideas whose time seems to have come, and inventions that spread like wildfire; but behind all of these forces lie their originators, the inspired men, the creative and imaginative geniuses. If these men can reasonably be seen as history's most influential, then perhaps a look at the creative imagination at work may offer further preparation for looking at God's shaping of history.

The Art of Drama

Human history is an ongoing drama, the beginning hidden from us and the finale not yet reached. If God is the origin, sustainer and completer of this drama, then the work of a human dramatist should offer a significant pattern of symbols for pointing beyond to God's relationship to history. In this section a human author's creativity within limits will be explored, as an extension of the previous discussion on making history and as a prelude to the depiction of God the Author of History in the next part of the chapter.

The striking paradox of authorship is that while the author appears to outsiders to be the absolute master of his material, the author himself knows that he is not. The heart of the artist's effort is his vision, his idea, the mysterious impulse within that comes from the imagination in interaction with the surrounding world. The artist uses materials of that world, its language, ideas, events, stories, characters and so does not have absolute control over the results. Dorothy Sayers, who was a novelist, dramatist and theologian, put her experience this way in *The Mind of the Maker:* "The only way of 'mastering' one's material is to abandon the whole conception of mastery and to cooperate with it in love: whosoever will be lord of life, let him be its servant. If he tries to wrest life out of its true nature, it will revenge itself in judgment, as the work revenges itself on the domineering artist."

It seems, therefore, that the author is to a certain extent a channel for reality expressing itself through him. His creative imagining is not simply an imposition on the world but is a new insight into that world and so he cannot mold his insight simply to suit his fancy. Authors often tell of the way characters get away from them, so that as they develop in their own natural direction they refuse to fit the story of which they are a part. Any attempt by the author to coerce the character, to make an unnatural, unprepared change in him, will undermine the authenticity of the work. As soon as the reader says to himself, "That's not very likely," the story will have lost its power.

But this danger does not mean that the author ought to try to keep rigid control over his characters, for if he does they will not live. Miss Sayers says from her own experience that "the creator's love for his work is not a greedy possessiveness; he never desires to subdue his work to himself but always to subdue himself to his work. The more genuinely creative he is, the more he will want his work to develop in accordance with its own nature, and to stand independent of himself." In a significant way a book or a play or a poem is an author's "child," having grown out of himself but now standing on its own. He wants people to read it, to enter into its meaning, to be influenced by what it is regardless of who the author was and what he is now doing.

In particular the author of a play creates something living, because he cannot control the way the actors will interpret the characters and their lines. The dramatist provides the story, the seemingly absolute control of the very lines to be spoken, but within them there is extraordinary freedom for the actor which can be extremely fulfilling for the author. As a dramatist Miss Sayers speaks authoritatively of this experience when she says: "To hear an intelligent and sympathetic actor infusing one's own lines with his creative individuality is one of the most profound satisfactions that any imaginative writer can enjoy; more—there is an intimately moving delight watching the actor's mind at work to deal rightly with a difficult interpretation, for there is in all this a joy of communication and an exchange of power. Within the limits of this human experience, the playwright has achieved that complex end of man's desire—the creation of a living thing with a mind and a will of its own."

This living creation reflects the author's mind but is not to be confused with the author's mind, for that transcends all his writings. The play and the characters provide insight into his views, his experience, his goals, but these all remain somewhat hidden behind his creations unless he chooses to reveal himself in an autobiography. If he does that, then this particular work (or act in the play) is not only one in the series of his works but is the key to them all. An autobiography reveals the way an author sees himself. His self-portrayal is not as much a separate, living creation as it is a representation of his ongoing self-understanding, something that will put all the rest of his works into better perspective.

An author is the creator of his play, but if it is to be a successful play, one that will engage, enlighten and deepen his actors and viewers, then he cannot be arbitrary. The story must conform to its own inherent vision. The characters must be allowed to have their own lives, even though they will be constrained by the author's plan for the whole play. The essential vision is the author's own, as are the setting and the plan of the whole. The story will turn out as the author intends, but along the way many unexpected twists and turns will take place. The author of a successful drama will be hidden behind the whole, reflected in every part of it but obvious nowhere. If he ever does become obvious, except as an autobiographical character, then he distracts his audience from the drama itself.

Conclusion

This section on man as the agent of history has been an attempt to suggest that man is an agent, that is, an actor, and not just a pawn in the hand of forces completely beyond his control. Further, it was suggested that it is precisely in his imagination that man transcends his past and the forces that mold him in the present. By imagining what might be he can shape what will be, as the dramatist creates characters and a story that become influential in the lives of many. Finally, this imaginative (yet somewhat restricted) creativity of the dramatist was explored to see how the author is related to his characters, in anticipation of developing the symbol *author* as a way to see into God's relationship to history.

God in History

The biblical writers use a vast array of different images of God's involvement in history. Almost all their symbols pointing toward him (those excluded are the reflections of his otherness, his transcendence) offer suggestive insight into ways we may imagine him being involved in the human drama. Down through the history of the Church, however, a few of these symbols have been selected and made central by different Christians and so a look at a few of the most popular ones may be useful. In particular we will consider God as puppeteer, repairman, person and wisdom; each of these comes from the Bible and is emphasized by some group today.

The aim of this section is to suggest that each of these symbols does represent something significant in the biblical witness to God, but that their limitations are such that none of them should be our central image. For our central image I propose God as the Author of History, for it includes much of what is central in the other four symbols and does not have as obvious limitations as they do. It is still a symbol, however, and it does have limitations which will be pointed out. If at the end of this chapter the reader concludes that we can imagine a little of the way God is involved in history but that finally he remains the attracting mystery we cannot explain, then the goal will have been reached.

Useful Symbols

The four symbols chosen for elaboration here represent much of the range of views held in the Church today. At one end is the puppeteer symbol, based especially on the potter imagery of Jeremiah and Paul, which is taken to mean that God absolutely determines the life of his creatures. Not a great many hold to that view any more, but the repairman image, based on the biblical references to God's intervention at those points where things go wrong, is very popular. Equally popular is the image of God as a person, influencing others only by personal involvement within them, but having no power over natural forces. Finally we may use the image of God as the wisdom (or order) permeating the universe, not only in the minds of man but also in every nook and cranny of the physical world.

Puppeteer

The image of God as absolutely in control of human life is found in speaking of God as a potter and man as his pot. The potter is master of the clay, making of it whatever he wishes, one pot of beauty, another for menial work, one to keep for himself, another to sell. The pot has no wishes to take into consideration, only the potter's will matters. Thus the power of God over his people is expressed by his words "like the clay in the potter's hand, so are you in my hand" (Jer. 18:6). This power is absolute, so if the pot turns out to be useless the potter breaks it, throws it on the refuse pile and starts again.

There is much of significance in this symbol for it touches human imagination and artistry, allowing intuitive insight into God's way with man. Most of all it points to the infinite difference between man and God for we recognize that a pot and its maker are quite different levels of reality. This symbolizes man's origin in and dependence on the one who has made him, the one he cannot escape no matter how much he may try. It emphasizes God's authority over man, so that it is the divine will that will be done, no matter how the pot may go astray.

The puppeteer symbol seeks to extend this basic potter image by saying that the thing made, a puppet, is the image of its maker, and the result aimed for is a story, a puppet show. The puppeteer creates his characters, dreams up his story along with them, and then makes the story happen with his own hands. When children look at the show all they see are the puppets, for the strings and hands and mouths are hidden. In much the same way God creates his characters, dreams up his story, and stands behind, hidden within, acting as the source and ruler of all.

The limitation of this symbol is obvious: pots and puppets do not have the life and mind and spirit that man does. Pots and puppets cannot object to their place, cannot ask why, cannot destroy themselves and so they cannot literally represent man in relationship to God. That is what is wrong with a completely deterministic theology: it takes this imagery too literally, not recognizing adequately that there are other important symbols that need to be combined with it if a rounded vision of God's way with us is to be gained. Above all this deterministic image provides no insight into the problem of evil, for if a puppet is useless it is wholly the puppeteer's fault.

The conclusion toward which we have been heading is now clear: the puppeteer symbol offers very significant insight into God's otherness, his power, his creativity and his role in bringing the story to its proper fulfillment. But at the same time this symbol is limited for it makes no room for man as spirit, for man as creative being, for man as the agent shaping history. Thus it must be supplemented, limited, corrected, by other symbols.

Repairman

The obvious limitation of the puppeteer symbol has led many people down through the ages to a compromise view. The Bible tells stories of God's involvement in history at particular points when he changed the course by his involvement, and this could be taken to mean that most of the time he lets man and nature go on their own way, interfering only when necessary. This theory was helped along in the Church by the growth of natural science from its Greek foundations. If some things could be explained as the result of natural processes expressed in natural law, then it did not seem possible to speak of God as doing them. Therefore God was assigned the inexplicable phenomena, the miracles, with everything else being assigned to natural causes. I suggest this is essentially a picture of God as repairman.

A repairman keeps his hands off any machine that is running well. His task is to be available for the rare occasions when the motor runs roughly or something completely fails to work. Then the repairman removes any broken parts, adjusts anything out of place, puts new parts in where needed and sends the machine on its "natural" way until he is needed again. This image does not present God as the direct cause of all events, but only of the supernatural events that change the course of history. In those events he acts with irresistible power to destroy the useless parts and to repair those that can be helped. Room is left for man's choice, for the source of evil in man's wrong choices; and yet God's overall sovereignty is not undermined.

This image is clearly related to the biblical story of God's involvement in history. We see the machine start going in Genesis 1, but when Adam and Eve cease working properly God intervenes to prevent them from completely subverting his intentions. Later he has to intervene in the flood when things get really bad, but he repairs the machine in rescuing Noah, calling Abraham, rescuing Israel in Egypt, elevating David. Gradually the machine begins to deteriorate despite the occasional intervention of prophets, so God junks most of the parts in the destruction of Jerusalem and starts over again with a rebuilt motor after the Exile. This too gradually fails so finally the grand repair takes place, for Jesus comes as a new creation. At most of these central points God's involvement is described in stories of wonders, events far beyond the normal, seemingly inexplicable in terms of the way things usually happen.

The symbol has real significance as an expression of the biblical story, but it has important limitations also. First, it squeezes God into the gaps in our knowledge, and as those gaps are filled God is further removed from history. For example, Newton's simple laws of celestial mechanics did not completely explain what was observed to happen so he said God occasionally intervened to put things back on course. Later, more complex laws were developed and God was no longer needed. A similar process took place in pointing to mysterious healing as evidence of God's intervention: today the role of psychological condition on physical health has shown that "miraculous" healings may be seen as natural psychosomatic healings.

An even greater limitation of the repairman imagery is that it cannot express the biblical image for God as everywhere, involved in all of history. He is not involved in the same way everywhere, but if he is the source of love, of creativity, of community, then he cannot adequately be imagined just as repairman. He is in addition the designer whose idea holds the whole machine together, the energy that makes it go, the order in nature that supplies the framework for the whole.

Finally, of course, the repairman image does not do justice to history as a human story, for it treats it as a mechanical operation that is entirely under the control of the repairman when he decides to intervene. Even though at other times, while it is running on its own, man can be seen as responsible agent, when the divine repairman intervenes, man and history take on machinelike characteristics. Thus this symbol stresses something significant in the biblical message, but its limitations are great enough so that it should not be taken as central.

Person

The growth of science in the modern world has led many people to believe that everything in the physical realm can in principle be explained by natural laws, leaving no room for God as the direct cause of events, even those so far unexplained. The stories of God's direct intervention in nature—Exodus and Resurrection, for example—are seen as primitive ways of expressing the "real" truth, which is that God touches man in his inner life, as a person influences another person by their mutual involvement. Many biblical stories can be presented to show that God does indeed work this way—speaking to the prophets, befriending Abraham, reaching out to people by Jesus' life and teaching.

The great advantage of this symbol over the previous two is that it makes central the deepest aspect of human life—person or spirit—and the core of the biblical experience of God—a personal, spiritual relationship with him. Throughout the Bible God is depicted talking to individuals as a man talks to his friend. His words are not overwhelming because they always leave the hearer room to speak or not to speak. Even in Jesus, united to God more closely than anyone else, we hear of his own instinctual desire to let the cup pass from him; his decision was "not my will" showing that it could indeed have been his own will if he had so chosen.

Imagining God as a person provides insight into the deep mystery of God because person, spirit and imagination are the most mysterious aspects of human experience. We do not know how influence flows from one person to another, not only when two people confront each other, but also when they are separated by centuries—as Plato, Augustine, Michelangelo and Shakespeare still influence us today. The whole realm of ideas developed by man's creative imagination can be seen as a significant source of God's involvement in history. If imagination may be divinely inspired, and if ideas are the greatest forces in history, then it is clear that God's personal involvement in human creativity offers great insight into God's role as the ruler of history.

The limitations of this symbol of God's involvement as wholly personal is that it divides man's inner life from his outer life, contradicting man's experience of being a unity. Only if man is made up of two separate parts, body and spirit, is it reasonable to suggest that God's involvement is only by means of man's spirit. But if spirit and body are two aspects of a single whole, then God's influence must reach into the whole of human life, the physical as well as the spiritual. This of course is what the biblical writers constantly assert, for they speak of God as within natural, physical phenomena (clouds, light, fire, storm) just as much as within man. His *Spirit* is a word that means wind and breath as well as inner life, a suggestion that God's involvement is in the weather, in basic animal life, as well as in human personhood.

Wisdom

The last biblical symbol for God's involvement in history given prominence in the Church is a little harder to grasp because it is more subtle: the symbol of God as the wisdom that permeates and integrates the whole universe. This suggests that God is related to the world as we are related to our bodies—intimately, completely, and spread throughout the whole as the guiding principle. In addition we are not completely confined to our bodies, for in thought and imagination we can soar to heights unknown, to other times and places; in this way our person transcends our body and is intimately involved with it.

While the early Church occasionally stressed this symbol in discussions with Greek intellectuals, it is mainly in this century in Process Theology that it has come to prominence. The basic image offered pictures all of creation as an organism in process of becoming, an organism that has mind as the heart of its process.

The biblical basis for this symbol is found in the suggestion that God's wisdom is the foundation of the world (Jer. 10:12), that his Word or reason or mind was his agent in creation (John 1:1–5) providing the order and integration for the whole of reality. Then further, of course, God's wisdom and Word enlighten mankind, to provide all the understanding exhibited by great men (Prov.). We usually think of wisdom or mind as simply an attribute or capability within, but both the Old and New Testaments speak of God's wisdom and Word going out from him, forming the world, sustaining it, enabling those who receive it, filling them with God's own mind.

Thus God's mind penetrates and undergirds everything but is supremely expressed in man, in particular in those who are open to receive God's gifts.

This symbol for God as the wisdom or mind of the universe has great significance and value as a way to express the biblical insight that God is intimately involved in human history. First, it allows no division between man's inner and outer selves, between spirit and nature, for it suggests that God is the inner power and guiding spirit in nature as well as in man. This expresses the biblical writers' view that God is the master of nature as well as the natural sovereign of man. Second, this view suggests how God's guidance in human lives takes place, because it sees man's mind as a reflection of the divine Mind; therefore communication between them can be instantaneous, not blocked by the need for external signs that are the only ways human minds can communicate. Finally, it provides ample emphasis on the mystery of God and his ways with man, for our minds are profoundly mysterious and can well symbolize God as the unseen depths, the ultimate influence, the order and mind pervading everything.

Naturally this symbol has its limitations (which its advocates often overlook). Its most important limitation is that it does not adequately express the biblical insistence on the otherness, the apartness of God. Our minds are completely integrated with our bodies, thus "no body, no mind," but the biblical view is that God's reality is not inevitably tied to the universe he has made. Second, this symbol does not adequately stress the experience of a personal relationship between man and God, for the difference between God and man is necessarily underplayed when we think of the unity of mind and body. Finally, while this symbol expresses well God's continuous involvement in the world it does not leave much room for his intervention in history at particular times and places. Thus this symbol like the other three has considerable value, but must be seen as one symbol among others because it too has limitations.

Conclusion

The four symbols just presented all have profound roots in biblical stories, all thus can be called biblical. But over the centuries of the Church's life they have each come to prominence at one time or another and were held as the central symbol, perhaps even held literally. In the Middle Ages God's absolute control as puppeteer was the dominant view, due to the influence of Augustine. Later, when the significance of scientific explanation was recognized, the repairman symbol of occasional interference was emphasized as a compromise with science. In the nineteenth century, with the rise of the theory that science can explain everything in the physical world, the symbol for God as person—working only in man's inner personal life—was presented as a way to accept both science and God. Now in the twentieth century the view has arisen that nature is not a determined machine but a living organism and so a different symbolism, God as the Mind of the universe, has been stressed.

At the present time all four of these symbols are used by different groups and writers as their central understanding of how God is related to the world. Many take their symbol literally, oblivious to its limitations, providing most of the debate about God found within the Church. A more appropriate view is to see that all four of these symbols have something of value to express if we wish to convey the biblical message today. But they all also have limitations, which become obvious when we put them together. Therefore we ought to put them together, letting each make its contribution. Then we will not fall into the trap of taking one literally and so distorting a great deal of the biblical message. As a guide to the way we can put these four symbols together we can look finally at the symbol *author.*

Author

In a number of significant ways the symbol for God as the Author of History, a drama in process of unfolding, provides an integration of many of the central points made by the four symbols just discussed but without all of their limitations. Naturally it has its own limitations, which will have to be pointed out, but it may well be an integrating symbol that can provide a starting point for interpreting the other four just described.

Characters and Actors

Let us think of the author of a play that is in the process of production, the author being involved in the production but not in complete control of it. Earlier in this chapter we suggested a number of the ways in which the author is related to the play, taking Dorothy Sayers's expression of her own experience as the evidence. Now we shall summarize that relationship and go on to point out what this suggests about God's authorship of our story.

Miss Sayers says first that while the author's idea is the inner reality coming to expression, thus the story in his story, yet he does not experience himself as absolute master of his material. Rather he sees himself as its servant, loving it in a caring way, not in a possessive way, trying to bring it to its own independence. Here the author is much like a father. Perhaps we can see our heavenly father as in some ways like this too: it is his idea that is being carried out in our history, but the way it is being developed is in a loving, fathering, guiding way, not by the hammering coercion that a blacksmith uses on horseshoes. It would not be surprising to find that one who called his sons to reflect him in service to others, and expressed himself ultimately in One who gave himself up to death for others, was an author seeking to serve rather than to master.

A significant aspect of the author's service of his characters is that he does not coerce them, but helps them to develop in their own way. When the author has allowed a character to develop in its own direction right out of the story, then the play will break down if he is arbitrarily coerced back into line. The actors will sense that the jump is poor writing and so the story will not have its intended effect. By analogy God too allows his characters to develop in their own direction, not overwhelming them because that would undermine the story that he is telling. Like an author he works with his characters, trying to influence and mold them so that they make a contribution to his story. But if in the end they fail to fit, they may have to be discarded.

The influence of the author on his play can be imagined in thinking of the actors speaking his lines while the author listens with the opportunity to comment. They are his lines, it is his play, but the actors and the director have their own choices to make on how they will play it. The author can discuss, suggest, tell what he meant, but the play will be done the way the players choose. Likewise our history is a story God has laid out, but the players choose their own way to act, to read their lines, to express themselves. The given lines and the author's presence are influential, but not absolutely decisive in the short run. In the long run, of course, the story will come out as the author intends, even though in the short run it may go astray.

The author of this ongoing drama of history has the advantage that the author of a serial has: in the next episode he can write in lines to modify an interpretation already given, or he can remove the character completely. But here again this cannot be done arbitrarily, for if the serial is to reveal something significant it must stay within the bounds laid down by the basic idea of the play. If God's idea is to develop sons who independently love him and so reflect him, then the course of the play must make that possible.

How the play makes that possible depends on the author's understanding of reality, and while he may do things that seem unreal or impossible to some actors it may well be that that is precisely the point of the whole play.

C. S. Lewis in his classic *Miracles* stresses this point in speaking of the propriety of God's action in history. We may think that the incarnation, death and resurrection of Jesus as described in the New Testament are arbitrary breakings of the laws by which God has designed the universe. But in reality they are the deepest order of all, the laws undergirding everything, and revealing them in Jesus was precisely the idea behind the whole story the author is telling. Lewis says: "If they have occurred, they have occurred because they are the very thing this universal story is about. They are not exceptions (however rarely they occur) nor irrelevancies. They are precisely those chapters in this great story on which the plot turns. Death and Resurrection are what the story is about."

Autobiography and Trinity

In particular the central event, God's coming in human form as a Galilean carpenter, can be seen as the author's autobiography. Miss Sayers stresses a number of significant insights to be gained by seeing the Incarnation this way. First, this actor in the play is like others, fitting in with all the conditions under which they live, yet he is unique in being the author's direct self-expression. He is thus a unique combination of author and character, being really both. But of course this character cannot express all that the author is, only what he deems significant to be conveyed. But if the author has imagined and written well, then his presence in the play will provide the key to interpreting the whole. When we wish to know what the idea in the author's mind is we will go first to his autobiographical act, and then read the rest of the play in the light of that. In all these ways Jesus can helpfully be thought of as God's appearance as a character in his own play.

With any play there is always the possibility of corruption, in particular the refusal of actors to play the part as the author intended. Even though the author may appear as a character the other actors may refuse to recognize him and interpret their lines and roles in accordance with the key provided. The trouble comes that others may wish to play author, to make their lines or roles different, and that leads to distortion of the Idea and the story itself. So also men try to play God, to rearrange reality to suit their own whims and desires, with a similar effect upon history.

Finally, to crown this analogy between the creative mind of the dramatist and the role of the author of history, we can valuably hear Miss Sayers's symbolization of the trinity, which is the thesis of *The Mind of the Maker.* She suggests that in the author's work there are three intertwined but distinguishable realities: there is first the idea that is the source of everything, hidden deep in the author's mind; but then this idea may be expressed in creative activity—the thinking out of the story, writing it down and presenting it in a communicable form; then finally, when the play is read or acted it exhibits a power to touch people, to enlighten them, to influence them, to motivate them.

The idea is completely unseen, unknown except through the visible written work and its effect. The activity is observable, its result can be seen in a script. The power can only be experienced, but it is tied completely to the observable work, being its effect on those who hear the story. The idea is a symbol of the unseen Father, the Source of everything. The activity is a symbol of the Son, the historical, observable expression of the invisible Father. The power is a symbol of the Spirit, which is the continuing effect of the Son on the world. The three together make up the Author, his vision, its expression, and its effect, each distinguishable in thought but inseparable in reality.

With this final creative trinity we have offered a somewhat different symbol for the Son than suggested in previous paragraphs. Here it is the author's whole activity, his complete writings, that are offered as a symbol interpreting Jesus' relationship to his Father. Previously Jesus' story was symbolized as the author's autobiography, his putting himself forward as one character within his play. We do not have to choose between these symbols, they are both valuable, but for different purposes. The Son as the expression of the idea is a way to imagine the trinity. The Son as the Father's autobiography is a way to understand the relationship of Jesus to the whole of history.

Plus and Minus

God as the Author of History is a symbol that provides significant insight into the whole of God's way with the world, summarizing many of the valuable intuitions of the other symbols described above. First, like the puppeteer it expresses the transcendence and power of God. An author is revealed to some extent in his writings, but he far transcends them, for he is something of quite another order of reality than a story. He is the source of his writings, their master in one sense, yet unlike the puppeteer he is creating independent characters, not marionettes dancing at the end of his fingers. Thus author overcomes the chief limitation of puppeteer—that it does not leave room for the human experience of responsibility.

Like the repairman symbol author too suggests the way recalcitrant characters may be guided toward the end result that makes for the best play. In particular, when we think of an author at play rehearsal, making comments and offering interpretations at particular points we have an expression of the biblical pointing to special events as God's action. Yet the author underlies everything and so does not have the limitations of the repairman image—that God seems to be absent when all goes well.

The strength of the person image is that it allows for constant human responsibility and for a personal involvement of man with God. The actors in a play have the responsibility of interpretation and expression, and can work out how best to do it in conversation with the author. The person image is limited in not providing any emphasis on the great difference between God and man, but an author decidedly transcends his characters as acted on stage, for he gave them life, provides for their story and has a full human life that a character in a play can only symbolize, not equal.

Finally, like a pervasive mind the author too has a role in all that takes place on the stage. He dreams up the settings, provides descriptions of the colors and objects and shapes and sizes that will then come into existence at his word. The author's mind in fact permeates everything, providing the basic idea, the outworking of the script, the integration of the whole and guidance for interpretation where needed. In addition, however, author as a symbol does not have the limitation of mind, which is its virtual imprisonment in the body, the play. Mind does transcend body, somewhat, but it does not begin to express the extraordinary otherness of God over the world that author-play expresses.

In many ways therefore we can see that author, a symbol that combines two major biblical symbols, Creator and Ruler, is an immensely significant symbol for expressing the biblical understanding of God's relationship to the world. But it remains a symbol. It has its particular limitations, among which are the following: author may not be felt by many people to be close to their experience, so it is a symbol with less than universal personal impact, because many do not feel within themselves what it is like to be an author. All of us probably have written letters, and many of us have made up stories to tell, so we do have an intuition of its meaning; but we look upon authors as people we do not know and so this symbol may at first be largely intellectual rather than personal for many.

Any reader who desires to overcome this experience barrier can do so by reading Robert Coover's novel *The Universal Baseball Association, J. Henry Waugh, Prop.* The UBA is a league imagined and created by Henry Waugh, played with dice on his kitchen table. The players come to be real people at times, the novel moving back and forth between Henry's dull life and the multiple lives of his players. Though they are all his inventions they have a life of their own, with batting averages and winning seasons and success and failure. The climax of the story comes when Henry's favorite player, a young star pitcher, is killed by a batted ball (which is the result of three consecutive throws of triple sixes on the dice). The analogy of Henry Waugh, the creator and proprietor of the UBA to God the Creator and Ruler of the world is the fascinating thought that gives this novel its central importance for any Christian trying to imagine God as the Author of History. By reading this novel we can overcome some of our lack of acquaintance with the experience of a creator-author.

Second, the relationship of author to character is considerably more loaded on the author's side than is the biblical expression of God's power over man. Man really experiences himself as responsible for his choices but we have to see it as much less normal for a character to run away from the author. Even when we are talking about an actor we have to imagine the extreme case of one who refuses to speak the lines given to him, but develops the character as he wants. In the theater actors normally conform too much to the author's words and intentions to be quite accurate as representations of how man deals with the "lines" given him by his "author."

Thus God as the Author of History is a significant symbol for summarizing much that other symbols say and for pointing to deeper insights not available in other symbols. If its limitations are remembered, so that it is always used in conjunction with other symbols that provide significant corrections (e.g., love), then it can be a valuable starting-point for imagining how God is involved in the ongoing human drama of history.

Conclusion

The goal of this chapter has been to continue our understanding of the biblical witness to God by seeing the symbols that have been suggested for imagining God's involvement in history, a central biblical thesis. As a foundation for that we continued our exploration of human experience, for it is human experience that the Bible uses to symbolize God. In particular we saw the central role that imagination and choice of ultimate allegiance have in the making of individual life and the history of the race, suggesting how we can begin to think of God's role as the ruler of that history. On the basis of that understanding of human experience we were then able to consider the four symbols for God that have been taken as central in Christian thinking of God and history. We saw that each truly expresses some of the biblical witness but in addition has significant limitations. Thus our final suggestion was that the symbol *author* is the least inadequate of those available to us, for it says much of what the others say, but with fewer limitations. One of its limitations is, however, that it does not adequately suggest man's rebellion, nor God's response, the subject to which we now turn.

Suggested Reading

Birch, L. C. *Nature and God.* Philadelphia: Westminster, 1965.

Coover, Robert. *The Universal Baseball Association, Inc., J. Henry Waugh, Prop.* New York: Random House, 1968.

Danielou, J. *The Lord of History.* London: Longmans, 1958.

Dewart, L. *The Future of Belief.* New York: Herder, 1966.

Haroutunian, J. *God with Us.* Philadelphia: Westminster, 1965.

Lewis, C. S. *Miracles.* London: Macmillan, 1947.

Oman, J. *Grace and Personality.* Cambridge: Cambridge University Press, 1917.

Sayers, Dorothy L. *The Mind of the Maker.* New York: Harcourt, 1941.

Chapter Four: Rebellion and Reprisal

Introduction: "Three Boys on a Tightrope"

The Tightrope

PRESSURE

INFERIORITY

INSECURITY

IT WAS GOOD

Rebellion

PRIDE OF PERSON

JOINING THE ANIMALS

WILL TO POWER

CONCLUSION

Reprisal

GUILTY FACADES

DEFENSIVE BLINDNESS

ALIENATION

SLAVERY

CONCLUSION: "THE KING'S STATUE"

Chapter Four

Rebellion and Reprisal

Introduction: "Three Boys on a Tightrope"

Once upon a time three boys climbed up on a high wire to learn the rudiments of tightrope walking. They were circus children, sons of high-wire artists, and this was the day the master had offered to begin their education. The high wire team was the crown jewel of the circus, its members being the lords of all they surveyed. They were heaped with honors, found great meaning in what they did to awe and entertain, and were exhilarated by the excitement of their calling. So their sons were first in line to try out as apprentices, for no calling could be greater.

The practice wire was set up outside, about ten feet above the ground so that no fall would be disastrous. On the right-hand side of the wire was the paddock where the circus horses ate and slept and occasionally fought and were molded into a team that was totally under the control of the trainer. On the left-hand side was the practice wrestling pit, where each wrestler tried to gain dominance over the rest but found that a winning streak made him a special target. Above the wire, to the left, was a walkway where the master moved along with his learners, holding out a pole to them to help them keep steady.

The three boys got up on the wire together, with two short poles hooked to the belts between the middle one and each of the other two. These poles enabled them to help each other, to gain stability by standing together, but the poles could be unhooked from their belts if they wanted to get loose. In addition the master held out a pole that one or another could grasp to keep them firmly on the wire.

As they start out they have a feeling of confidence, because they have seen others walk easily much higher and without the support they have. But soon they begin to wobble, for they start looking down at the ground and worry what it would be like to fall. Knowing this the master calls out, "Don't look at the ground. Keep your eyes on the wire." But just as he says that they find they look more at the ground than before and become afraid. They see all at once that it is not easy, that they are really inferior to this master above them. Worse still they see that they are terribly insecure, that any one of them could fall from fright and drag the others down. To those feelings of insecurity and inferiority they react in different ways.

The first says to himself, "I'll show I don't need his support or his instructions. If I just escape the tie to those clumsy elephants behind me I'll be fine." So he unhooks the pole connecting him to the boy behind, rejects the master's support and steps out boastfully on his own. The result is inevitable: after five quick steps he finds he cannot balance himself. He falls down on the wire, hanging on barely by his fingers and his crossed feet. Now he is alone.

The second boy responds quite differently to the same feeling of inferiority and insecurity. He decides that the goal is not worth the struggle, that the tightrope artist's exhilaration and honor are not worth the cost of learning to live with and conquer these feelings. So he looks for an escape and sees it in the paddock: along with the horses there are a few men and boys sleeping in the hay, living much like the animals—day by day satisfying their most pressing needs, working for the circus in the jobs requiring no experience or concentration. The second boy gives up the goal of joining the high-wire team by jumping down into the paddock hay and joining the animal life there.

The third boy decided on a third way to escape the feelings of inferiority and insecurity that swelled up in him. He decided to pull himself up to the master's walkway, to show him that he will sit under no one's thumb. So he grasps the master's pole as tightly as he can, jumps up pulling on the pole and trying to swing himself up to the master's place. But as he pulls, the pole is jerked out of the master's hand and the boy falls from his place on high down into the wrestlers' pit where people like him who want to fight to get to the top can get all the fighting they want.

The tightrope is the human condition—the way man exists in the world caught between his animal life bound to the earth and his spirit that soars. The choices the three boys made are some of the major forms of human rebellion, attempts to escape their precarious calling. The results of these attempted escapes depict the reprisal that God has designed to fall inevitably upon those who refuse to live the life that has been given to them. Each of these central issues of human life in God's world will now be examined.

The Tightrope

Our previous discussion of the nature of man stressed the unique situation in which man finds himself: he is a body, bound to the earth, an animal among animals; yet he is an enspirited body, a person, one who transcends himself by imagination and self-consciousness. On the one hand, he is of the earth and may decide to live as other animals do by concentrating only on satisfying his immediate desires, for food, sex, self-preservation. On the other hand, he may take his earth-transcending aspect as the whole story, and then he may try to escape his animal life, his dependence, trying to become the Master himself, either by going his own way or by trying to take the Master's place. Whichever road he takes, the initial impetus to it is found in the natural human condition itself. But this condition is only an impetus, not a predetermining cause. Therefore, pointing out the inherent tension in human life, the tightrope man finds himself on, is not an explanation of why he chooses to rebel; it is simply a help in seeing why there is a certain reasonableness in his really irrational rejection of the life God has given him.

Pressure

Man's basic condition includes internal pressure from his passions and instincts, and also external constraint imposed by his environment. He finds that his body demands to be fed, and when it is not, all other questions are largely driven from his mind until food is found and the inexorable demands of the body satisfied. He finds that when he is threatened, feeling danger, his organism reacts to preserve itself, either by escape when that is possible, or by fighting. And sexual instincts cannot be ignored, for they provide their own pressure, seek their own outlets, breaking down any flimsy barriers set in their way. These are the internal pressures of man's body, a condition he shares with the other animals, a situation he cannot escape.

But in addition to these internal pressures—instincts seeking outlets, demanding action—man also lives in communities which provide external, i.e., social, restraints. He forms communities in order to satisfy his animal needs for food, protection and sexual partnership, but he finds that the community provides as much tension as it relieves. At the core of any community is a set of laws, the regulating conditions of communal life. While these do help in providing food, protection and sexual order they do this by damming up some of the instinctual behavior in these areas. Food cannot simply be taken whenever found. Killing a threatening neighbor cannot be allowed. Promiscuous sexual behavior will not go unchecked. Thus the community is a necessity in order to help satisfy man's animal needs, but it does this by stifling them to a certain extent, trying to arrange a compromise between the desired results (food, protection, sex) and the original instinctual demand.

Many writers have seen this tension between society and individual needs as the explanation for the evil man does. Rousseau and the romantics believed that in the state of nature man is good, that only social institutions have made him bad. Marx agreed, pointing specifically to the capitalist economic system in industrial nations and arguing that abolition of that system would make men so good that government could wither away. Freud too emphasized this general view: he believed that man's basic problem is that his natural instincts (in the id) are thwarted by social inhibitions (in the superego) so that the instincts are repressed from consciousness and are allowed to rule man's life subconsciously.

There can be little doubt that a significant aspect of the tightrope on which man stands is the pressure of his instincts coming into conflict with his social needs. There is no escaping this tension, for it is inherent in the human condition created by God. Bolitho described this condition imaginatively when he said in *Twelve against the Gods:* "We like the eagles were born to be free. Yet we are obliged, in order to live at all, to make a cage of laws for ourselves and to stand on the perch. We are born as wasteful and unremorseful as tigers; we are obliged to be thrifty, or starve or freeze. We are born to wander, and cursed to stay and dig." The condition is inherent, but our response to it is not predetermined, as we shall suggest below.

INFERIORITY

A second aspect of the human condition, the way man came from the hand of God, can be labeled "inferiority." This is not an "inferiority complex," a denigration of the self so that action is paralyzed. Rather it is a fact recognized by everyone: there are realities more powerful than he is. Initially this fact is recognized in contact with nature: the wave does not stop when King Canute tells it to; the hurricane does not notice the human beings it destroys; the elephant will always be stronger than any human being. On his own, man is puny, weak, almost helpless against the forces of nature. Only when he gets together with others, and begins to create machines, does he begin to alleviate some of that weakness.

But these new sources of strength turn out to be further comments on his inferiority, for if there is strength in numbers then the individual sees himself as inferior to the group. If machines can give man undreamed of strengths and abilities, they also make him aware of his inability to think as fast as a computer or work as hard as a jackhammer. So he stresses that these machines are offshoots of his brain so that he is really superior to them in one way. But he has quickly come to see that technology can become his master, a force gathering momentum and ready to obliterate him at any moment.

The more man has learned, the smaller he has felt, the more ignorant he has recognized he is. With every advance in knowledge of the universe man's infinitesimal place in it became more and more apparent. With every secret uncovered in nature two previously unrecognized questions are raised so that nature's secrets keep increasing day by day. Every year as we discover more and more about the ways social groups and individuals operate we recognize how deep the mysteries of human life really are.

Most of all, anyone who has opened his eyes to the realities that impinge upon him recognizes that the universe as a whole is beyond his understanding, let alone his control. We can ask where it came from and why it is but we can only enter more deeply thereby into a mystery that engulfs us. As we stand beneath a starry sky, or watch a baby grow into a child and more, or meditate on the origins of life, we know we are inferior in many ways to what surrounds us.

Perhaps our greatest source of inferiority recognition is in our imagination which dreams of many things that might be, but never are because we have not done what we could. We know that many different pathways are open to us, but we cannot take them all. In our dreams we can have fifty different careers but in reality only a few. Our reality is inferior to our imagined possibilities, and always will be as long as we continue to imagine. Our inferiority is inherent because life is short, we are going to die, we cannot do everything we wish.

Insecurity

The reality of death toward which we are getting closer every day not only accents our inferiority but provides for basic insecurity in our lives. This does not mean we necessarily feel insecure any more than we necessarily feel inferior. Rather it is simply a statement that we *are* insecure, that we cannot count on being alive tomorrow. We *do* count on being alive tomorrow; however, in fact, most of us count on being alive to the average age at death for our sex and nation. But when we put our mind to it we know that our lives are precarious and can be snuffed out at any time by accident, disease or violence.

The facts of life are that we may not be around to finish what we have started—a college education, a child's upbringing, a house, a painting. When we become involved with another person we cannot know how long we have, for the other may be dead before we have reached the limits of our possibilities together. What shall we do? Take a chance or hold back? We will never know until it is too late, so our central decisions are seasoned with the inherent insecurity of our mortal condition.

A further complication in this insecurity of death is that it puts to question any answers we give to the meaning of life. Like all the animals, man dies; but unlike them he seeks for meaning while he lives and cannot escape the tension of these two aspects of life as long as he wishes to remain human. The meaning of life simply is not apparent, it cannot be uncovered by using the right techniques. Man's search for meaning cannot be satisfied as his hunger and his sexual drives can be, because the search is an ongoing attempt to see the depths of life despite the surface incoherencies that no one can miss.

Together with the insecurity inherent in our having to die, and in the lack of certainty in our search for meaning, we must see the insecurity inherent in individuality. I am I and not you, and I know it. I know that I do not see as you see and speak as you speak, so I am never sure how close our contact can be. Even when two people have lived together for fifty years, if they are alert they will continue to discover the gap between them. For all the other people in our lives the gap is yawning, for no one really understands what I am feeling, striving for, imagining, dreaming. In a very significant way we recognize that we are alone and that accentuates our insecurity.

We *are* insecure, whether we feel it or not. A central fact of human existence is that our place is shaky because of the threat of death, the yawning possibility of meaninglessness, and the reality of our aloneness, our separation from everyone else by the fact of our identity, "I am I." This insecurity cannot be escaped, for it is inherent in the human condition, but there is no inherent necessity that it lead to disaster.

It Was Good

Even though man's natural condition is one of pressure, inferiority and insecurity, still it is good in God's eyes. God created man to be the link between himself and the rest of creation, so man had to be an animal as well as an angel. If he were only an animal, not knowing the difference between good and evil, then he would be innocent but unable to relate to God personally and rule the world for God. Yet man's likeness to God in knowing good and evil provides fertile soil for sin to grow. The connection between the soil and the growth is mysterious, but the reality of the connection is clear.

"Coming of Age"

The jungle of eastern Borneo is a strange place to think of as paradise, but it was that to the infant boy and girl who later were named Abnah and Emmah. At first they had no names, at least names that they knew about, for they were jungle babies. Their tribe of ten families, living primitively in the heart of the jungle, had fled a forest fire and mistakenly left the two infants behind when they were both less than a year old. Fortunately the fire missed the spot where they had been lost, and even more fortunately they were found by a chimpanzee band and were adopted by two mothers.

The two children grew up as chimpanzees, not knowing any other kind of life. They wore no clothes, ate the roots and berries their family gathered, learned to use the trees as their highway, and learned to imitate the grunts they heard around them. They were as happy as chimpanzees, for that is what they were.

This paradise remained their home until age thirteen when the crash interrupted it. One day a hard, shiny, burning rock fell out of the sky and above it floated down a figure who seemed strangely familiar. It was a pilot whose plane had lost power over the jungle and who had bailed out. He landed in the treetops not far from the chimpanzee band, and the boy and girl went and helped him down out of the trees. Of course they could not converse immediately, but before long the pilot had begun to teach them to speak, and inevitable changes overtook them unnoticed.

The greatest change crept over them when the pilot said one day, "It is not right for you to live here in the jungle. It is wrong for human beings to live like animals." The words *right* and *wrong* introduced them to a world that ended their innocence. Gradually they could no longer live by their instincts and the practical methods of a chimpanzee band.

The young pair were exhilarated by learning to talk, to think, to know right from wrong, but their new knowledge inevitably brought trouble in its wake. Instead of the strongest ruling naturally, as among chimpanzees, questions had to be discussed about what was right: along with love they learned of hate; along with rights they learned of domination; instead of the naturalness of a boy and girl living unashamed in nakedness they learned of shame and secrecy and competition for affection.

The end came when the pilot decided it was time to try to find civilization. He told his two young friends of all the wonders of the world outside, especially wanting to talk Emmah, as he had named her, into coming with him as his guest. But Abnah had learned jealousy with his language and decided to go with them also.

As they traveled, the conflict among them gradually became more and more intense until a fight broke out between the two men on the edge of a cliff. The pilot slipped while they were struggling and barely hung on at the edge of the cliff. Abnah stepped up to him and stamped down hard on his fingers, bruising his own heel but making the pilot fall to his death on the rocks below. Then Abnah and Emmah continued the journey that they had begun: paradise was left behind, they had now joined civilization.

Rebellion

If God created man to walk the tightrope between himself and the rest of the animal world then man's refusal to do so is rebellion. Previously we pictured man's refusal to accept his tightrope as taking at least three different forms: he refuses to accept the Master's offered hand and the support of his neighbors, attempting to go alone to show he needs no one; a second possibility is that he may join the animal world, refusing to accept his spiritual potential;

finally he may strive for power, trying to equal the Master.

The heart of the story is the conviction that the tightrope walkers really have a choice, that their responses to their precarious situation are not forced upon them. The biblical emphasis upon man's responsibility to choose his basic attitude toward life is the key to the picture. Jesus' walk on the tightrope even at the cost of his life is a sign of God's intention for man and the possibility put before him. One choice will keep us in our place as the lords of the circus —the decision to serve and depend on the Master and our brothers with us on the high wire. Any other choice is rebellion, the prelude to disaster. But mankind has always made one of the other choices.

Pride of Person

The first apprentice high wire artist in our story responded to the pressure, the insecurity and the realization of inferiority by attempting to deny them. His response was to unlock himself from his neighbor, reject his master's support and try to walk alone unsupported. His major impetus is refusal to accept his inferiority, his need for help from others. Instead of seeing his inferiority as a possibility he takes it as a threat and tries to overcome it by a bold self-assertion. He is the individualist, the man of intellectual and moral pride who believes that he stands above the crowd, needing no one.

The beginning of this boy's rebellion is in his false conclusion that physical, intellectual and experiential inferiority mean personal inferiority, that he is of less value than others. It does not. But the mistake is an easy one to make. Thomas Harris in *I'm OK—You're OK* says the conclusion in the child that "I'm small and weak so I'm not OK, not valuable" is universal and thus the prelude to many actions taken to try to feel valuable.

The action taken by our individualist is a denial not only of the false conclusion—"I am not valuable"—but also a denial of the true premise—"I am dependent, I cannot stand alone." There are many ways we can work out this decision but in the Bible there are two basic forms that stand out—the legalist and the nationalist. The legalist is a man who believes that by himself he can obey the law, can pull himself up to the perfection God desires. This is moral pride, a conviction that we do not need God's forgiveness or his spiritual power because we can make it on our own. If we think we can perfect ourselves then we find no need to depend on others, to become involved in the caring and sharing of communal life, so our moral pride produces a lack of love. Like some of the Pharisees we do the external deeds that can be seen, but our hearts are "curved inward upon ourselves," as Luther said.

The pride of the nationalist was denounced by Isaiah when the king of Judah believed that the nation did not need God's guidance and strength but could survive and prosper on her own. Involved in this is intellectual pride, the foolish conviction that we can see ahead into the unknown and can gain our desires without trusting in the Author of our story. In order to overcome our feelings of personal lack of value we boost ourselves on high, fooling ourselves and so believing that we really are what we have dreamed.

Finally, and perhaps the most basic of all, is the assertion of freedom. Dependence on the Master and the other apprentices may seem like prison, a denial of freedom, so some people may burst out simply to try to be free. Dostoevsky elaborated on this choice in *Memoirs from Underground:* "Man loves to act as he *likes,* and not necessarily as reason and self-interest would have him do. Yes, he will even act straight against his own interests. Indeed, he is sometimes *bound* to do so. Such, at least, is my notion of the matter. His own will, free and unfettered; his own untutored whims; his own fancies, sometimes amounting almost to a madness—here we have that superadded interest of interests which enters into no classification, which for ever consigns systems and theories to the devil." Our imagination may lead us to envision a greater freedom than the one that God intends for us, and so we reject his gift, try to grasp independence, and find, as we shall see, that we lose out in the end.

One significant way of rebellion is thus the attempt to walk alone, to deny dependence, to boast of our individual superiority. It may take the form of moral pride in the Church, someone boasting of his own achievements, refusing close involvements. It may be intellectual pride, not only in the man with intellectual achievements to his credit, but in anyone who holds himself better than others and ignores his debt to all from whom he learned. Most puzzling and terrifying of all it may be pride of freedom, the boast "I can do anything I want, I do not need your society, your laws, your help." Whichever form the rebellion takes it leads to personal disaster, which will be depicted later in the chapter.

Joining the Animals

The second apprentice tightrope walker took a different route to escape the pressure, inferiority and insecurity of his position. He abandoned his high potential, jumping down to the paddock to join the animals and the circus bums who lived like animals. Instead of accepting the tension between inner pressure and outer constraint he abandoned himself to one or the other, either to sensual indulgence in animal passions, or to conformity to social demands and loss of individuality. Instead of recognizing his inferiority in some respects as a necessity for his place in the universe, he takes it as the full story of his life and forgets about his high potential. Finally, instead of living with the insecurity inherent in human life he seeks the security of the earth, of the animal life or the mass-man life, abandoning his responsibility and creativity.

We may join the animals first of all by taking our inner impulses as the great standards of life. Self-preservation and its needs for food and shelter may become the center of life. Viktor Frankl saw how this happened to many people in concentration camps: "On the average only those prisoners could keep alive who, after years of trekking from camp to camp, had lost all scruples in their fight for existence; they were prepared to use every means, honest or otherwise, even brutal force, theft and betrayal of their friends, in order to save themselves" *(Man's Search for Meaning).* In the world outside the camps the same choice has been made by those who live for sensual pleasure alone, seeking food and drink, sexual exploits, pleasures of any kind, constrained only by the pain imposed by society or coming out of their own bodies.

A second form of abandonment of potential seems quite the opposite but is in reality quite similar—abdication of responsibility to a group with which we identify. Communism provides the most extreme recent example, described for example by Arthur Koestler in *Darkness at Noon:* "In a struggle one must have both legs firmly planted on the earth. The Party taught one how to do it. The infinite was a politically suspect quantity, the 'I' a suspect quality. The Party did not recognize its existence. The definition of the individual was: a multitude of one million divided by one million." The crowd is the reality, the individual loses his individuality in it in order not to experience the insecurity of responsibility. He becomes the soldier who knows nothing and does not want to know anything.

Down through history religion has been the chief mass in which man has sought to lose himself. The Grand Inquisitor in Dostoevsky's *The Brothers Karamazov* knew this when he said to Christ returned to the earth: "I tell you that man is tormented by no greater anxiety than to find someone quickly to whom he can hand over that gift of freedom with which that ill-fated creature was born" for "man prefers peace, and even death, to freedom of choice in the knowledge of good and evil." Modern Americans by the millions would probably scoff at such an idea but the Grand Inquisitor knows that full well: "today, people are more persuaded than ever that they have perfect freedom, yet they have brought their freedom to us and laid it humbly at our feet." In the United States today *us* is not necessarily the Church, but may be the masters of the economy, the executives in advertising, teachers in the great universities and the manipulators of the mass media. For millions the security provided by these modern "priests" is all that is desired, so individuality and creativity and imagination are abandoned.

Possibly this choice—to join the animals in sensuality or conformity (or both)—is the most common form of rebellion. Materialism and the desperate need for community approval are its most often-mentioned examples today but the lives of "quiet desperation" lived by millions are common also. In substance this rebellion is a failure of nerve, an abandonment of confidence in oneself and the potential God gave us. It takes our natural insecurity as an absolute threat and so seeks security at the price of humanity. The irony of it all is that it is not security we find, but simply blindness to our continuing insecurity.

Will to Power

The third apprentice tightrope walker took another way out of the position of inferiority, insecurity, and tension in which he found himself. He attempted to grasp for equality with the master, to abandon the high wire for the even higher walkway; but he too fell. This boy symbolizes the attempt of many people to grasp for power, to rule over other people, to reject their own inferiority and try to hide it by showing themselves superior to others. Not all people who work for positions of power in government, industry, education and the church are acting in this way for it is possible to work for power as a means to serve others. However, many people may start seeking to serve and find that power corrupts their motivations so they cling to it for its own sake. Others fool themselves and others into believing they seek to serve when in reality they seek the ego boost that domination of others brings. In fact such deception is common among the powerful, for as John Adams once remarked, "Power always thinks it has a great soul."

While reaching for political power in a democracy must be camouflaged as serving the people, there are many other types of government and many other power systems within a democracy in which people can grasp for power as a way to overcome their inferiority. A child may rule over his younger siblings or over neighbor children. A bully in school, or the leader of a gang, or an ambitious executive may all provide their own examples. Parents can relish power over children, as ministers and teachers may bask in their opportunities to manipulate others. It might even be close to the truth to suggest that everyone at one time or another, in one situation or another, tries to lord it over someone else, boosting himself up by standing on top of others.

Most people, however, never reach the extreme expressed by Nietzsche when he said, "I couldn't bear to think that there were gods and I wasn't one." That word became political flesh in the Nazi and Stalinist parties and is depicted in its ultimate logic in George Orwell's *1984:* "The Party seeks power entirely for its own sake. We are not interested in the good of others: we are interested solely in power. . . . We are different from all the oligarchies of the past in that we know what we are doing. All the others, even those who resembled ourselves, were cowards and hypocrites. The German Nazis and the Russian Communists . . . never had the courage to recognize their own motives. They pretended, perhaps they even believed, that they had seized power unwillingly and for a limited time, and that just around the corner there lay a paradise where human beings would be free and equal. We are not like that. We know that no one ever seizes power with the intention of relinquishing it. Power is not a means; it is an end . . . God is power." Here is a clear expression of the attempt to play God.

The temptation to grasp for power is found in the human situation itself. Our position is insecure, death does confront us, so we may try to make a name that will endure, or to build pyramids that will give us "life" after we die, or we may grasp for power to fend off threatening forces as long as we can. We recognize our inferiority as well as our superiority to many other forms of life, and so may be tempted to get as high up the ladder as we can, so we can think better of ourselves and be more comfortable within. Almost all power is seductive, for it makes us think that we are bigger than we are, more alive because our strength is greater, more able to fulfill our animal needs for food, sex and safety. Once we begin to play the game of power-grabbing we become addicted, for we deceive ourselves into believing that life really is a power struggle in which you win or lose; thus we lose sight of the possibility that life is intended to be a cooperative task in which everyone may "win" because loving relationships are the highest goal.

Conclusion

The three apprentices rejected their master's instructions in different ways, one trying to stand alone, another trying to lose himself in the mass of animal life, the third seeking to take the master's place. Some people fall quite clearly into one of these three categories of rebellion, but many others exhibit more complex combinations. For example some people, like the Roman aristocracy, grasp for power in order to be able to indulge themselves in their passions. Others, like good party members, or good patriots, lose their individuality in their strong party or nation so they can identify with the power dominance of their group. Many other combinations are possible, all of them emphasizing that man's rebellion against God can take a multitude of different forms. The three basic forms presented here are thus a beginning suggestion and by no means an exhaustive description.

Whatever the path taken, the biblical proclamation is that all men have walked down into this valley into the depths of sin. This view is tersely summed up in the words of Willie Stark, the governor of a Southern state in Robert Penn Warren's *All the King's Men.* Willie was sending an aide to try to dig up something compromising on the judge, a former political friend who had just opposed him. The aide suggested that the judge might be completely upright, but Stark sent him off with these words: "There's something. There's always something." And there was. Each one of us, looking deep within, knows "there's always something."

Reprisal

When the three boys reject their places on the high wire, retribution is inevitable. They lose the presence and guidance of the master who alone could help them learn to become artists themselves. In rejecting each other they lose the cooperative community, the personal relationships, which are essential for true human life. They find that their choices have meant the end of their possibilities, for now they become helplessly trapped in the life to which they have fallen. They thought they could escape from a situation of tension but in their escape they fall into much worse—loneliness, constant power struggle, or a denial of their deepest spiritual potential.

The inevitability of this fall into intolerable situations is God's reprisal, his wrath executed upon them. In Romans, Paul says that God's response of wrath to man's rebellion is that he "gave them up" (Rom. 1:24, 26, 28), having made them in such a way that rebellion would produce its own painful results. Thus we can see in the pathway man walks to destruction something further of significance in the way God made man: God wants man to respond in living obedience to him, and so he has created the world in such a way that life lived apart from him is unfulfilling. As Augustine wrote so memorably, "Thou hast made us for Thyself and our hearts are restless till they find their rest in Thee."

This means that *man* is an agent of God's wrath against himself, for every man brings destruction upon himself by his rebellion, and contributes to the general evil of the world which then weighs down on everyone. As we shall explore further in the following chapter, the biblical images of powers of evil in the world are tied directly to man's sinfulness and God's judgment found intrinsically in that sin. In a significant sense the demonic powers are the results of man's sin, the agents of God's wrath, and the causes of deepening sin—all at once.

In this section we will concentrate on the divine wrath exhibited in the inevitable results of our own rebellion. We need to see clearly the message Pogo sent back from the front-lines of the human struggle: "we have met the enemy and he is us." We discover early that we are guilty, responsible for failing to be our potential selves and so we build façades to hide behind, to try to fool others. The trouble is we cannot keep up the façades unless we build inner defenses to hide our higher aspirations by becoming blind to the truth about ourselves. Façades and defenses produce alienation from others around us and disintegration and struggle within. The end result is that we become slaves to forces beyond our recognition and control, unable to help ourselves out of our chains.

Guilty Facades

The beginning of man's trouble comes when he falsely concludes that since he is not equal to God that he is not worth much, that is, when his factual inferiority leads him to a feeling of moral inferiority. The feeling may well come when the Master says "hold on. Don't look down. Do what I say." It comes when we hear, "Do not eat of the tree" (Gen. 2:17), or "Do not covet" (Rom. 7:7 f.). For most of us it began with "stop crying" or "don't touch that" or "eat your food" or "stay off the road." The law handed down by some monstrous person towering over us emphasized our weakness and insecurity and provided the perfect opportunity for something alien to spring up within us. Paul says that the immediate result is a desire to do just what is forbidden, to rebel. Everyone does it in one way or another. Everyone rebels, refuses to remain on the tightrope, strikes out for greener pastures.

Unfortunately we carry our past with us, for when we feel ourselves morally inferior and so rebel against the One who has put us where we are, we come to feel guilty and cannot escape. Whichever form of rebellion we take we intuitively know that we are not living up to our potential, that we have not uncovered the best that life has to offer us, that we are responsible for our plight. No matter how much bravado may accompany our power-seeking or our pride or our sensuality and conformity there is always underneath an echo, loud or dim, of what might have been.

Our immediate impulse when we feel ourselves guilty is to hide it from others, because if others can see what we have done wrong then we will feel even more morally inferior than before and this will accelerate our downward spiral. We hide our guilt from others by building a façade, putting up a front that is the best we can do to make us acceptable in our group. A child will hide his misbehavior by doing it out of sight. An adult will hide it by the same means, adding a camouflage of words and deeds to fool others into thinking all is right within. Families appear cordial in public even when they fight like cornered rats at home. Some parents put up a front of loving care in front of their children, saving all their real feelings for their private battles.

The value of a façade from our point of view is that it keeps our failures private, so that—we hope—we will not be rejected by the significant people in our lives. The disaster of a façade is that it becomes a way of hiding guilt rather than dealing with it, and it builds a barrier between us and other people because when façades confront each other the persons behind them are kept apart. That accentuates our troubles, because then our desire for loving involvement is thwarted; we feel guilty that we are not able to become close to others so we build our façades thicker to make believe we have, and the beat of the drum of inner destruction goes on.

Defensive Blindness

Once we have begun to construct our façades, to try to make others feel that we are valuable, we find that we cannot live with the falsehood we have created. Life is just too painful to be lived trying to cover up what is going on within us, our feelings of guilt and failure. So we erect inner defenses to try to cope with the tension within. The basic defenses are these: a barrier suppressing, as well as we can, the deep human needs that we have not been able to satisfy; a filter distorting reality as we view it so that we do not have to recognize the depths of our problem. We hold down our memories and intuitions of the possibility of really loving others, of responding to the Spirit undergirding the whole universe; we do our best to deny that the exhilaration of the high wire really beckons us. At the same time we blind ourselves to the reality of the world, to the judgment on our behavior made by others.

Paul in Romans 1 accented this very point, for he saw the result of man's rebellion, his refusal to honor, thank and trust God, as this: "They became futile in their thinking and their senseless minds were darkened. Claiming to be wise, they became fools" (vv. 21–22). The worst of it is not just that we are blind, but that we are blind to our blindness! We think we are acting reasonably but our reason is corrupt, other forces are in control. Paul Tournier expresses this view clearly in *The Meaning of Persons:* "We are controlled by feelings not by logic, though we fondly imagine we are being guided by our reason. What happens in fact is that reason supplies the arguments with which to justify our behavior."

Our inner defenses keep us from recognizing that our actions are not based on a rational evaluation of what is best for us in the long run. If we knew how much our actions are based on uncontrolled passions, we would feel even more guilty than before, and also helpless. So we hide the truth. We do our best to put everything in the best light, to try to believe we act in our own best interests. But that is a self-delusion, as Erich Fromm clearly saw in *Man for Himself:* "At the end of his life he recognizes that he had deceived himself; that while following the principle of 'self-interest' he had failed to recognize what the interests of his real self were, and had lost the very self he sought to preserve." It is precisely in living for "self-interest," in opposition to the interests of others, that the blindness is darkest, because our real interests coincide with those of others; we need loving, caring relationships most of all and they can never come at the expense of others.

Our inner defenses are the judgment God lets fall upon us when we refuse to be involved with him and try to overcome our guilty conscience by building a façade. The façade does not really fool those close to us, but it does fool us. We become convinced that we are right and the world is wrong. We are blind to our real needs and aspirations because we have blocked them out as a way to escape their incessant revelation of our failure to be what we really could be. Without the external insight provided by others and the internal motivation provided by our deepest needs and longings, our hearts become hardened, our necks stiff, our eyes blind, our ears stopped. Our punishment is more than we can bear.

Alienation

The spiral staircase leading us down into our own private hell has not been fully exposed even now. The guilt over our rebellion produces external façades and inner defensive blindness but it also has devastating effects in all our relationships, something hinted at several times already. We find that we are not only guilty and blind, not only have outer façades and inner defenses, but are also alienated, estranged, at loggerheads, feeling like enemies, with the significant persons in our lives. We find that we are enemies of God, estranged from our neighbor, divided even in our own inner selves.

When we refuse the Master's outreached hand and decide to go our own way without him he does not simply remain available on the shelf like a bottle of medicine we decided not to take just yet. We can never reject another person and not have the rejection create a gulf between us wider than the Pacific Ocean. My act of rejection comes between us, creating as much a block in my own mind as it does in the mind of the one rejected. In the case of our rejection of God we try to cover our guilt by various measures of suppression: we may deny that he exists, among the worst things we can do to any person; we may deny his moral and personal nature, saying that all he really wants is public display to uphold his reputation and prestige, so we provide ritual displays on Sunday and ignore him the rest of the time. Whatever form our reaction takes, we see and feel God as our enemy because his offer of love makes a demand for response that we continually refuse to give. A chasm as deep as the Grand Canyon yawns between us and him, and we cannot cross it even in those wistful moments when we imagine "maybe . . ."

Intrinsically tied in with our alienation from God is estrangement from our neighbor. When the apprentices rejected the master they rejected each other also. Since God is love, rejection of him means refusing to see loving relationships as our greatest potential, need and calling. As soon as we feel morally inferior and attempt to overcome that feeling by rebellion and façades and defenses we have turned to our selfish concerns and abandoned our communal, cooperative calling to find our true lives in involvement with others. The instincts of parental care, sexual bonding and self-preservation still drive us to a significant amount of involvement with others, so the race continues. But the deepest possible involvement, in self-giving love that is the presence and power of God, *that* we have lost in our rebellion.

Finally, we are alienated from ourselves, disintegrated within, because our habits and defenses drive us one way while our irrepressible spiritual longing urges us another. Goethe's *Faust* expresses something of this inner alienation when he says:

> Two souls, alas! are lodg'd within my breast,
> Which struggle there for undivided reign:
> One to the world, with obstinate desire,
> And closely-cleaving organs, still adheres;
> Above the mist, the other doth aspire,
> With sacred vehemence, to purer spheres.

Paul knew this same inner disintegration, the striving on the one hand to fulfill the desires of the flesh, the passions within, and yet at the same time aspiring to something far transcending this world: "I do not understand my own actions. For I do not do what I want, but I do the very thing I hate. . . . For I delight in the law of God, in my inmost self, but I see in my members another law at war with the law of my mind and making me captive to the law of sin which dwells in [me]" (Rom. 7:15, 22–23).

Slavery

Paul's description of the inner power that makes him a captive brings us to the final general characteristic of the state of man suffering under the wrath of God. We may have started off with the possibility of freedom, but when we abandoned our natural position on the tightrope we rejected that possibility. Our freedom is so great that we were even allowed to escape it, to turn away from the relationship to God and neighbor that is the only road of inner freedom. Edmund Burke epitomized the whole human condition when he said, "men of intemperate minds cannot be free; their passions forge their chains." Though they may have great political and financial liberty, indulgence in the immediately pressing instincts for power, or pleasure, or prestige means the creation of inner defenses that become prison walls.

The image of man enslaved within is a way to emphasize that he cannot save himself. His feeling of moral inferiority produced rebellion, which led to guilt and the building of façades; in order to live with this false front, inner defenses were contrived to blind him to uncomfortable external truth and to suppress his higher needs and aspirations within; by these means he became alienated from God, his neighbor and himself. His only way out is through the care of others showing him the truth and helping him to come to grips with himself. But once alienation is the truth about his condition, he has locked the only door out and thrown the key out the window.

Since the whole rocky downhill slope was started on first to overcome inferiority and insecurity, the increased feelings of guilt and the tenuous hold on inner life of the alienated man reinforces the initial feelings and drives him further down the road. On the surface, in his outward life and his conscious mind, he has made the best truce he can: he ignores his guilt as best he can and agrees not to probe behind his neighbor's façade if his neighbor will make believe in the same way; the insecurity of life is repressed by holding firmly to something perishable—power, pride or pleasure—and working at them enough to convince his conscious self that they really provide meaning for life.

The result is that he has come to identify himself with his façade and his defenses and so is enslaved by them. He is hardly even aware most of the time that the prison walls surround him for he has built the walls himself as the best protection he could manage at the moment and so every other choice seems intolerable. It was only after Paul was released from this inner prison that he could describe it so powerfully in Romans 7. For most of us our bars look like windows keeping out the wind and rain, and our handcuffs are taken for decorative bracelets. We are unable to free ourselves because we lost the vision of freedom when we lost the vision of God as the Master by whose hand alone we can walk as we were intended.

Conclusion: "The King's Statue"

Once upon a time in the country of Patagonia two small villages flourished within five miles of each other without any significant conflict between them. Most of the time they simply kept out of each other's way, for the primary impulses in both towns were for food, water sources, and self-protection, though once a year they joined in a harvest festival together as a means of finding wives and husbands. Whenever external threats loomed, however, they turned inward, holding onto their own resources, rejecting cooperation.

One day word came from the distant capital that the king, who demanded complete allegiance to himself, had heard suspicious rumors from travelers that the proclaimed loyalty of one village was insincere. In fact, the story had reached the capital that the village was jealous of the king's power, prominence and wealth and was verging on rebellion. The truth was that there had been such talk, but the villagers thought that it had been kept quiet enough. Now they knew they were in trouble because of their disloyalty of heart. A dire threat seemed to be conveyed by the king's call for loyalty, and feelings of weakness and insecurity overcame many in the village until action had to be taken.

The villagers decided first of all to erect a huge statue of the king at the entrance to the village, with inscriptions of undying loyalty on its base. Every day in front of it sacrifices were offered, intended as signs of the villagers' desire to offer the king whatever he wanted. In addition, strong walls were built around the village and all the outlying homes were abandoned for the safety within. The walls were built because the villagers knew that trouble with their neighbors, five miles away, was going to come because the deer for the sacrifices could only come by hunting further afield, in the territory their neighbors called their own.

Within the village there were those who denounced the changes as foolishness. They said the king would not long be fooled and the neighbors were people they needed and so offending them was disastrous. But the majority of the village saw such talk as treasonous, liable to inhibit this proper defensive action, and so opposition was banned. The ban was enforced by locking up the few troublemakers in an underground prison where no one was allowed to talk with them.

Before long, war with the neighboring village broke out over the deer and the village had to tighten its belt. There was less food so compromises had to be made: the strong (soldiers) and the important (leaders) got all they needed and found the war exhilarating, but everyone else suffered. Gradually internal dissension began to grow like a cancer until there was as much fighting within the walls as outside.

At that point the king came with his army, for he had been told that his most important law—the one forbidding fighting between villages—had been cast aside. He knew that the monstrous statue was only a front, an attempt to hide disloyalty. So his army broke down the walls, destroyed the town and scattered the villagers, some fleeing as refugees, some ending up as slaves. As peace settled back down on the scene there was nothing left but rubble, and a gigantic statue left as a reminder of one village's folly.

Suggested Reading

Conrad, Joseph. *Heart of Darkness.* New York: Airmont, 1966.

Dostoevsky, Fyodor. *The Brothers Karamazov.* New York: Random House, 1950.

———*Memoirs from Underground.* New York: E. P. Dutton, 1913.

Golding, W. *Lord of the Flies.* New York: Putnam, 1954.

Kümmel, W. G. *Man in the New Testament.* Translated by J. J. Vincent. London: Epworth, 1963.

Harris, Thomas. *I'm OK—You're OK.* New York: Bantam, 1967.

Menninger, Karl. *Whatever Became of Sin?* New York: Hawthorn, 1973.

Niebuhr, Reinhold. *The Nature and Destiny of Man.* New York: Scribner's, 1941.

Roberts, D. E. *Psychotherapy and a Christian View of Man.* New York: Scribner's, 1950.

Robinson, H. W. *The Christian Doctrine of Man.* Edinburgh: 1911.

Rogers, Carl. *On Becoming a Person.* Boston: Houghton Mifflin, 1961.

Stacey, W. D. *The Pauline View of Man.* London: Macmillan, 1956.

Chapter Five: God's Servant–Enemy

Introduction: "The Children of Light"

The Powers and God

CREATED COLLECTIVE
LAW AND WRATH
PARASITIC CORRUPTION
OPPRESSION AND SLAVERY
CONCLUSION

Demonic Powers in Modern America

THE PLAGUE OF VIOLENCE
Evil Spirit
Roots of Violence
Mortal Disease
CONCLUSION

THE CANCER OF PREJUDICE
Natural Roots
American Growth
Destructive Demon
CONCLUSION

CHAPTER FIVE

God's Servant-Enemy

Introduction: "The Children of Light"

Once upon a time a man named Joseph Light had a blinding, overwhelming vision in which he believed he saw God, as Isaiah did, and was called to an extraordinary task—organizing a purified remnant of God's people. Joseph was renowned as a mystic who found his fulfillment in meditation, in reading the sacred books and passing on the message he received. But he heard a call to set up an organization that would carry on the purification of the "Children of Light" (as he called his followers), without his direct involvement.

So he created four structures, four departments, each of them making a contribution to the unity and purity of the Children. The one everyone knew about was the bureau of order, for it provided the government for the Children, organizing them into a unit and enabling cooperation. The second Bureau developed law, and it was less well known for it worked behind the scenes, deciding what laws to impose and then imposing them as the law of God, absolutely binding on all the Children. Naturally Joseph knew some Children would stray so the third structure was the bureau of punishment whose task was to bring the straying Children back by helping them experience the full consequences of their disobedience. Finally, the most secret of all, Joseph created the bureau of testing, an organization that secretly operated to test the allegiance and purity of the Children so that hypocritical facades could be discovered.

Joseph set up these structures with their own rules and powers and ways of operating and appointed his sons to run them. His eldest son he kept apart from these powers and authorities, for he was Joseph's spokesman who visited him in his mountain retreat and brought back his father's word. So Joseph put his other four sons in executive positions in each of the bureaus, leaving it to them to carry out each bureau's intended purpose.

Before too long it became apparent that the Children fell away quite easily. The Tester (Tempter) found no difficulty in uncovering strains of selfishness and rebellion. In fact the Tempter and the lawgiver learned to work in tandem, for new laws could be written that provided testing of allegiance and thus were effective as temptations to disobedience. At the same time the punisher and the ruler came to team up because the punisher needed the legitimacy of the governing order and the ruler needed the threat provided by his partner. Thus before long it was hardly possible to distinguish wrath from government, for government came to be defined almost as "the bearer of the sword."

The punishments imposed were designed to bring the sin home on the head of the sinner by making him feel the inevitable results of his chosen way. Thus anyone who stayed away from the assembly of the Children without good cause was punished by not being allowed to attend the next two meetings. Those who were sensually overindulgent were required to double their overindulgence—this time in public. Those who were aggressive were forced to work out with the boxing squad organized for just that purpose. The result was that sinners did feel the effects of their sin, but in order to feel superior they told themselves they liked the results and so individual habits soon became widespread community practices.

As this downward spiral developed, the four sons in charge of the bureaus became more and more united under the leadership of the Temptor, who seemed clearly the most effective and powerful of all. He was proud of his success, as was the punisher who had driven many Children much deeper into sin than they had intended. Those two had subordinated the ruler and the lawgiver to themselves already, so the final result was a unified hierarchy. Instead of the tempter and the punisher enforcing the law and so upholding order, the result of the Children's sinning was a complete perversion of Joseph's intention: now the ruler and the lawgiver supported the growing evil promulgated by the success of the tempter and the punisher. The structures created for good had become evil because of the sinning of the Children.

In the end Joseph saw that his created institutions were subverting his intentions. So he sent his eldest son to break the hold of the now-oppressive structures and to create a new, communal form of life, one in which the powers would not become powers of evil.

The Powers and God

This story of the "Children of Light" is a parable expressing something of the biblical understanding of the way God's good, created, superhuman "principalities or authorities" (Col. 1:16) became the demonic enemies of both God and man and so had to be conquered by Christ (Col. 2:15). Since there is no one place in the Bible that the whole story is told, it has to be pieced together from many scattered references, so many Christians do not know the great importance of the powers of evil in biblical thought. An attempt will be made here to remedy that ignorance. In this first section we will note the main characteristics of the powers: they are envisioned as created, and as collective forces hidden within and behind society; they are pictured as agents of God's wrath, his way of punishment; but they become corrupted by man's sin, their evil being a parasite feeding on what is still good in them; in the long run they become oppressive, enslaving man and thus being God's enemies instead of his servants.

Created Collective

The Old Testament speaks of the powers ruling in the nations of the world as sons of God, or angels. In Deuteronomy 22:8 f. each nation (except Israel) is imagined as ruled by one of the "sons of God," and in Daniel 10:20 f. the nations (including Israel) each have their angelic "prince" as the superhuman power lying behind the nation. In both the Testaments God's wrath is exercised at times by a subordinate, the "angel of the Lord" in the Old Testament (2 Kings 19:35; 2 Sam. 24:15 ff.), and Satan in the New Testament (1 Cor. 5:5). In both Testaments Satan is the Tempter, shown as a perfectly respectable task in Job 1, but one that has somehow become demonic in the New Testament, though it is still under God's ultimate control (1 Cor. 10:13). Finally, we find in the New Testament that religion and law are earthly expressions of the powers: pagan religion is worship of demons, slavery to "elemental spirits of the universe" (1 Cor. 10:19 f.; Gal. 4:8); but Jewish religion is the same kind of thing for the law was "given by angels" (Gal. 3:19). The Jews are blinded by Satan's use of the law (2 Cor. 4:4), and so they can be called slaves of the elemental spirits of the universe also (Gal. 3:23; 4:3).

Lying behind all these diverse references seems to be the general notion that God has created orders or structures or powers that lie behind the organizations and institutions seen on earth. This suggests that there is a deeper reality in an organized group than just the surface phenomena we can see. For example, there is a spirit that transcends the present United States, a dynamic process or movement that would continue on even if the government were wiped out by a nuclear bomb. Even though generations come and go, laws and programs change, there is still something that we personify as "Uncle Sam" or refer to as "the American Way" or "the Spirit of '76" which is a collective reality lying behind and within the nation.

The biblical writers suggest that God has created structures, ways of organizing human life, which can be pictured in personal form as "Sons of God" or the "Prince of Persia," or can be seen more abstractly as "thrones, dominions, principalities and powers." These refer primarily to the governments and religions of the world, for in the ancient world those two structures were never completely separated since the gods of the nations were seen as their supernatural rulers. Law was usually seen as having a religious source even if it dealt primarily with civil matters, and punishment was an expression of the god's displeasure even when exercised by the civil government.

It seems that the biblical writers saw the human developments of government, religion and punishment as expressions of the structures created by God, symbolized as angelic beings subordinate to God. Basically then, these structures are created and good. They are the forms man needs in order to live a human life. But unfortunately they may turn out to do more harm than good. In no case is this paradox more evident than in God's wrath, since Satan is the servant of God's wrath and as such is also God's great enemy.

Law and Wrath

An essential function of the structure of human society is the promulgation of law and the exercise of punishment. These do not have to be thought of as just the official forms practiced by organized groups such as states and religious bodies; there is unofficial law, or custom, that regulates all societies and along with it there are sanctions of various sorts imposed on its violators. Thus law and punishment are intrinsic to all groups, and so they can be seen as parts of God's created ordering of the universe. Man did not just happen to form ordered groups maintained by law and punishment; the biblical writers suggest that God has made man and the universe in such a way that this ordering of human life is as natural as eating and sleeping.

In the Bible there is a certain studied ambiguity concerning God's punishment of man. There are numerous times when God himself is said to have inflicted punishment, one of the most picturesque being Isaiah 63:1–3. Here God is pictured as a man with clothing all splattered red like a grape-treader, but in this case he has trodden down the nations: "I trod them in my anger . . . and their lifeblood is sprinkled on my garments." Yet at other times biblical writers explicitly point to someone other than God as the worker of wrath. It is an angel who is said to kill by plague 70,000 Israelites (2 Sam. 24) and 185,000 Assyrians (2 Kings 19:35). It is Satan who brings all the misery to Job, who is called the one who has the power of death (Heb. 2:5), and is the one who executes punishment according to one Pauline statement (1 Cor. 5:5). Thus Satan and wrath are in some way combined.

In a somewhat parallel way Satan and law are combined. Satan is the one who accuses men before God (Job 1; Rev. 12:10) but Paul sees the law as exercising this function (Rom. 3:19; Gal. 3:10 ff.). In addition the law leads man into sin (Rom. 7:7 ff.) just as Satan does. Third, Paul sees the law as something imposed on Jews by angels (Gal. 3:19), making Jews slaves of the elemental spirits of the universe (Gal. 4:2) who must be seen as part of the structure under Satan's lordship.

In both these cases, the association of Satan with wrath and with law, we have a paradox that offers some insight into the evil of the world. Wrath and law are good things, created to uphold order and life. Yet in the world we know they are now "servants of Satan," meaning that they produce evil so that salvation for mankind means salvation *from* wrath and law. Wrath is God's own, yet it is God's enemy, something that he wishes to rescue man from (1 Thess. 1:10). Law is God-given yet it too has become his enemy, for it is the means by which sin comes to power over man (Rom. 7:5), and indeed Paul can even say that "the law brings wrath" (Rom. 4:15).

Therefore we can see in the biblical writings that God's wrath and his Law have become his enemies, that the Satan seen as God's servant in Job 1 has become the dragon, the supreme enemy of God in Revelation. Somehow corruption has set in on God's good creation, evil has become parasitic on good.

Parasitic Corruption

How could it have happened that God's good created structures of rule, law, testing and punishment could have turned into his enemies? First, it is important to note that they are seen as something good that has been corrupted, turned on the wrong path, and not anything intrinsically and absolutely evil. It is essential that we recognize that evil is a parasite on good, a hidden corruption that has a façade of good but inner workings that produce evil. On the surface government and religion and law appear reasonable and valuable and good but each of them contributes to the sinfulness of society.

We shall see this in more detail in the second half of this chapter, but here we might note the way evil is hidden within good. Governments use violence to punish wrongdoers—both individuals within the state and also enemy states—but in doing so the violence is almost always over-done producing more violence in return. Religions act to promote worship of God but at the same time they engender prejudice against outsiders who worship differently, and this prejudice contributes to the evil in society. Law regulates life but tempts people to think that they are just fine if they have lived by obedience to the law; and law always expresses the interests of lawmakers rather than some absolute truth; in addition it leads to evil both in tempting to disobedience and also in tempting to self-righteousness. At the core government, religion and Law express good created structures, but in practice they hide evil demonic powers within them.

Where did it all go wrong? The answer seems to be that these created structures were taken by man to be God himself and were given the allegiance that was to be given only to God. The root of all sin is that man "worshiped and served the creature rather than the Creator" (Rom. 1:25). Pagans worshiped the "sons of God," the "rulers and authorities" lying behind their states and religions. Jews "worshiped" the law, boasting in themselves and their own religion, thereby serving something created rather than the Creator. When government or religion comes to hold a man's primary allegiance, then they become demonic because they begin to act as if they were God. A totalitarian state tries to order the news, history, economics and everything else. A totalitarian church reaches into the bedroom and into the depths of the mind as well as into public behavior. Those who give allegiance to these creatures playing Creator provide the continuing impetus to their demonic status.

In every society numerous examples of something secondary trying to make believe it is absolute can be found, both in government and in religion. The prophets of Israel spoke often of the way God's "servant-punishers" overstepped the bounds laid out for them and thus became his enemies. Isaiah sees Assyria as the rod of God's anger against Israel, but Assyria believes itself to be master of the world, destroying any nation it wishes (Isa. 10:5 ff.). So God must finally conquer his own servant-punisher, acting graciously towards Israel to rescue her from the agent of his wrath. The zeal of punishers often becomes demonic, for the servant-punisher must harden his heart against appeals for mercy and so often becomes one who enjoys punishing. Fatso, the stockade sergeant in *From Here to Eternity*, was just that sort of man; he had become a demonic, almost inhuman, bearer of pain to all in his charge, especially those who could not bend to his will. It was the role itself that molded him, so eventually he became a killer rather than the preserver the stockade was intended to be.

A further source of the corruption of God's good structures is found in the corporate nature of human life. Punishment is due only to those who have rebelled, yet there is no way to punish one man without hurting others around him. A man who tries to escape his personal problems in alcohol finds God's wrath in the downward road to alcoholism. But his family and friends and society as a whole also pay. Every man who is driven further into sinning seeks company and so becomes a source of temptation and seduction to others —a carrier of the plague. No one can escape completely the forces of evil in society, forces to be described more fully below, so it happens that one man's sin leads to the corruption of others and to the corruption of the whole of society. Thus God's good order becomes the front for an inner order of evil that can be enslaving.

Oppression and Slavery

So far we have suggested that the evil forces at work in the world were God's creatures, in particular his law and wrath exposed in government and religion, which have become corrupt. Their evil is a parasite sucking life from the good that still exists. Now finally we need to suggest the strength of these forces at work in our world, for too many Protestants hold a strongly individualistic point of view that conflicts with the biblical witness. We often think that doing right or wrong is a choice left wholly up to us; but the biblical writers proclaim that there are oppressive forces at work within society that enslave us without our knowing. For example,

Orthodox Jews in Jesus' day really had little choice in rejecting him because their minds had been sealed by their misunderstanding of God's desires for them (a blindness Paul attributes to Satan in 2 Cor. 4).

Most of our slavery to evil forces is that kind of cultural conditioning that is largely beyond our control. For example, during the presidency of Andrew Jackson, 17,000 Cherokees were forced to migrate in the dead of winter from Georgia and Tennessee to Oklahoma because white men wanted their land. How could Americans be so brutal and inhumane, forcing the deaths of 4,500 on the way? It was easy: Indians were not seen as human beings, but as wildlife like the buffalo. President Jackson approved this vast larceny, mass murder and cultural destruction, "because I am not going to let a civil war start over some Indians." Americans in general (though certainly not all, for the Supreme Court ruled—ineffectively—against the action) were blind to the humanity of these "savages" and so their blindness made them treat the natives like cattle.

Evil forces work not only to produce blindness to reality but also as the kind of spirit that gets into a mob and starts a riot or a lynching. George Orwell gives a gripping description of this kind of compulsive power of evil when in *1984* he describes the daily ritual of party members: "The horrible thing about the Two Minutes Hate was not that one was obliged to act a part, but that it was impossible to avoid joining in. Within thirty seconds any pretense was always unnecessary. A hideous ecstasy of fear and vindictiveness, a desire to kill, to torture, to smash faces in with a sledge hammer, seemed to flow through the whole group of people like an electric current, turning one even against one's will into a grimacing screaming lunatic." Most compulsive evil forces are less obvious than that, but equally devastating.

The evil forces depicted by the biblical writers deprive man of the inner freedom described above regardless of whether or not he has the external liberties that most men seek. In fact the presence of external liberties fools many into thinking they have all the inner freedom they need, so they may acquiesce completely in the demonic processes of their society. Conversely it may happen that complete absence of liberty, such as Frankl experienced in concentration camps, may bring to mind the real possibility of inner freedom which can then be cultivated. Citizens of a democracy are therefore no better off with regard to the inner oppression of demonic powers than are slaves in a totalitarian dictatorship. Right here in the United States we need to learn to unmask the oppressive forces of evil for they are largely hidden within the body of society.

CONCLUSION

The previous chapter suggested the way individuals rebel against God and then are driven deeper into their sin as appropriate punishment. In this chapter the focus of attention is on the collective nature of human sin and punishment. Just as God's wrath in the individual drove him on to further sin, so also God's wrath in society is the working of God's servant Satan who tempts, accuses and punishes. All of these were initially legitimate business, but they have become illegitimate. They were the ways God ordered the world, but those good bureaus have become fronts for corruption that has become demonic. These powers of corruption are not theoretical creations we can believe in or not; when we take a clear look at society we can see the powers at work on us and can begin to accept the biblical proclamation that all men are enslaved.

Demonic Powers in Modern America

The first half of this chapter has presented an outline of what seem to be the biblical assumptions concerning God's relationship to the powers of evil. There is not an absolute dualism with God and Satan being eternal enemies, but instead a corrupted monism, for all originates in God though in various ways the powers become corrupt. This whole developed picture of Satan and powers of evil was not simply speculation and superstition but was the way the ancient writers made some sense out of the mystery of evil they experienced. Human experience is the foundation for all this theory, for people experienced forces of evil in society yet also experienced God as the ruler of everything. The general story developed in the first section above was the way these two aspects of experience were pictured as making some sense when combined.

In the modern world, especially in the United States, there is a blindness toward forces of evil that makes many people think the whole biblical imagery of evil is primitive superstition. We are so individualistic in our philosophy that we falsely believe we are almost entirely responsible as individuals for our successes and failures. In particular, members of the white middle class—most of whom have done some hard work to achieve their goals—falsely give themselves most of the credit for their achievements and thus blame the poor and minorities and other nonachievers for being lazy and irresponsible. American Christians, who are mostly white and middle class, thus need to recognize the forces of evil at work in society if they are truly to understand God's work in the world.

In this brief discussion of demonic powers at work in our society we will suggest how good structures in society may contribute to the forces of evil. The government, first of all, is good and necessary, but it is one of the chief purveyors and supporters of violence, an especially powerful spirit in America. Second, religion makes a significant contribution to human life, yet it promotes prejudice, another demonic force sapping our nation's strength. Both of these demonic powers will now be investigated.

The Plague of Violence

The assassinations and bloody riots of the 1960s and early 1970s brought home to many Americans the truth that there is in their society a greater tendency to try to solve problems by violence than is found in other Western European nations. This does not mean that we have a monopoly on violence, but the imbalance between our situation and that of our friends is striking. Political assassinations are almost unknown in Western Europe yet we had five in five years after 1963, and in the 1970s attempts were made on the lives of George Wallace and two incumbent Presidents. The total number of murders in England, Germany and Japan (population together about 200 million) one year recently was 500, whereas in the United States with the same population it was 16,000.

As individuals, Americans are not a great deal different from Englishmen and Germans and so it is difficult to account for our high level of violence simply in terms of individual choices. We have to look to the nature of American society, the traditions of American history, and the values permeating the nation if we are to understand (and so hope to overcome) this plague. In other words we need to see that violence is not only something people choose, but is also an insidious disease that invisibly penetrates the vital organs of the body of the nation and can only be overcome by collective action to block its advance.

Evil Spirit

By calling violence an evil spirit or a demonic power my intention is to suggest that in many ways it is very like an infectious spiritual disease. This is not a complete denial of human responsibility, but a suggestion that our evil choices are to a significant extent determined by the forces at work in our society. Even if we have external liberty we may lack the internal freedom that is God's gift to us, so we may be to a great extent victims of powers beyond our control.

It is not possible to demonstrate conclusively that violence can usefully be understood as a disease, but there are a number of observations that can suggest the value of this analogy. The most basic evidence is the fact that violence almost always produces more violence. We see in our children that when one gets angry and hits out, the almost inevitable result is the victim gets angry and violent also. When students start to riot and throw rocks at the police, the police get angry and start shooting back. When the United States began escalating the war in Vietnam, the communists raised the level of their violence. Wherever we look, violence seems to be the kind of phenomenon that reproduces itself, almost forcing its victims to be violent in return.

The image of an "evil spirit" at work in violent mobs proclaims the apparent truth that such events are much more like the natural phenomenon of disease than like the human experience of rational choice. The riots in American cities in the 1960s were spontaneous eruptions of frustrated youth who felt themselves to be the victims of the institutional violence of racism and poverty. The riots were hysterical fits, despairing rages, the release of bottled-up frustrations which came as explosions that fed upon each other. There was no planning involved, just a spirit of violence spreading from ghetto to ghetto as the response to the perceived violence of the established order.

Roots of Violence

If we wish to find the roots of the criminal violence we abhor today we must look for it in the "good" things of our history, our government and our traditions. Just as the biblical writers see the powers of evil as corruptions of good structures, so this demon violence must be traced back to the sources of which we are proud.

The first source of American violence is in our unique history. For the 300 years that are now just over, we have been advancing across the wilderness of our continent, living on the frontier, trying to bring order. But on the frontier there was never any consistent state power that could control those who would deprive others of their rights. So the tradition arose of men using guns to protect themselves, their families, their small bridgeheads of civilization. This frontier tradition of every man being his own policeman has never fully been outgrown, for it lives on in the heroes of western movies and television shows. These shows, especially when they are most realistic, indoctrinate us in the theology of Mao Tse-tung, that "power comes out of the barrel of a gun."

A second source of the American disease of violence is the government and the way it has acted in the past and the present. We have gone to war many times when a considerable element of the population thought it was unjustified—e.g., Congressman Abraham Lincoln thought the Mexican-American War was a crime. But until Vietnam we have always won and thus have continued to propagandize ourselves with the belief that when Americans use violence justice triumphs. So our police forces use violence at home and get away with it most of the time. The police kill five hundred people each year and few policemen are indicted for it. The National Guard killed four students at Kent State and no one has been punished for it. It remains to be seen whether the people of the nation will put a stop to the official violence that is one of the sources of violent response by citizens.

That the American government is one of the chief sources of violence is not unique, for strong governments throughout history have been demonic in just this same way. From the biblical perspective God has created "government," in the sense of embedding in man the need and the will and the ability to form governments to provide for the common good. "Order" is thus divinely given. But when "*this* order," a particular government, is seen as absolute, as God's will for man, then it has become demonic. Whenever man sees his own nation or government or form of government as worthy of absolute support because it is the best possible, then man is worshiping the creation and the creation becomes an evil power.

Rome in Jesus' day saw itself as absolute; the Caesars called themselves divine; and so Revelation sees them as the Beast and the Whore of Babylon—Satan's agents. Hitler and his Nazis believed completely in the divinity of their cause and so the German government became a satanic power of greater destructiveness than any in history. After World War II both America and Russia came to absolutize their own forms of government, seeing democracy and communism respectively as the ultimate perfection in politics, the one to bring to all the nations of the world. Each feared the pretensions of the other and for twenty-five years promoted violence at home and abroad in anti-communist and anti-imperialist crusades.

In our anti-communist fervor we have seen our way as God's way, to be upheld or imposed by the sword around the world wherever communism rears its head. Thus we absolutize our system at home also, and when the students rose up against "the system," at

Jackson State (against discrimination) and at Kent State (against our attack into Cambodia) the system kills, with impunity so far. The extreme hostility of police and National Guardsmen in these cases is a sign of the way challenge to our system is seen as a matter of life and death.

Only a government, or an established order, that believes itself to be divinely ordained can believe that it has the right to kill whenever it is challenged. What Americans need is a good dose of the Book of Revelation where Rome, the great policeman of the ancient world, is depicted as the fountainhead of violence. We have not fallen nearly to the level of Rome because we have never had the absolute power Rome had. But to the extent that many people do think of the American system as God's greatest gift to politics they will be purveyors of the demon of violence.

Mortal Disease

If we are to understand violence as an impersonal force, a disease, a demon, one of the "principalities and powers," then we must suggest where its power lies. How does it work in society so as to overwhelm us? Through our blindness to it, our anxiety about death, and our self-righteousness in using it.

All the demonic powers pointed to in the Bible work insidiously, blinding people to the real evil that is being done. Satan is seen tempting Jesus to do things that appeared good on the surface but were evil underneath. That is precisely the way violence works. We foolishly believe that when we use violence it is a surgeon's scalpel that will cut out evil and encourage good. The truth is that violence is a blunt club that mainly angers our opponent and incites him to violence in return. We went to war in Vietnam with very good intentions, to protect the liberties of the non-communist countries in the region, but it led to the absurdity of "we had to destroy Ben Tre in order to save it." The low-violence guerrilla war we entered in the early 1960s could have continued for 100 years and not approached the destruction and death we caused in seven years. The war we left behind was more widespread and destructive than the one we found; our violence produced more violence. Our blindness to that likelihood was our undoing.

A second source of the power of violence is the anxiety and selfishness of individuals and groups. Our individual anxiety over our mortality leads us to overreact to any threat we perceive. Our individual guilt coupled with that anxiety leads often to feelings of hostility that are completely unjustified. Since we fear death we fight for life when violence is directed towards us. If the threat is against our group in which we take pride then any threat to the group is a threat to our identity. Our hostility and selfishness are usually unknown to us for we camouflage them as justified indignation and protection of the right. So our individual and group passions are allowed to run free, to contribute to violence.

We feed our hostility by self-righteousness, believing that our cause is right and so violence in its aid is righteous. Black Panthers saw the police as murderers and so believed themselves acting rightly in killing them. The police have responded in kind, as we would expect. The United States has believed for a generation that it was the world's policeman, that its views on appropriate national behavior were to be imposed on others. So we promoted counter-revolution in Guatemala, supported an attack on Cuba, joined in an uprising in the Dominican Republic and continued to sell arms to tyrants in Greece, Spain and Portugal. The most disastrous case of course was Vietnam, in which we believed that our goals ought to be imposed by force.

Conclusion

Violence has flourished like the plague within American society from the beginning, though it has stood out in obvious bursts at particular times such as the decade beginning in 1963. Today it seems to have quieted down somewhat but we need to know that this plague is quite similar to the physical disease of that name, to remember "that the plague bacillus never dies or disappears for good; that it can lie dormant for years and years in furniture and linen-chests; that it bides its time in bedrooms, cellars, trunks and bookshelves; and that perhaps the day would come when, for the bane and the enlightening of men, it would rouse up its rats again and send them forth to die in a happy city" (Albert Camus, *The Plague*). We may think violence has died away in our society, but it goes its insidious way at its "normal" destructive level.

Violence is therefore a modern expression and manifestation of the "spirit that is now at work in the disobedient," the work of the "god of this world." It rules us, it destroys us, it frustrates us, it changes our history for the worse, it robs us of life and happiness, it dehumanizes us. It is all that Satan was seen to be and much more because it cannot be laughed at and ignored, for it will not go away.

The Cancer of Prejudice

One of the forces that contributes to violence in our society is prejudice, a form of violence that is covert and psychological rather than open and physical. The same thing was true in New Testament times. The Pharisees' prejudice against the common people led them to attack Jesus, who befriended these outcasts. Thus prejudice led to violence, marking the Pharisees as "children of the devil" (John 8:44 ff.). In the United States today the major targets of prejudice are colored minorities and women, for the nation has always been run by and for white males. Just as most people do not make a conscious, rational choice to commit violence, so also they do not intend to be prejudiced. Instead they grow up in a society in which prejudice is firmly embedded, justified and camouflaged so that they take in the prejudice virus with their mother's milk. Only if we understand this virus will we be able to find a cure.

Natural Roots

Prejudice in one form or another is an almost universal human phenomenon. All people seek one or more social groups for their own protection and fulfillment as human beings, coming thereby to find part of their identification in their community. The feeling naturally arises that life within the group is better than life outside it, for otherwise they would not belong. The beginning of prejudice is found in the proud, sinful deduction that we who are *in* must therefore be wiser and better than those who are *out*. This sinful self-righteousness is always subtly promoted by the group because it cements the group bond and aids in institutional self-preservation. Thus a certain amount of prejudice in favor of one's own group and against all other groups is to be expected as long as men are sinners.

A second cause of prejudice is the fact of human finitude and man's consequent desire for simplicity. We cannot understand everyone in the world as an individual so we identify them by their groups, as we often identify ourselves by our group. This means that when the less desirable characteristics of a group become public knowledge we generalize about its members. We say that all Englishmen are snobs, all Frenchmen are unfaithful lovers, all policemen are corrupt, all politicians can be bought and so on. Prejudice means "pre-judging" a person by his group identity, and we do this in order to have some beginning insight into people we meet.

Religion has been one of the primary sources of prejudice throughout history and continues so today. Surveys taken of the attitudes of people who belong to religious groups show that on the average church members in the United States are more prejudiced than nonmembers (see Gerhard Lenski, *The Religious Factor*). The reason for this appears to be that religious people feel strong commitments to the truth of their religion, and so they see nonmembers as espousing falsehood and sinful behavior, both of which appear to be threats to the religious group. It is much harder for a person who is committed in this way to be open and accepting of the views of people with other commitments. Prejudice thus is the greatest temptation religion offers.

We thus can see religion in general and the biblical religions in particular as divinely created "authorities" which have become demonic because of the sinfulness of their adherents. The religion of Israel was slavery to demonic powers because Israel had absolutized the law. Israel believed that her tradition, her ritual, her law, her religion, were the absolute truth, open to no change, so she crucified her king instead of welcoming him in repentance.

Throughout history the Church has absolutized herself in precisely this same way so that she too has become time and again the agent of evil powers. Whenever Christians believe that they *possess* the truth, that their ritual and doctrine and behavior are precisely what God desires, then they have elevated themselves to God's rank. We do not possess the truth but are possessed by him who is the Truth, and our witness to him is always, *always* obscured by our sinfulness.

By elevating our version of Christianity to the level of God's Word we are able to see ourselves as the truest of the true, the purest of all mankind. So we could slaughter Muslim infidels in the Crusades and pagan red men in North America and fellow Christians during the Inquisition and European religious wars. Religion —which in our case is our disfigured Christianity—is the perfect vehicle for pride, self-assertion and hypocrisy, all of which are sources of prejudice.

Further, religion is always conservative, for it always hands down the message and practice of previous generations. Thus the social prejudices of previous generations which were united with their religion tend to be accepted uncritically also. This is clearly the case with sex and race prejudice in America. The Judeo-Christian tradition has supported for centuries the almost universal belief in the second-class status of women, and so the Church today (including women in the Church) largely continues to believe that women would not be adequate or acceptable as pastors and priests. European Christianity in addition long justified the third-class status of colored peoples, calling them descendants of the accursed Ham (Gen. 9:22 ff.). So the Church has until recently supported prejudice against Blacks, Indians and Orientals.

American Growth

The cancer of prejudice has natural roots in human grouping and finitude and religion but it has come to luxurious growth in this country. This is not a judgment that it is worse here than elsewhere, but just a concentration upon the log in our own eye. In both cases—racism and sexism—prejudice has become firmly embedded in society because "facts" are seen as supporting it.

In the past blacks were considered mentally inferior by whites and so allowed to perform only manual labor. Two hundred years of slavery based on that theory produced the American black who had no history, no national identity, no pride, no traditional motivation to inspire young men and women to achieve. All of these necessities for successful achievement were denied them by the structure of slavery and then by the system of segregation. The result has been black underachievement in educational, employment and political spheres.

The underachievement is then taken as proof of black inferiority! At the same time the present situation of blacks and minorities in society is the picture taken in by children growing up. If a child in a white neighborhood sees blacks only as maids and gardeners then it is no wonder that the white boy looked into the baby carriage a black mother was pushing and exclaimed in all innocence to his mother, "Look, a baby maid."

Similar factors have been at work in suppressing women. Their traditional subjugation made impossible any considerable achievements in education, business, politics and the arts. This underachievement then was used as evidence that women were incapable of voting properly or using an education, let alone having any power over men. By this means powerful males eliminated half of the available competition for their places of eminence. In addition they gained a lover-nursemaid-servant who made their lives even more enjoyable. There is thus nothing surprising in the continuation of male prejudice against women whenever it is possible.

But women have largely acquiesced in their second-class citizenship, showing how insidious and effective this particular cancer of prejudice has been. All of the children's opinion-shaping media—mostly parents, schools, religion and books—have supported the male superiority propaganda. By pointing to the obvious (women alone bear and nurse children) and offering a few crumbs of privilege (laws against women working more than 12 hours a day) most women have traditionally been indoctrinated into the male rule mythology.

Destructive Demon

Obviously prejudice is destructive in the lives of those it is aimed against for it provides unnecessary obstacles that prevent all from fulfilling their potential as God intended. The publicans and sinners of Jesus' day suffered as outcasts just as much as minorities suffer today. Knowing oneself as an outcast causes frustration, anxiety and hostility when the prejudice is recognized and wasted lives even when it is not recognized. The number of black and female geniuses whose talent was lost to the human race because of prejudice will never be known but it probably is immense. We have all suffered from that loss and will always suffer from it because they are dead and gone and their contribution is lost forever.

Even worse than that is the fact that upholding a system of prejudice is destructive in the lives of those who carry it on. A great deal of energy and intellect must be wasted to keep up the front, and that allows the prejudiced to hide from their real problems. James Baldwin has made it clear that racism is the outer cover on deeper evils: "The white man's unadmitted—and apparently, to him, unspeakable—private fears and longings are projected onto the Negro. The only way he can be released from the Negro's tyrannical power over him is to consent, in effect, to become black himself . . . White people in this country will have quite enough to do in learning how to accept and love themselves and each other, and when they have achieved this—which will not be tomorrow and may very well be never—the Negro problem will no longer exist, for it will no longer be needed" (*The Fire Next Time*).

In a similar way male prejudice against females is destructive to males also. The most important reason for this is that prejudice requires a sharp distinction between maleness and femaleness and so to be "masculine" has come to mean repressing all the traits that are "feminine" such as tenderness, patience, emotion and wonder. Many men in our society are so fearful of appearing anything but super-masculine that they have lost touch with almost half of their potential self.

Prejudice is a cancer. It is insidious in its action because it works unseen and unknown to its perpetrators, deep within the living cells of society. It feeds on what is good—religion as man's highest endeavor, motherhood as a privilege only given to woman, parental desire to give their children a good education (which means in a school with "our kind"). This cancer is compulsive, for people do not reason about it. They irrationally continue to espouse it even when their attention is called to it, for it is deeply woven into the fabric of their upbringing and the social structure they knew. For all these reasons prejudice can well be understood as a modern manifestation of the powers of evil depicted in the New Testament.

Conclusion

The goal of this chapter has been to try to suggest a few experiences within our society today that can appropriately be understood as the powers of evil depicted by the biblical writers. The correspondence between biblical witness and present experience is striking. The Bible depicts structures created by God—government, religion, society—which are good servants but become the forces of evil when man gives them the allegiance due only to God. In our world today we have no trouble recognizing the evil spirit of violence that has been let loose by governments and nations that saw themselves as the ultimate creation of God or history. We can see the prejudice that eats away at society, fed to a significant extent by religion that claims absolute validity for itself rather than for the One it serves so sinfully.

The recognition of these "evil spirits," these "principalities and powers," the "god of this world," shows how we can still today see that the predicament man finds himself in is one of his own making. The biblical proclamation is clearly that God made the world and its powers and authorities, and they were good. But he made them in such a way that if man refused to worship *him* and came to worship *them* they would become the instruments of God's judgment and wrath, not of his gift of order. God gave rebellious man up to the powers he chose to serve and so man became a slave of these servants of God's wrath. The powers of evil are the morphine in the bloodstream of society: morphine has a good use as a pain-killer; but if it is used indulgently, allowed to become a central necessity of life, it becomes addicting and destructive of life. It becomes punishment to anyone who gives it first place.

God intended the corruption to be punishment. But the corruption of the world has become so extensive that God's ultimate goals are threatened, the servant powers have become enemy powers. Thus the New Testament proclaims that man's slavery is both justified punishment *and* tragic oppression. Its good news is that in Christ the powers have been conquered, a message that is woven into the fabric of the remaining chapters of this book.

Suggested Reading

Caird, G. B. *Principalities and Powers.* Oxford: Oxford University Press, 1956.

Cullmann, Oscar. *The State in the New Testament.* New York: Scribner's, 1956.

Graham, H. D., and Gurr, T. R., editors. *Violence in America: Historical and Comparative Perspectives.* New York: Transworld, 1969.

Kallas, J. *The Satanward View.* Philadelphia: Westminster, 1966.

Langton, E. *Essentials of Demonology.* London: Epworth, 1949.

Langton, J. G. *Jesus and the Power of Satan.* Philadelphia: Westminster, 1968.

Niebuhr, Reinhold. *Moral Man and Immoral Society.* New York: Scribner's, 1932.

Chapter Six: Conqueror of Evil

Introduction: "The Gang"

Preliminary Victories

MOSES AND THE EXODUS

DAVID THE IDEAL KING

JEREMIAH THE SUFFERING PROPHET

Salvation in Judgment

Suffering Joy

Jeremiah Lives

Fulfilling the Promises

LIBERATING LIFE

Binding the Strong Man

Unbinding the Law

PURIFYING LIGHT

Real Royalty

All-Including Arms

CONCLUSION

Chapter Six

Conqueror of Evil

Introduction: "The Gang"

One sultry summer day half a dozen boys were lounging around the streets of their concrete jungle, the decaying inner city that was the only world they knew. Across the street the owner of a small market watched them and felt sorry for them so he called them over and said, "How would you boys like it if I got a basketball and backboard and set it up in the alley beside my store?" Having nothing else to do the boys jumped at the chance. That was the beginning of their team, their gang, which they named "The Kings." They were initially really grateful to "the Man" as they called the store-owner, for in forming their gang they found not only something to do but also a community which provided protection and identity.

In the winter the gang found itself in an escalating conflict with a larger gang that did not relish the idea of competition. Eventually the Kings were surrounded and imprisoned in a basement by the Cheetahs and threatened with the worst beating they had ever imagined if they did not dissolve their gang. The store-owner heard of the crisis and sent a former gang member, John Brown, to lead an escape. He tried to bargain with the Cheetahs, but when that failed he sneaked in and freed the Kings and set up an ambush for their enemies. When the cocky Cheetahs returned to the scene they found themselves attacked from all sides with garbage, water, sticks and bricks. The result was that the Cheetahs acquiesced in the liberation, so the Kings had their very own turf.

The second crisis the Kings faced was internal, for a leader took over whose aims were all self-centered. He struggled to the top in order to feel superior to others, and so his way of leading was to demand that everyone do exactly as he commanded. He forced two young boys to steal a car. He ordered every new boy to bring him back a purse snatched from a woman. He was tolerated because he kept the gang strong, but one young gang member, George Washington Carver, slowly became alienated from him and so went to the Man to talk over what might be done. That talk gave him determination to stand up and oppose the tyrannical ways of the leader. Naturally the result was that George was driven from the gang; but gradually he collected around himself a growing number of the disaffected gang members so that eventually they were able to go back and depose the tyrant. George then became the new leader, and even though he made many mistakes he was remembered in the gang as the greatest leader they had ever had.

A few years later George had gone and the gang had become almost indistinguishable from all the other gangs in the city. They still occasionally went back to the store and played basketball. Now and then they would go in and talk to the Man when nothing was happening, but when they left it always seemed as if a few apples and other edibles had left with them. Shoplifting and even burglary in other stores in the area began increasing, along with assaults and muggings in the streets. So the store-owner, aware that the gang was involved, found a messenger to send to them. He sent a boy named Jerry, who knew the gang but had not belonged to it, with a message of warning: either the crime in the stores and streets dried up or the police would wipe them out. Through Jerry he invited the boys to begin again on basketball, but they laughed in his face. Beyond laughter they played tricks on Jerry, including locking him in a cellar where the water was up to his knees. They thought that they could avert the day of reckoning if they silenced this critic. But shortly the police came in answer to many store owners' complaints, sweeping up the whole gang and getting them sent off to reform school.

Eventually a few of the gang returned from reform school and the Kings began to form again. The group's memory of the disaster of arrest and imprisonment kept it out of bad trouble for a while. But slowly it began to deteriorate again, for an adult organized crime mob appeared on the scene and corralled the gang by a combination of promises and threats. Thus the gang members began to serve as spies, numbers runners, drug pushers and enforcers of the mob's "law" on all the young people of the area.

Naturally this did not go unnoticed by the store-owner who had brought the gang into existence and helped it out of trouble many times over the years. His old store had been demolished in an urban renewal project so he now was located several miles away, but he kept in touch. This final disaster of coming under the influence of organized crime led him to send his son, whom none of the present gang members knew, to join the gang and try to free it from the clutches of the mob. It quickly became apparent to the gang leaders that this new boy would be a source of trouble, for he spoke up against the alliance with the mob and began to lure some of the others to his side. The gang leaders brought this threat to the attention of the mob and a few days later the son was run over by a car and killed.

The shock of this killing forced the son's followers to see they were playing with dynamite, so they abandoned the gang and found a new life a few miles away under the care of the victim's father—the founder of the gang many years before. The son's willingness to stand openly and freely for real life inspired them to do the same together. Before long the rest of the gang and the mob fell out over the killing and so the mob wiped the gang out, driving the boys away. The name "The Kings" was forgotten in the old streets, but a few miles away, it lived on in a new gang called "The King's Sons."

The parable just told is based on Jesus' story of the Wicked Husbandman and elaborated in the light of the whole biblical account of the way God has gone about overcoming the evil that has crept into his good world. It offers a number of modern analogies that may help us to enter imaginatively into the story of Israel. Before we go on in the main sections of this chapter to elaborate on God's victories, a few of the main principles underlying the whole chapter need to be mentioned for they provide the basic orientation that will help to make this approach meaningful.

First, all we need to see that the central biblical image of God's action in the world is of him as conqueror of evil. In Christian thought too often a narrowing has taken place so that God's goal is seen solely as the atoning for man's sins, or the reconciliation of individuals to himself. These are certainly part of the whole, perhaps the central part, but the whole of God's action must be seen as the context. The last chapter made clear that man's problem is not simply that he is guilty for what he has done and so cannot come back into God's presence. Man *is* guilty; but in addition he is blind to the truth, and is enslaved to forces that are beyond his control.

To a substantial extent man is thus a victim. He is a victim of forces at work within society that mold his mind to accept half-truths as whole truths; he is seduced into accepting as reasonable the imprisonment within corrupt structures that he was born into. God's action in the world to save mankind must thus be more than alleviating guilt. He must in addition help men to see and overcome the subtle and not so subtle tyrannies at work throughout civilization. All evil is God's enemy and so his work is the conquest of every form of evil.

The Bible as a whole is a story that reveals to us that in Israel and in Christ God has decisively initiated the conquest of evil by creating an expanding island of freedom in love surrounded still by a hostile sea of tyranny and hate. The Bible does not offer us theories of this conquest, so that we can convince ourselves logically and rationally that we ought to believe this or that. Quite the contrary, the biblical writers tell us a story, a series of historical events understood as God's action to free his creation from the evil to which it had become subject. The biblical writers did not tell the story because they lacked the philosophical tools to construct a theory. They tell the story because a story is something we can identify with, something that gets down into our imagination, intuition and the seat of our motivation. We live by stories that provide our identity. We do not live by theories, however much value theories may have in helping us understand the stories and relate them to other areas of life.

The story of God's conquest of evil is a long one, beginning with the story of creation and reaching forward to the vision of the consummation in the new heaven and new earth still to come. Christians, especially Protestants, have often missed much of the story because they have focused entirely on the death of Jesus as God's saving action, thinking of the Old Testament as simply predictions of the coming salvation and Jesus' life as simply a prelude to his death. The biblical writers, however, saw the history of Israel as a history of God's real, if preliminary, battles against evil. God's conquest of evil was a long-term battle and the Old Testament was a real beginning, even though its culmination came in Jesus.

The culmination of God's battle with evil must be seen in the whole of Jesus' life, not just in his death. His death was an integral part of his life, the final battle in a series of battles that marked the whole of his ministry. Only when we see how he fought evil during his life can we properly understand what finally happened in his death and resurrection. The stories we find in the Gospels are thus much better vehicles of the victory of God in Christ than are the theological theories developed in later centuries to try to make the biblical message philosophically respectable.

The stories of Israel and Jesus are stories out of a distant past, however, and so if we are to find our identity in them today we must assimilate them to stories in our more recent past that have evocative power in our lives. To feel the power of the Exodus story we must associate it with a story of liberation with which we identify, the American Revolution or the Emancipation Proclamation, for example. To grasp the way Jesus' nonviolent death could be a victory over evil we must talk about the martyrdom of Lincoln or Gandhi or Martin Luther King. These more recent stories, we shall suggest, provide more immediate impact for many, but in addition are examples in our own time of God continuing his battle against evil.

Seeing the story of God's involvement in human history as the conquest of evil helps to solve a paradox that has agitated Christians for centuries. How can God be both loving and just? The answer is that in his conquest of evil he is always both, for his attack on evil is always judgment for evildoers and rescue for victims. The last chapter showed the way that biblical writers saw God's wrath exercised by Satan and powerful nations. But these powers always went beyond the punishment due their victims so God then came in battle against the punishers, overcoming the oppressor, rescuing the victim. For those in society who are on top, the oppressors, God's action comes as destruction. For those in the world who are the victims, the people Jesus spent his life with, God's intrusion comes as a rescue. How we experience God's coming depends to some extent on whether we identify ourselves with the oppressors, the supporters of evil powers, or with the oppressed, the victims.

In the two main sections of this chapter we will now weave these themes into the biblical story of God the Conqueror. The first section will bring out three central instances of God's victories in the history of Israel. The second section will show how Jesus' life is to be seen as the culmination of the battle. Then in the next chapter we will take up the New Testament images of the Cross, the metaphors used to point to the meaning of Jesus' death.

Preliminary Victories

The Old Testament story of God's battles against evil in the universe is *our* story; it is not a past that is over and can be forgotten by Christians. It is our story because it concerns our God, our present Author of Life. It tells how he began long ago the process that reached its decisive point in Jesus' life, death and resurrection, a decision, a victory, that is now being worked out in our own lives today. In one sense the victories of God in Israel's history are like the preliminary Allied victories in the Egyptian and Libyan deserts in World War II: in both cases the victories were important but not decisive, though they pointed ahead to what was coming—the invasion of Europe, the overwhelming victory in Jesus.

In a second sense the stories of God's victories over evil in Israel's history are more important for his story than were the North African desert battles for the story of World War II. Those tank battles in the desert helped raise Allied confidence, but the real test was still to come; knowing the story of Montgomery at Alamein and Patton at Casablanca does not help us much to interpret what is to come. But God's conquests in the Old Testament are directly revealing of who he is, what kind of work he is doing, and so they point forward to the time when these preliminary victories will be fulfilled in the great victory. I shall try to show that only in the light of those Old Testament stories do we adequately see what God was conquering through Jesus.

We cannot survey the whole of the story of Israel because the major thrust would be obscured by the details. So we will present three significant episodes in God's battle with evil, those associated with the careers of Moses, David and Jeremiah. God's victories in the lives of these three men can justifiably be pointed to as among the highlights of the drama God was working out. But in addition each of them in a different way from the others points ahead to the Coming One, to the decisive battle, and so illumines what happened in Galilee and Jerusalem centuries later.

Moses and the Exodus

The first Israelite Declaration of Independence, made in Egypt under Moses, was the central story in Israel's memory, the guiding light in its continuing life, the symbol of her identity as the people who were given freedom by a loving, conquering Father. For more than a century the descendants of Jacob in Egypt had been oppressed by the Egyptians: they were forced into slavery, and became the victims of attempted genocide when Pharaoh ordered all their male babies killed. They were evidently a people of initiative and talent and communal responsibility because the Egyptians saw their gradual population increase as a distinct threat to the status quo.

The most amazing part of the Israelite memory of their liberation was the fact that they had only to trust God's promises and obey his orders to get up and leave. They were not to organize guerrilla bands. Nothing was said about infiltrating and undermining the Egyptian government and army. No fighting was called for, only faith, which was hard enough. Moses called the people to follow him out into the desert, to stand up and vote for liberation with their feet. And though the sensible people said this was the road to destruction, it turned out to be the way home. The victory over evil turned out as promised to Moses in his vision in the desert: "I am the Lord, and I will bring you out from under the burdens of the Egyptians, and I will deliver you from their bondage, and I will redeem you with an outstretched arm and with mighty acts of judgment, and I will take you for my people, and I will be your God" (Exod. 6:6 f.).

The adoption took place out in the desert, once God had conquered the Egyptian lust for slaves, bringing freedom to Israel as he brought judgment upon Egypt. At Mt. Sinai Moses the liberator became Moses the mediator, the one who led his compatriots into a covenant with their rescuer and with each other. They recognized that their liberty was a gift of love from beyond them and that an appropriate response was thanksgiving, honor, allegiance and service, forming a nation that would reflect in its laws the One who was its Creator.

The story is simple: a group of slaves is wondrously freed from a power greater than they could ever hope to conquer, and this event binds them into a nation living out of that great gift. Future generations told the story as their own, for the way it was remembered was in these words: "the Egyptians ill-treated us, humiliated us, and imposed cruel slavery upon us. Then we cried to the Lord of our fathers for help, and he listened to us and saw our humiliation, our hardship and distress; and so the Lord brought us out of Egypt with a strong hand and outstretched arm . . . It was not with our forefathers that the Lord made this covenant, but with us, all of us who are alive and are here this day" (Deut. 26:6 ff.; 5:3). Down to the present day Jewish people repeat these words, remember this story, identify with the liberating victory and so experience anew God's conquest of Egyptian evil.

But Christians generally refuse to accept that story as their own. The wondrous events, the miracles and plagues, are brought forth as evidence of God's power. But the heart of the matter—that God's loving deed is liberating victims of slavery—that is too often forgotten. It is ignored first because Christians have generally been slaveholders not slaves in the modern era. But secondly Gentile Christians, we who have our own national allegiances, find it difficult to know what to make of this political memory when we have our own political memories. Somehow we need to associate our own national feelings of identity with this ancient story, but not fall into the trap of saying our Declaration of Independence supersedes the ancient Hebrew one.

The truth from a biblical standpoint seems to be that the Exodus story is the creation of liberty, the charter for liberation movements, the declaration that the God of All is one who seeks political freedom for the enslaved as one of his goals. Therefore whenever people have stood up against enslaving tyrants, in the Magna Charta, the American and French and Russian Revolutions, the Emancipation Proclamation, we have an outworking of the flow of liberty that began with the sending of Moses to Egypt.

For Americans the national memory of George Washington is often a helpful way to try to enter into the story of Moses. We remember Washington as the leader of the ragged army of liberation; as the one who presided over the formation of the covenant at Philadelphia; as the man whose honesty, shrewdness and lack of prejudice and ambition enabled him to hold together thirteen separate colonies until they were a union. If we can associate our empowering memories of the story of our liberty with the story of Moses and mankind's liberty we may begin to be moved by the Exodus story the way ancient Hebrews and early Christians were.

From the Christian standpoint of course the victory over Egyptian tyranny was the beginning, but not decisive. Political liberty comes and goes, and there is no guarantee that political liberty, good as it is, will bring inner freedom that comes from trust in the Giver of liberty. The Hebrews remembered the story but ignored the warnings that went with it and so eventually slavery came again and again. The covenant at Sinai was a great step forward, an agreement to live for and by the One Lord. But it was only a beginning too, for it was an external covenant, laws governing external behavior for the most part and so it did not reach down to the depths of the peoples' hearts. The form was kept and the spirit often forgotten, so eventually even the form was often ignored.

Thus Moses and the Exodus stand as an eternal memory for God's people, a memory of both success and failure. We must remember that liberty, the freeing of political slaves, is God's deed, one he continues to carry on, in Germany and Africa, Greece and Portugal not too long ago; in Eastern Europe and Southern Africa in the not too distant future. But the failure of political liberty to provide full life points forward to the One whose victory would provide the inner freedom, the inner covenant, that alone fulfills the promise of the Exodus.

David the Ideal King

The nation Israel reached the peak of its worldly glory under David, the king remembered throughout the people's history as the ideal, the original model of what God desired a king to be. Two significant events took place through David, the deposition of Saul and the freeing of the nation from threats on its borders, in particular from the Philistines. Saul had earned the Lord's displeasure by disobedience, giving in to the wishes of the people instead of following the command given through Samuel (1 Sam. 15). Saul was a man given to fits of madness after the Lord's favor and spirit left him (16:14), the worst of it being his completely unprovoked jealousy of David in his success as Saul's general (18:17 ff.). This jealousy drove Saul to exile David and thus weaken the nation enough so that the Philistines beat the army and killed Saul and his three sons.

The story of David presents him as a complete contrast to Saul, and thus the Lord's anointing of David as king is a victory given to the whole nation, not just to one man. In Egypt the tyrant was Pharaoh, but in Canaan it now can be seen that Israelites too may be tyrants, for evil may be found even in the anointed one of Israel, the king. David's exile is the means by which the Lord brings an end to Saul and his tyranny, for David is then anointed king upon his return. The Lord is with David and so the enemies of Israel all go down to defeat and the nation's boundaries reach their greatest extent ever.

If it had been only the *national glory* for which David was the agent, that would have made him a central memory in Israel. But there was much more. David's character stood out and made him more than a military hero, for he was an ideal of what a king of Israel needs to be. He was first of all remembered as quite humble. He spoke of himself as a flea, as nothing, when Saul offered him marriage to his daughter, and later tried to kill him (1 Sam. 18:23; 24:14). When the Lord promised that his line would last forever David took it as completely undeserved (2 Sam. 7:18) for he knew that the Lord rescues the humble and overthrows the proud (2 Sam. 22:28). David gave all the credit for his victories to God, seeing that all that was needed was to depend on him (2 Sam. 22).

Second, David was infinitely loyal. Even though Saul was trying to kill him he twice refused to kill Saul when he could have. David remembered the friendships of his exile when he became king, treating Saul's family far beyond what they deserved, for the sake of Jonathan, Saul's son and David's friend. David was kind to those who did not deserve it, and gracious to enemies when they were defeated (2 Sam. 19:22). Unlike the typical oriental monarch who treated everyone in the nation as his possession, David saw himself as God's servant to lead and serve God's people, obedient to him and dependent upon him. Thus the image of a servant king first began to surface in David.

In this king the Lord united his nation, freed it from its enemies, gave it a chance to develop its inner life so as to reflect him. But the victories won in David were only preliminary, not decisive, for David was a sinner too. David committed adultery with Bathsheba and then had her husband murdered to cover up; so disaster struck the nation as a result. David's son Absalom started a civil war, and though he was defeated, the seeds were sown there for the future division of the nation and the destruction of both parts in the centuries to come. Yet even in his sinfulness David was a model, for he acknowledged his guilt, repented and returned to the Lord. Characteristically David once cried out to the Lord: "It is I who have done wrong, the sin is mine; but these poor sheep, what have they done? Let thy hand fall upon me and upon my family" (2 Sam. 24:17).

In David's failure we see how that great victory over the Philistines and Israelite disunity was only preliminary, not decisive. Great victories were won through him, but he too had his weaknesses, and finally he died and a tyrant arose again in the person of his son Solomon. For the next centuries the people looked forward to a new son of David, one who would bring a decisive victory over the enemies of Israel—without and within—one who would be a second David but without David's weaknesses.

In the American memory probably Abraham Lincoln is the

closest parallel to the Hebrew memory of David, for Lincoln is remembered today (at least in the North) as the model president, the one by whom all others are measured. Like David, Lincoln was a man of humility, loyalty, and graciousness to enemies, one who cared for the common people because he was one of them. By Lincoln's hands God ended the inner strife that threatened to destroy the nation. He too had his faults and the willingness to acknowledge them and seek a new path. Finally we find that his victory too was only preliminary, not absolutely decisive, for discrimination has not ended and slavery of subtle power has remained until this day. But if we wish to feel how we might enter into the memory of David as one of God's great but preliminary victors, our memory of Lincoln is a good place to start.

The object of telling David's story (and pointing to our memories and feelings about Lincoln to evoke a deeper intuition of what David was like), telling both the victory and defeat, is to give a further, different, image of the divine Conqueror of Evil at work. The Exodus points to God as victor over the tyranny of an international oppressor. David's story shows that evil may appear in the person of the leader of God's own people, as when self- and family-preservation rather than service become Saul's dominant motivation. Here individual evil became collective disaster. Thus God's victory comes through the judgment on Saul, a victory by which David unites the nation and becomes the model king for generations to come. Here it is clear that God is very much concerned with the character and actions of kings and presidents, for their individual evil can bring nation-wide, and in these days world-wide, catastrophe. Yet even this Davidic highpoint is not decisive in God's drama, for David fails and in his failure points forward to one who will not fail.

Jeremiah the Suffering Prophet

In Jesus' lifetime there were three great men from the story of Israel's wanderings with God who were suggested as foreshadowings of his coming. The first was Moses the liberator, mediator and lawgiver with whom Jesus was associated in a number of ways: in the Sermon on the Mount (a new law), in the Transfiguration in which Jesus' death is called a new Exodus, and in the Last Supper in which Jesus is the mediator of a new covenant. David of course was in the people's mind when Jesus was called Messiah, King of the Jews and Son of David.

The third great servant of the Lord whom the early Christians saw as a foreshadowing of Jesus was the prophet Jeremiah. Matthew specifically says that when the people wondered who Jesus might be they spoke of the return of "Jeremiah or one of the prophets" (Matt. 16:14); but in addition there are striking parallels between Jesus' life as the persecuted suffering Savior and Jeremiah's life of pain. In telling Jeremiah's story, therefore, we will suggest one more preliminary victory won by the Conqueror of Evil that pointed beyond itself to the decisive battle still to come.

Salvation in Judgment

Jeremiah was sent by God to bring judgment and salvation to the people of Judah. Jeremiah did not simply present ideas, he had divine power to conquer evil, for at his call God said: "This day I give you authority over nations and over kingdoms, to pull down and to uproot, to destroy and to demolish, to build and to plant" (Jer. 1:10). Jeremiah bore God's word within him, a word that scorched like fire and splintered rock like a sledge-hammer (23:29), because the kings and their ministers and the people responded to Jeremiah's word—usually by rejection.

The central significance of Jeremiah's mission is found in the fact that he helped overthrow Judah by demoralizing the corrupt leaders; thus he helped save the people from the complete destruction a siege would have caused. The people were saved by being taken into exile where a remnant lived on, a spark remained alive, so in two generations the light could be relit in Jerusalem. Jeremiah brought judgment, punishment, destruction on the evil that Judah and her kings had lived for so long. By his prophecy he prepared the people for the judgment, and so enabled them to see their exile as a purifying, refining, chastening source of new life. Without Jeremiah Israel's religion would probably have died, the supremacy of Babylon's gods having been proven. So Jeremiah brought judgment and salvation together, the conquest of Israel's evil and the possibility of new life.

Moses' story pointed to the evil of pagan tyrannies. David's story brought out the evil even in Israel's own leadership. Jeremiah's story shows us how the disease can permeate the whole organism of God's people, with only one or two individuals like Jeremiah and Baruch remaining largely uninfected. God may have to destroy his people outwardly in order to save the spark that may start a new fire when the wood is dry again. There were hints in the lives of Moses and David that God's chosen servant will suffer in his role, but this reality reaches its peak in Jeremiah.

Suffering Joy

Jeremiah stood in the Temple and proclaimed that the Lord would destroy it because of the oppression, bloodshed and idolatry of the nation, foreshadowing Jesus' words in the second Temple six hundred years later. As a result Jeremiah was arrested and threatened with death (Jer. 26:8). At that time he escaped but his life was constantly threatened; "I was like a gentle lamb led to the slaughter" for his enemies hatched plots to destroy him, even to wipe out his name (11:19); he was flogged and put in the stocks as a public disgrace (20:2); he was imprisoned by the king himself (32:2 f.), arrested for treason, flogged (37:12 ff.) and imprisoned in the bottom of an old well where he was left to starve (38:6) and only barely escaped. He was taken into exile in chains by the Babylonians but then freed (40:1). Finally, in the worst humiliation of all, he was forced to disobey God by going down to Egypt with Judah's survivors, expressly against God's word (43:7) and there he probably died, sharing the pain and death of exile.

The pain Jeremiah suffered was not only this unjust persecution that followed him constantly but also his sympathy for his people, for he says (perhaps in God's name): "I am wounded at the sight of my people's wound" (Jer. 8:21). He wished he could refuse to speak destruction, to save his people and himself, but when he kept silent God's word became "like a fire blazing in my heart, and I was weary with holding it under" (20:9). In addition God's proclamations often did not come out as Jeremiah expected so he accuses the Lord of duping him, of deceiving him (4:10; 15:18) for the wicked prosper and the faithful prophet knows endless suffering (12:1) so that he regrets that he was ever born (15:10; 20:14).

Yet right in the middle of his life of suffering Jeremiah had something that made up for it all, for he says to God: "Thy word is joy and happiness to me, for thou hast named me thine" (Jer. 15:16). God's presence is all he needs ultimately, for the divine promise is "they will fight against you; but they shall not prevail against you, for I am with you . . . to deliver you" (1:19). In God's presence Jeremiah experienced beforehand the salvation that began in destruction: he foresaw the overthrow of Babylon in seventy years, and the return of a purified remnant at that time (25:11; 29:10 f.); he saw a new king, a just, benevolent, true Son of David (23:5); and above all he saw in his own experience of God's inner relationship with him the promise of a new covenant, when all God's people individually would know the Lord in their hearts (31:31 ff.).

Jeremiah Lives

By Jeremiah the Lord conquered the evil of Judah in such a way that good came out of the destruction. Jeremiah's own endless suffering was the price he had to pay for his faithful serving of God, a suffering that joined in and exceeded the suffering of those upon whom punishment was due. He brought about the judgment and suffered it himself; but he was not able to do more than provide a hope for new life by means of the pictures he painted of the future and his own experience of personal involvement with the Lord.

Few people in American history provide the feel of Jeremiah better than Martin Luther King, Jr. He was a prophet who proclaimed the same word Jeremiah did: "Amend your ways and your doings, . . . execute justice one with another, . . . do not oppress the alien [i.e., ethnic minorities], the fatherless or the widow [i.e., the poor and powerless], shed [no] innocent blood, . . . do not go after other gods" (Jer. 7:5 ff.). King stood in opposition and suffered persecution, imprisonment, plots hatched against him and was finally led as a lamb to the slaughter. His nonviolent word brought out much violence in the cities as blacks became incensed at the oppression he pointed out. Yet he was an innocent, nonviolent, victim of the power of the oppressors. He too had a dream, as Jeremiah did, and was not able to bring that dream to fruition himself but had to leave it as his gift to us who follow. If we enter into the story of Martin Luther King, Jr. we will find out a great deal about Jeremiah, the prophet who brought God's conquest of evil, bearing the pain in his own body, handing on a dream that was a significant power in God's hands over the following years.

God's victory in Jeremiah was only preliminary. The worship of physical idols that had been practiced by God's people was rooted out forever. The overt oppression of the weak by aristocrats was never again as central a problem in Judah. A beginning was made in seeing each individual man (but only men, not women) as directly involved with the Lord. Jeremiah's life of suffering brought to life the image of God's man as one who suffers externally and finds his prosperity only within, in loving relationships. But these things happened only in a preliminary way, for idolatrous legalism was developed, oppression of the religious nonconformists arose, individual relationships to God were encased in ritual requirements, and suffering as God's way to victory was seen only as a rare oddity. Only in Jesus was the decisive breakthrough made, when the victory begun in Jeremiah's suffering prophecy came to its fulfillment in the suffering prophecy of One in whom God's Word was incarnate.

Fulfilling the Promises

The victories won by God in the history of Israel were real conquests of evil, but they were only partial, pointing forward to a fulfillment yet to come. Our Declaration of Independence was like that, for it was an act of liberation based on the premise of the equality of all, and it has since become a powerful symbol for independence movements. But the American Revolution brought equality only for white, male landowners, thus the next centuries have been a continued battle to bring equality to the nonwhite, females and the poor. A promise was made in the real victory of 1776, and that promise is still being brought to reality. Conquest of the evil of inequality is still a painful battle.

Liberation came with Moses, purified government with David and the refining out of the nation's evil in Jeremiah. Those were real victories, and as such are essential symbols showing how God was at work conquering evil and where he is at work in our world today doing the same thing. But our Christian impetus toward serving God as those Israelite servants did does not come just from their stories, ambiguous with both victory and defeat as they are. We now see in Jesus the end of the line of Israel, the fulfillment of the promises made in those stories and their failures. The New Testament proclaims that in Jesus God has fought the decisive battle against evil so that those who inherit his Spirit can experience the liberation, purification and power over evil that he did. For while the decisive battle is over and final victory is certain (we believe), still the war goes on and indeed the whole of the Christian life as the Church can and should be understood as carrying to the depths of human life, the roots of society and the ends of the earth the victory won in Jesus.

The way that victory is carried is by our purified, liberated, loving, suffering lives. The one essential source of such lives is the *story* of Jesus. The gospel is not a theological-philosophical theory about the nature of God and man and atonement. The gospel is a story, for stories have an evocative power of their own, and that is why the early Christians remembered stories about Jesus and put them at the beginning of their collection of Christian writings. If we are to see how God's decisive conquest of evil took place in Jesus we must tell the stories and they will touch those who are open to their insight. In this second half of the chapter I will tell some of the stories of Jesus' life that make present God's conquest, and then in the next chapter I will take up his death and Resurrection that are the consummation of his story.

Liberating Life

Moses was the liberator of Israel, but he only began the task that was brought to its decisive turn in the time of Pontius Pilate. In the Exodus story the evil conquered was a political tyranny; but that is only one manifestation of the powers of evil and so a much greater victory over the source of evil must be gained. Second, Moses was the mediator of a covenant and its attached law which provided basic identity and direction to Israel. Unfortunately such externals can be made into tyrants, and that was precisely what happened, for in Jesus' day the law itself was the instrument of Pharisaic tyranny. Finally, Moses was a violent man, having murdered an Egyptian in his youth, and so his example supports the ancient demon of violence that whispers, "Get them before they get you." Here too Jesus is God's ultimate Word, his decisive victory.

For several centuries now the New Testament emphasis upon unseen powers of evil as the real enemies of mankind has been discounted as primitive superstition. As a result of that intellectual censorship the Church has generally lost touch with the central biblical theme of God's victory in Christ over the demonic powers. In the present century, however, especially since the advent of Hitler, Stalin, nuclear weapons, television and computers it has become apparent to many that evil does work as insidious, powerful, often unseen forces that run and ruin many lives. The last chapter showed that the biblical emphasis upon government, violence, law and religion as fronts for demonic powers makes a great deal of sense of modern experience. Therefore we can return to the biblical good news that in Jesus these powers have been decisively defeated and see whether that too may help to make sense of Christian experience.

Binding the Strong Man

A central theme of Mark's Gospel is that Jesus is man's champion against Satan, who is the image embodying all the forces of evil arrayed against man. Jesus hints that his acts of freeing the demon-possessed are the sign that Satan (the demons' master and owner) has been bound: "No one can enter a strong man's house and plunder his goods, unless he first binds the strong man; then indeed he may plunder his house" (Mark 3:27).

In a small Southern city Herb Strong was the man to see for everything. He controlled the mayor, the police chief and the district attorney because he possessed compromising pictures of them caught unawares in the illegal local brothel. Their own illegal, unacceptable behavior had made them his pawns.

One day Herb invited Josh Knight, a young, politically ambitious attorney in the district attorney's office, to have a political discussion at his big house on the hill. In the discussion Herb offered the young man the district attorney's job at the next election and who knows what thereafter. But Josh asked warily, "How will you get the DA to retire?" Strong replied, "I have ways." "Show me," Knight said, "I'm not going to join you unless I know you can produce." The boss then opened a safe and took out an envelope which he handed to Josh. Inside were the pictures of the DA that could destroy his reputation in a day if they were made public.

While Strong was opening the safe the young attorney had daringly dropped a knock-out pill into the other's drink, for he had come prepared for just this, having been warned by a friend. In a few minutes the boss passed out and Josh tied him up with curtain pulls before ransacking the safe. Every picture and negative he could find he took and immediately mailed anonymously to the victims at their offices, with the envelopes marked "Personal."

The strong man was bound, his kingdom plundered, his victims liberated (as long as they did not go back to their old sinful ways). But of course the young attorney did not become the district attorney, for he saved others at the cost of making a mortal enemy for himself.

The one gospel story that symbolizes Jesus' binding of the strong enemy best is the vivid dialogue between him and Satan in which he refuses the reasonable but corrupting temptations offered:

S: Do you seek disciples? Give them all the bread they want, show them your fantastic powers of production.

J: No thanks; even bread can be corrupting when given too much prominence.

S: Are you really someone special in God's eyes? Will he really protect you? Try him out; jump off the Washington Monument and see.

J: Not a chance. Trusting him is the only way to be sure of his strength, so testing him is self-defeating.

S: Well, how about achieving your goal of becoming King of the world? Come my way, use my methods and my power and your task will be complete.

J: I cannot. Your way is the tyranny I have come to end.

In refusing to go the way of the world, the way of power over people, the way of manipulation and self-aggrandizement, Jesus brought to human history a small island of real freedom from tyranny. By accepting the burden of refusing the world's way, Jesus made real the possibility for all mankind to become a part of his island of freedom.

Unbinding the Law

The hardest part of his burden was standing in opposition to the Law, to Israel's religion, for here his refusal to bow could be taken by many to be a rejection of God's calling, judgment and victory in Israel. The dominant power in Judea in Jesus' day was the religious system divided between the Sadducean priests who controlled the Temple and the Pharisaic rabbis who taught the law in the synagogues. They were the inheritors of God's victory over Egypt, the preservers of the covenant and law. They thought *they*, not Jesus, were the agents of God's liberating power, but in reality they were pawns in the hands of the powers of evil. Paul spoke of the Jewish religion as the slavery practiced by the "elemental spirits of the universe," just as pagan religion was (Gal. 4). Jesus saw the law in the hands of the Jewish leaders as the chain binding all Israel: the publicans and sinners were kept unacceptable, frightened, unable to believe God loved them; the "righteous" were kept proud, hypocritical, ritualistic and unloving.

So Jesus refused to take the easy way, to conform and so rise to the peak of the Jewish rabbinate as he certainly would have. Instead he stood and resisted. He touched lepers, accepting their uncleanness in order to cleanse them. He refused to allow an adulteress to be stoned, accepting in himself the anger deflected from her. He deliberately healed on the Sabbath to proclaim in his deeds that the Sabbath is for man's welfare and is not a burden to be added to his daily load. He denounced the externalism of the self-righteous, the hypocrisy of caring that men rather than God praised them, the oppression that their legalism became for the outcasts of society.

Religion, even the divinely inspired religion of Israel, can very easily be a tool in the hands of the powers of evil, but Jesus once for all time by his life exposed and so disavowed those powers as far as his followers are concerned. The victory was in his resistance, but it can become a present victory in anyone who follows him, commits himself to Jesus' cause and receives his Spirit. This victory is thus one that is fought within us and the weapons are not swords or dollars or votes or doctrines. Jesus was God's conquest of the powers of evil, a conquest that was grounded in his life and was consummated in his death as the next chapter will suggest.

Purifying Light

In David God had made a great step forward in his battle against evil, for in that young shepherd-warrior-king God had elevated humility, loyalty, kindness, graciousness, justice and service to the heights where usually only self-assertion, greediness and violence were found. In David Israel began to see what a king really was and so came to see more truly the King of the Universe whom David served. Yet David was not immune to the corruption power brings and his children were even less immune for they had never been anything but powerful princes. So David's story is only a first step in opening the world's eyes to reality. In fact, as the centuries passed and David sank further into the distance, the blindness of God's people increased. Until one day their King came as a brief flash of light that illumined their darkness and purified the minds and lives of those who were willing to have their eyes opened.

Real Royalty

Jesus was called King of the Jews, and like previous kings starting with Solomon he was called Son of God (2 Sam. 7:14). Both these titles were meant to show that in Jesus we see the way God is our King, for the son in Hebrew thought is a reflection and representation of his father. If God is King, as Jesus is King, then a revolutionary new image of what it means "to rule" came into history. It was hinted at in David, who cared for and served his people much more than oriental potentates (like Solomon) usually did, but David only hinted at the amazing servanthood of God that was the Light we can see in Jesus.

Throughout his ministry Jesus showed time and again that those who imitate the perfection of their heavenly Father serve rather than dominate. When the disciples sought power Jesus replied, "If any one would be first, he must be last of all and servant of all" (Mark 9:35). While the world's "great men" lord it over their subjects, treating them as objects for manipulation, in God's eyes "whoever would be first among you must be slave of all. For the Son of man also came not to be served but to serve" (Mark 10:44 f.). No story symbolizes this greatness, this kingship of Jesus better than John's account of the Last Supper. Jesus took a basin and a towel and washed his disciples' feet, the task usually performed by a servant or the lowest-ranking of the disciples. But Jesus emphasized that this was the mark of his Lordship and the way his followers could also be kings.

Jesus' second revolutionary insight into the mind of God is tied to the first: since greatness like God's comes in the form of great service for others, therefore wealth and social standing are not signs of God's blessing but vehicles of man's self-assertive sinfulness. There were hints of this flash of light in the Old Testament, for Amos denounced the oppression of the rich (2:6; 4:1); but for the most part Israel's prophets proclaimed that prosperity was the reward of righteousness. Jeremiah began to see that suffering may be the good man's reward but it was left to Jesus to overthrow the universal prejudice in favor of the rich, when he said "it is easier for a camel to go through the eye of a needle than for a rich man to enter the kingdom of God" (Mark 10:25). That was Jesus' conclusion to his encounter with a rich young man who obeyed the commandments but knew that he did not have life. Jesus offered him life by telling him to give away his wealth to the needy for then he would have eternal riches as one of Jesus' community. But the price was too high. Worldly wealth can be seen and counted on, but who knows whether this radical Jesus really tells the truth when he offers the opposite as divine wealth.

All-Including Arms

Not only did Jesus overturn the traditional understanding of kingship and wealth, but he also brought a purifying light to bear on the religious realm and its proclamation of how God's people are to react to sinners. The traditional view was that God demanded the ostracism of all those who did not obey the law. In the Old Testament this was often expressed in the demand that people be executed for such things as gathering sticks on the Sabbath, cursing one's parents and adultery. In Jesus' day the most common ostracism was for the "righteous" to avoid all contact with publicans, sinners, lepers and all the other unclean "people of the land." Jesus acted in a quite contrary way, spending almost all his time with just such people, on the grounds that they were the ones who needed help. However there was undoubtedly considerable irony in his tone when he allowed the prejudiced, self-righteous legalists to see themselves as the healthy "who . . . need no physician" (Mark 2:17).

Jesus expressed himself more fully in his parable of the wheat and weeds. When the farmer's workers wanted to uproot the weeds deceptively planted along with the wheat, the farmer forbade them because he knew that the uprooting would take the good with the bad and leave both good and bad. That was precisely what the judgmental practice of the "righteous" did: it turned away people whose hearts were set on God's way, while keeping hypocrites whose hearts were set on their own way. Religious people have always ostracized nonconformists and called God's wrath down on them, but Jesus objected. Apparently God allows both the healthy and the sick into his hospital. There are none who are completely healthy and so do not need him, just as there are none who are beyond help. Instead of God's community being a society of beautiful people (as most of them then and now seem to think), in Jesus God called it a rescue mission for grateful bums.

In all these ways Jesus brought the dazzling light of God's presence into the middle of darkness that was largely unreceptive. Society has always been built on power and hierarchies so Jesus' abrogation of the ancient authoritarian image of God's Kingship undermined the position of the political, economic and religious oppressors of mankind. The common ancient image of the king focused on an oriental despot who demanded his own way to satisfy his own whims, surrounded himself with the upper class from society and religious circles and used his power to manipulate his subjects like pawns.

If Jesus is Israel's King, God's Son reflecting his way with man, then that oriental potentate image is largely false. For Jesus brought God before man as one who serves and supports, not one seeking servants and self-aggrandizement. Far from enslaving men as human leaders do, God sets them free from the conditioning of their culture and its standards of success, thus allowing them to be themselves. Ever since that Light dawned there has been no excuse for the power-seeking, money-grubbing, nonconformist-excluding behavior of God's people. Even though we still act that way our memory of Jesus washing feet, having no money, excluding no one, burns in our conscience as a spark that cannot be extinguished.

Conclusion

Jesus was the fulfillment of God's promises of conquest of evil, promises that had been seen by Israel in the partial, preliminary victories that were the central chapters in her story. In Jesus, so his followers believed, God brought to all mankind the liberty and light that were the sources of the true life the people of Israel had glimpsed afar off. The clear differences between Moses and David on the one hand—men of great political, social and legal influence in Israel—and Jesus the outcast, crucified criminal on the other seem to make the claim that Jesus was the fulfillment of their promise an empty one. But from the Christian perspective the key to man's troubles is within him, no matter how influential his environment may be. Therefore the final freedom is spiritual, the true light is inner light, and so Jesus is the peak of the mountain Moses and David had begun to climb centuries before. By taking Jesus' story as our own we can today experience the victory his ancient disciples knew.

The way liberty and light can come through a man with no worldly power is seen in Randall McMurphy, the hero of Ken Kesey's *One Flew Over the Cuckoo's Nest.* The cuckoo's nest is a mental hospital where most of the patients have committed themselves voluntarily because they cannot cope with the outside world. The boss of the ward is Big Nurse, the epitome of the iron hand in a velvet glove, her appearance being reasonable and friendly but her basic viewpoint being not far from that of a slavemaster keeping slaves in line. McMurphy entered her prison and brought life to many of the inmates, life that had seemed to be a lost hope. His method was essentially to teach the men to laugh and play, to begin to enjoy life, to stand up firmly for what was good for them. This continually meant conflict with Big Nurse who cherished docility and obedience in the inmates, and so naturally McMurphy was the major target of her wrath. But gradually a number of the men began to believe that they could run their own lives, free from the straight-jacket of the asylum. In particular, Chief Bromden, an Indian who never spoke before McMurphy came, turned gradually back into a human being under the influence in his life. At the end the chief escaped and a number of the others left by uncommitting themselves, all of them now being essentially cured.

One point in the story remains to be told, however; the consummation comes with McMurphy's death, for Big Nurse was finally able to get him, legally of course. It was his carrying the battle to the ultimate clash costing his own life that decisively changed his friends. How this happened is the central theme of the story which thus is a modern parable of the meaning of Jesus' battle with evil. McMurphy's life had significant impact on his friends, just as Jesus' did, but it was his death that was the culmination of it all. In just the same way Jesus' death was the culmination, the completion of his battle, so to that story of Calvary we must now turn.

Suggested Reading

Cone, J. H. *A Black Theology of Liberation.* New York: Lippincott, 1970.

Cullman, Oscar. *Christ and Time.* Philadelphia: Westminster, 1950.

Danielou, Jean. *The Lord of History.* New York: World, 1958.

Greene, Graham. *A Burnt-Out Case.* New York: Viking, 1961.

Hendry, G. S. *The Gospel of the Incarnation.* Philadelphia: Westminster, 1958.

Robinson, Henry Wheeler. *The Cross in the Old Testament.* London: SCM, 1955.

Chapter Seven: Only a Suffering God Can Help

Introduction: "Theseus's Descent into Hell"

Sight for the Blind

The Black Hole of Humanity

The Window to Reality

Bridging the Gap

Peace at Last

Costly Forgiveness

God's Blinded Eye

Weakness Conquers All

Freedom Within

You're OK

The End of Death's Hold

"The Snake's Poison"

Shackling the Evil Powers

Conquering Violence

Overcoming Prejudice

Conclusion

"One Old Indian"

CHAPTER SEVEN

Only a Suffering God Can Help

Introduction: "Theseus's Descent into Hell"

Once upon a time, when history and legend were intertwined, the most beloved hero in Athens's memory was Theseus, son of King Aegeus after whom the Aegean Sea was named. Aegeus had made one bad mistake in his time as king: he had allowed a guest, the only son of the king of Crete, to go out on a dangerous hunt and the boy had been killed. The boy's father, King Minos, invaded Athens and threatened to destroy it completely unless every nine years the people sent him a sacrifice of seven maidens and seven youths. These sacrifices were sent down into the earth, into the labyrinth under King Minos's castle in Crete. Down there was the ruler of that underworld, a ferocious monster, half-man, half-bull called the Minotaur. He devoured the Athenians as punishment for the death of King Minos's son.

The sacrifices were usually chosen by lot, but when Theseus became of age he stepped forward and volunteered to be one—the only time that anyone had ever freely gone. The people loved him and praised him for his courage and nobility, but wept at the prospect of their future king dying. Theseus, of course, volunteered in order to do something permanent about the Minotaur. He was willing to risk his life for the chance to conquer the monster and so end its threat to his people forever.

When the Athenians arrived in Crete, they happened to be seen by the beautiful Ariadne, King Minos's daughter. She fell in love with Theseus and so approached the creator of the labyrinth, a man called Daedalus, to find a way out of that hell. There was no way out. The tunnels all led deeper and deeper down into the depths and in the past all the young living sacrifices sent down had eventually fallen into the clutches of the Minotaur. But there was the way *in*, and if somehow Theseus and his companions could get back to the barred gate then Ariadne might be able to free them. The plan Daedalus offered was for Theseus to take a ball of thread, to tie one end to the gate and unroll the ball as he descended. Then, if and when the Minotaur was conquered, they could get back out by following the thread.

Theseus formed his companions into a close-knit band, his own willingness to lose his life being the spirit that bound them all together. They had practiced working together as a group to bring about the conquest of the Minotaur. They found a place at the end of a straight tunnel of the labyrinth where a hard rock jutted out. There they used other rocks to sharpen it to a point. Then Theseus, taking the ball of thread, crept quietly down toward the Minotaur's lair. He woke him and got him to charge at him as bulls always do. Theseus then jumped aside at the last moment and gradually drew the monster up to the trap. Finally Theseus stopped in front of the sharpened rock, and just as the beast charged Theseus's companions yelled and jumped and threw things to confuse the enemy. Instead of stopping he charged even faster, and when Theseus jumped aside at the last split second the Minotaur killed himself by driving his skull into the sharpened rock.

So the sacrificed Athenians escaped and sailed back to Athens where Theseus became king. No longer did the threat of the Minotaur hang over every Athenian family. Now joy and thanksgiving and freedom became their heritage once more.

The story of Theseus is one of many ancient stories that depict the hero voluntarily descending into the lair of the great enemy to do battle and then coming out victorious to rule his liberated people. The story is a parable expressing a great deal of the early Christians' experience of Jesus' life, death and resurrection because they too experienced a liberation in him.

The foundation for all Christian thought is the experience some people had of God's presence, power and victory in Jesus. The first Christians experienced a new community, a new life, a new world through their personal contact with him. They found this new creation beginning in Jesus' lifetime, in his gathered community of disciples, in his teaching and his actions toward the weak and the strong. But after his death and resurrection they discovered that this new "spirit" that had animated any group Jesus was in had become the spirit within them all. It now animated Jesus' followers all the time. Therefore the first Christians came to believe that their new relationship with God and each other was a result of Jesus' whole story, his whole appearance and action, not with just one of its parts, his life or death or resurrection alone. When they said "Jesus" they meant the risen one, the suffering one, the one who had lived with them.

Later of course, as preaching and teaching developed, Christians began to reflect on their experience of liberation and the way it could be associated with different aspects of Jesus' whole story. They had come to see God and the world in a new light, they were enlightened, and so they spoke of Jesus as a *prophet* and connected this role with his life and teaching. Further, they had experienced forgiveness and reconciliation through him, so they spoke of him as *mediator* and priest, and associated this role especially with his death seen as a sacrifice. They also experienced him as a liberator from evil powers and so they called him a *conquering king*, and thought of this as especially symbolized in his resurrection and exaltation.

By these distinctions the early Christian preachers showed Jesus as the fulfillment of the great Old Testament servants of God and made the new creation a bit more understandable. But they knew that he was really prophet, priest and king in all phases of his story. In his lifetime he was not only enlightener but also reconciler, bringing God's forgiveness, and liberator, ending the power of demons. The same inclusiveness is found in the effects of his death and his resurrection. Thus we make a mistake if we say it was precisely and solely his death or his resurrection that is the source of God's victory. Instead we need to see that he suffered throughout his lifetime, and was the conqueror of evil continually, his gifts resulting from all he did and suffered, not just from one specific part.

The first Christians had a wide variety of experiences of God's victory because they came with quite various needs. Peter was a blustering coward who needed inner strength to stand firmly in the face of death; and that came to him. Paul was a self-righteous aristocrat who needed to see himself truly and to learn that life comes only through suffering; and Christ taught him that. The publicans like Zacchaeus needed to be reconciled to their neighbors, and to be rescued from their money-grubbing; and that victory was theirs. Others experienced God's victory as freeing from demons, or as forgiveness that rescued them from paralyzing guilt, or as a challenge to their upholding of the minutiae of the law.

The result of this variety of experiences of God's victory was a variety of symbols used by the first Christians to try to express what God had done for them in Christ. They took deep experiences from many different realms of life and used them as images of what they had experienced in Christ. None of these symbols expressed the fullness of God's victory, and like all symbols each of them had its limitations if taken literally. But when a number of the symbols are held together and each allowed to influence our imagining, then we can begin to grasp the mystery of the conquest of evil given to mankind in Christ.

Symbols were chosen from the world of nature, when the victory was called a new creation, new life, a new birth. Education was used and Jesus was seen as the new way of life and truth. The realm of medicine was used too so salvation could be seen as healing blindness, curing disease, or cleansing physical disfigurements like leprosy. The legal aspect of social life was used too, with God's gift being called acquittal (or justification). Even the economic realm provided a significant experience, the giving of a ransom to buy back a slave. Closely allied to that was the military symbol of liberation of the oppressed by conquering the powers of evil. A very common set of symbols naturally came from the religious world, so Jesus was spoken of as offering a sacrifice—the Passover lamb, the Day of Atonement bull, the new covenant blood, the first fruits, grain and several more. Finally, and most central of all, were the symbols taken from personal life, with God's victory in Christ being seen as forgiveness, reconciliation, a new relationship of love and trust.

All these symbols were used in the New Testament and each has something of value to suggest. However, not all of these symbols are as closely tied to our experience today as they were to the experiences of the early Christians. We do not have much personal contact with the economic symbol of ransoming of slaves, but the military symbol of liberation by the conquest of evil powers is still quite vivid. We do not experience temple sacrifices as ancient men did, but we do still know about the personal symbols of reconciliation and love shared anew. Not many of us know of blind men regaining sight, but most have experienced enlightenment through education, the painful growth into an adult way of life and an adult approach to truth. Thus in this chapter we will concentrate on the symbols that are still closely tied to our experience today, seeing Jesus' death and resurrection as enlightenment, reconciliation and liberation.

As I shall emphasize in the next two chapters the victory God won in Christ is seen by Christians as the *decisive* battle but not the final one, for the war still goes on. The analogy that became popular after World War II was the distinction between D-Day when Hitler's European fortress was decisively penetrated and V-Day day when it was overrun. The hardest battle was getting a toe hold on the Normandy beaches, so when that was achieved final conquest was assured. Similarly the early Christians believed that in Jesus the powers of evil had been decisively beaten so that the end is now certain even though the battle still rages in our midst. This future orientation will be further elaborated on in the last chapter, while this present chapter emphasizes what has already been won.

Sight for the Blind

We are blind, not seeing ourselves, life or God truly because seeing them would be too uncomfortable. Freud was absolutely right in recognizing that we are masters at repressing insight which would make us feel less secure, less certain, less comfortable. So we repress the truth of what we really are, covering our paths with a bland "I am as good as the next man." We cower behind a blank wall, hiding from the truth about life's meaning because true life is costly, and we find it easier to take than to share. And supporting the whole blank wall is a flying buttress of an idol we have created in our own image, a "god" whom we can accept so that we can hide from God. But in Jesus' death God has penetrated our darkness with a piercing ray of light.

The Black Hole of Humanity

The death of Jesus is a stark, revealing exclamation point after the judgment "Man the Inhuman Animal!" In the beginning this was not seen, of course, for the Jews and the Romans acted against him for all the best reasons. The high priests were concerned for their people, their nation and their religion, worrying that if a rebellion started among the followers of Jesus then the Romans might take drastic action. The Romans too acted from superior motives; they wanted to keep everything peaceful in the empire, so they dealt swiftly with troublemakers who could have disrupted the peace.

Excellent motives. Good men doing their best. Yet they executed the one Man who had ever lived a truly human life. They were confronted by the presence of God and tried to obliterate him. He came to them and called them to a new way of life but they judged him a failure, a troublesome mosquito they smashed and forgot. Here is condemnation. Their condemnation of him turns out to be condemnation of themselves.

By this act the leaders of Rome and Israel showed their true colors and condemned themselves for all time. *And us too.* We cannot escape the judgment that comes from that event because we too are revealed there. The Jews and Romans were not the worst of men, ancient versions of Stalinists and Nazis. Far from it, they were the best of men, the Winston Churchills and Franklin Roosevelts of the time. But just as Churchill sent bombers to wipe out Dresden and its civilians and Roosevelt ordered the imprisonment of innocent, loyal Japanese-Americans, so the high priest Ananias and Pilate the governor procured the judicial murder of Jesus.

We cannot blame just the Romans and the Jews, for they reveal what is also in us, even if we are the best of people. Even when our motives are heavenly our actions are hellish; in fact, the two often seem to go together. So when we look at the Cross, its first word to us is that we—mankind—acting for excellent reasons, try to destroy the truth when it comes to us. Our own national and individual methods vary, but we all act that way.

The American way of changing leaders often seems to be assassination, an event that brings judgment on us all. When Martin Luther King, Jr. and Robert Kennedy were assassinated the feelings of many Americans were expressed in a cartoon which showed the Statue of Liberty with a sign on her forehead: "Beware, Sick Society." These deaths were not condemnations of the victims, or just of the killers, but of the whole society that spawns and encourages violence. Likewise the Cross of Christ is a light filtering through our closed blinds telling us that we too—the best of us—are killers, especially in our support of, or lack of opposition to, our governments, churches and businesses when they act in inhuman ways.

The Window to Reality

Man's blindness extends to the deepest realms of all, to God himself. While every person has been touched by him, still our rejection of his touch has meant that a wall has been built up between us and him. We refuse to let him touch us, and are blind to his presence, but the Cross is a window in our wall letting us see once again.

The Cross says first of all that God is self-giving love. This may be a commonplace to some, but to many others it is a complete reversal of their views of reality. Whatever they profess, many people really believe, deep down in their hearts, that manipulating, impersonal power is the supreme reality. Power is what affects everything in our social, economic, political and ecclesiastical systems, so power must be the ultimate reality. God is thus seen as essentially the One who has unlimited power, doing whatever he decides to do.

But the Cross makes it abundantly clear that infinite power is an idol constructed by man in his own sinful image. God is instead to be seen in Jesus' death as the One who reaches out in love, a way of life that is occasionally seen around us. In Admiral Perry's expedition to the South Pole one man became frostbitten and had to be carried. He feared that his presence would prevent the others from getting back safely, so one night he simply walked out of the tent into the snow and disappeared, allowing his comrades to get home safely. That is self-giving love. That is the way God acts toward us—not in power that forces us his way, but in weakness that changes us.

Paul spoke eloquently of "the weakness of God" which turns out to be far more earth-shaking and history-making than any of the power plays of men. But this is a scandalous idea, that the weakness of love—weakness in that it does not manipulate or coerce—is a far deeper reality than coercive force. It reverses all our common assumptions to think that if we want to be in touch with the deepest foundations of life, with the reality that gives life, with the streams that provide refreshment, then we must find out where the weakness of love is, for there is God.

Jesus' life made it clear that this was his message; he did not come to us on a white charger leading a well-armed militia, but on a donkey surrounded by peasants bearing only palm branches. Likewise, when the story of the 1960s in the United States is written, it will be seen that people carrying flowers and signs had far more influence for good than Black Panthers or Minutemen or police guns.

The truth about God is seen only if we recognize that he reaches out to us not from a throne, but from a Cross. Medieval theologians saw God as an aloof King, and adopted the Greek philosophical view that God cannot suffer or change. The Cross refutes that view, for it says that God enters into the suffering of mankind, experiencing the hostility that man directs toward his neighbor and toward himself. God suffers from our evil.

God in Christ suffering from the evil of the world is a striking thought that goes right to the heart of the problem of evil. On the surface the death of Jesus seems to be one more example of the radical, inexplicable nature of evil in the world—a contribution to the problem rather than in any way a help. If the best man who ever lived is treated that way there seems to be no justification for the trust that love is the undergirding reality of the universe. Millions of examples of such innocent suffering can be presented as evidence that there is no loving Author behind this story but more likely a demonic one.

The Christian message of God's suffering in Jesus' death and God's victory in Jesus' resurrection does not offer an intellectual answer to the problem of evil. It does not explain why this evil is here nor how it can be reconciled with the Creator's supposed loving will. Just as the Book of Job leaves the source and cause of evil a mystery so does the New Testament. But just as Job finds a personal solution in God's speaking to him, so also in Christ we find a way to live with the evil of the world. In Christ we discover that bearing the evil we cannot explain can be the way to overcome it so that it no longer needs explanation. Once we know that God has entered into our situation and suffered with us, then our suffering becomes a way to know him, to join his cross-bearing, to find the way to overcoming evil, wherever it came from.

Bridging the Gap

Our blindness is a monumental problem, but it is only a surface symptom compared to the alienation that eats away at our hearts. We have rebelled against God, slamming the door in his face and rejecting our neighbor in one move. By our hostility toward God and our enmity toward our neighbor we have become divided within ourselves. Now we find that guilt over the past, hostility in the present and anxiety about the future are our constant companions, either consciously or subconsciously. Is there any hope?

Peace at Last

The testimony of the friends of Jesus was that he brought them a peace unlike anything they had ever known. It was not the world's peace—merely a break in overt hostilities—but divine peace that re-creates life. Not only those first Christians but millions of others down through the ages have added the weight of their stories to the great story, saying that knowing the crucified one means knowing an end to the war that has roared within us as long as we can remember.

Our internal civil war is a confrontation between our standards and our deeds, between our highest desires and our lowest actions, between our dreams and our reality. Each succeeding battle only makes the warriors more intransigent, as happens in wars between nations also. At the beginning of World War I, Europe's civil war, both sides thought it would be a six-week gentlemen's war with professional armies butting heads and the social structures of the nations remaining firm. But as the guns of August gave way to the battle of the Marne and on to Verdun, the two sides became completely locked in, draining the very life-blood of their nations but being unable to stop themselves. The end came only by the addition of an outside factor, the American Army. Likewise our internal war will not just be fought out, it will become increasingly worse unless and until there is One who is allowed in, to absorb the hostility and forgive the guilt of the past. The Cross is God's offer to be that One.

The Cross comes to us as God's resolution to our personal civil war. Our insecurity is overcome by his undergirding hands, his assurance that the universe is for us, not against us, since it is his universe. Our inferiority feelings from comparing our outward success to that of others are exorcized by his word to us that as his children we are all equal in possession of the greatest gift—his love. Our guilt is forgiven. Our hostility is absorbed. Our anxiety is transmuted into hope because One who is willing to suffer for us will see us through everything. Thus it happens that if we are willing to accept God's outstretched hand, ending our war against him, at the same time we come to the end of the devastating war within ourselves.

Once our war against God is over, his outreached hand having ended our rebellion and settled our inner strife, then our enmity toward our neighbor can cease too. We hate our neighbors because we hate ourselves. We see the inhumanity in ourselves and project it on others. Cathy, Adam's wife in *East of Eden* by John Steinbeck, was just like that: she knew she was evil to the core and so thought everyone else was that way too. So she spent her life as the enemy of all who approached her. She never experienced forgiveness, so eventually she killed herself. But millions of others have come to know that God has annulled the guilt of the past, opening a whole new book in which either good or evil can be written. For those who have experienced God's calming acceptance, the deepest reality in life is good not evil, love not hate. That good love is what they see in their neighbors, and feel toward their neighbors, ending the war and starting a new era. But this acceptance from God is never cheap, for it cost Christ his life.

Costly Forgiveness

The Cross was the symbol and summing up of Jesus' whole life of forgiveness. He was crucified *because* he forgave. In a very real sense the Cross was the cost Jesus paid for being One who forgave men in God's name. He forgave by explicit words, but even more he brought God's acceptance to the dregs of society simply by living with them. He did not condone their past, but when they confessed their failures he brought them a new start.

By accepting the bums, prostitutes and petty crooks he made them *feel* God's forgiveness. Thus they were able to accept themselves, and to accept their neighbors, ending the internal and external wars that had devastated their lives. It was Jesus' presence, reaching out in love, putting the legalities of religion aside and overcoming social barriers, that brought an end to the alienation of those who knew him.

For acting in this way he was called a troublemaker, one who set aside the law, one who could lead to a revolution, and so he was condemned. It was precisely his way of life, spending his days with sinners, bringing them to God's forgiveness, that brought the condemnation of the religious officials upon him. The same experience overcame Alexander Dubcek in Czechoslovakia. He brought in the first real Czech springtime in twenty years when he introduced many new freedoms in 1968, trying to present "the human face of socialism." He freed his people from the ignorance of a controlled press, the fear of secret police, the dehumanization of repressed free speech. As Jesus told the poor they did not have to be second-class citizens, so Dubcek told the Czech people that they too could be free and equal to the best.

The tragic result is well known: the high priests of communism exploded from their Kremlin temple, invading Czechoslovakia, killing unarmed students, destroying the new freedoms and banishing Dubcek. The Russians believed that any deviation from their rigid legalistic code would endanger the whole communist world, just as the Jewish high priests saw Jesus as a threat to their hegemony. They thought that they had the forgiveness business sewed up in their law and their sacrifices, but he undermined them. So they sought to get rid of him. The Cross was thus the result of his forgiving, the sign of the costliness of forgiving, and the seal of his intent to forgive to the uttermost.

The Cross did not make available forgiveness that had been lacking before. The Cross did not force God to forgive by paying the price that God demanded before forgiveness would be given. Forgiveness is free, and it always comes from God. The Cross is the work of God himself, not the work of man directed toward God. In the Cross of Christ God himself suffers the rejection of man, reaches out across the chasm of that rejection, and makes a new start for us all.

God's Blinded Eye

The experience of forgiveness among humans is analogous to the Cross in most of the important points that have just been brought out. When two people have become alienated from each other because of the actions of one of them, a psychological Grand Canyon looms between them which prevents real personal contact. The one who has done the wrong cannot possibly make up what has happened, for saying he is sorry will not take back the hurt. The only way for the estrangement to be overcome is if the one who is innocent makes the necessary move. The heart of that move is to forgive.

Forgiving involves judgment, admitting "I have been hurt by you." This does not have to be said out loud, but if it is not said at all, forgiveness cannot begin. If I say instead, "It really doesn't matter, it didn't really hurt at all," then I am refusing to face the truth, protecting myself by saying that I was not really vulnerable. By so doing I am refusing to go back into the arena of vulnerability with that person again. When I say "It doesn't matter" when it really does, what I am actually saying is "Our relationship doesn't matter, this is the end." Admitting the pain is therefore the vital first step toward forgiveness.

The only way the pain can be dealt with is if the one who has been hurt is willing to accept it and absorb it as the price he has to pay in order to re-create his friendship. When a wife discovers that her husband has been unfaithful to her there are three possible paths she can take. She can say it does not matter and then they will go ahead and live separate lives in a shell of a marriage. She can say she will make him pay, and then they separate and the marriage is dissolved, or they live in their local version of hell. Or she can confront him with it and if there is a desire on his side for the marriage relationship to be re-created, then she can bear the hurt and grief that he has caused her, for the sake of the relationship that can come out of the reconciliation.

Pain that is absorbed creates a relationship anew, and can greatly change the one whose fault it was. Herodotus, the Greek historian, tells how Lycurgus, the author of the Spartan Code, once acted in just this way. A young aristocrat, Alcander, objected violently to some of the reforms Lycurgus initiated, for they helped the common people at the expense of the aristocrats. Alcander attacked the old lawgiver and blinded him in one eye. When his assailant was presented to him for punishment, Lycurgus took him with him into his house, neither did nor said anything severely to him, but asked Alcander to wait upon him at the table. The result of this friendly association was that Alcander from being an enemy, became one of his most zealous admirers, and told his friends and relations that he was not that morose and ill-natured man they had taken him for, but the one mild and gentle character in the world. That transformation in Alcander came from Lycurgus willingly bearing the pain and disability of the loss of his eye.

The Cross is God's blinded eye. It is God accepting the hurt of our rejection of him. He says to us, "I have no pride that needs to be assuaged; I am willing to appear as a common criminal. I want you back with me, and I will accept the hurt of your rejection, reaching out to you through that hurt." The Cross does not take away his suffering for us before or since, but it stands before us as the historical embodiment of God's eternal hurt. From the Cross God says to us: "This is the way I am, now and forever accepting your rejection of me as the price I will pay to bring us back together again."

Weakness Conquers All

In the two previous sections we have looked upon man's problem as first blindness and then guilty alienation, but these two do not include one more large area of need: inner slavery and outer oppression. Within we are enslaved by our façades, our defenses, our habits, our fears. Outwardly we are oppressed by the great institutions that are the offspring of God's servant-enemy—religion and its prejudice, government and its violence, society and its machine-life. We may have learned from Christ's death to see clearly; we may have found forgiveness; but if there is not also liberation from oppressive forces without and within we will be back in our chains in no time. Actually these great gifts of enlightenment, reconciliation and liberation are substantially intertwined in the experience of Christians, so it is only for the sake of understanding that we discuss them separately.

Freedom Within

In chapter four I suggested that the inner slavery of man could be understood in terms of façades and defenses that were erected to compensate for the insecurity, inferiority and guilt that are every person's lot. We erect façades in order to hide our inner mess from those outside and in order to censor any incoming information that may challenge our attempt at equilibrium. But in order to keep the façade erect we must create defenses within us that will justify our thoughts and behavior and will keep out any impulses from God's Spirit that might lead us to act differently. By means of our façades and defenses we keep a tenuous hold on life, not letting ourselves be touched by anything we cannot assimilate. Locked in by our own creations we are more firmly bound than a man in chains for we do not even recognize our plight.

There is no way our inner slavery can be overcome by force. The surgeon's knife can change our inner life drastically by cutting into our brain, but it cannot free us. Brainwashing can alter our beliefs and actions almost beyond recognition but only by creating more oppressive façades and defenses. Our own will power is a magnificent thing but the experience of mankind from the ancient sages to modern psychotherapists teaches us that we cannot basically free our inner selves simply by willing to do so. There is no manipulative, coercive power that can cut those bonds, but they can be melted by something quite contrary—the weakness of love.

You're OK

The story told by the friends of Jesus was that in their association with him, through his life, death and resurrection, they found the inner freedom they had longed for but never known. They proclaimed far and wide that anyone who responded to Jesus' story as they themselves had done, in trust and love, would find that same Spirit of freedom that had animated Jesus and had come to his followers. The two great apostles John and Paul spoke of this gift of freedom as the conquest of the power of sin within (John 8:34 ff.; Rom. 6:17 f.). The way that this inner freedom comes through Christ is not difficult to understand.

The beginning of our trouble was in our feelings of moral inferiority, the recognition that we are less than we could be, and worse than others seem to be. In Transactional Analysis terms most people think "I'm not OK—You're OK." But in Jesus we hear a contrary message directed at each one of us—You're OK because God loves you, loves you enough to suffer immensely to bring you back to himself. In seeing how Jesus treated people and hearing that he backed his action with his life, we begin to see the possibility that as distinct, unique individuals we may be of infinite worth because God loves us.

If our guilty feelings of inferiority can begin to be dealt with the necessity for a façade begins to lessen. The story of Jesus comes to us through those who have experienced his freeing love and in our contact with them we begin to experience a community in which façades are less necessary. Those who follow Jesus know that they are sinners on the way toward full human life so they do not need to hide their sinfulness as much as they previously had. When we come into a group in which people are real and accepting we discover that our mask becomes increasingly loose until we realize that we can come out from behind it and do without it most of the time.

At the same time as we experience an overcoming of our guilt and inferiority, we also begin to feel stirrings deep within us. Most of us have created defenses to keep us from following impulses that may lead us to become too open, or too caring, or too accepting, since we are afraid of getting hurt. But the amazing thing that the story of Jesus' death does for us is to magnify those impulses and convince us that even if we die because of it we can never be too loving.

The End of Death's Hold

The threat of death is one of the chains creating our inner slavery; we seem instinctively to fear death and to flee from it. The evil of death comes when we turn everything to the pursuit of reversing the gradual debilitation that is our lot. When we try to make up for our mortality by increasing our power in other realms, no matter what the cost, then we have become trapped. But the story of Jesus' death and resurrection reveals that we need not fear death.

"The Snake's Poison"

In a small village long ago the people lived beside a beautiful forest they were afraid to enter. It could have supplied wood for their houses, and berries for their supper, and beauty for their appreciation but they never went in. A monstrous poisonous snake patroled the forest and so the people saw death engulfing them if they left their open fields. Even when someone got lost in the forest no one would go to rescue him because the threat was too great.

One day a stranger arrived in their village, a handyman who could fix anything, whether a broken plough, or a sick dog, or a crying child. When he discovered the villagers' fear of the snake in the forest he began to suggest that perhaps their fear was overblown, that perhaps the threat was not as great as their tradition led them to believe. But they scorned his suggestions, eventually warning him that he would be held responsible if anyone accepted his foolishness and wandered into the forest.

Before long it happened that a child did wander into the forest and got lost, his faint cries being all that marked his trail. All the villagers were frightened stiff and refused to try to rescue the child. Instead they found the stranger and unjustly blamed him, demanding that he go and rescue the child. They were surprised when he did not argue with them, saying instead that they need not fear the snake. Quickly he walked into the forest and before long returned with the lost child in his arms; but the price was written in the two fang marks in his hand and the blue color moving up his arm.

He told the villagers to take some of his blood and then give a small dose of it to everyone for that would make them immune to the snake's poison. They took the blood but were afraid to use it on themselves because they did not believe him, thinking instead that it would kill them. During the night they became certain of this as the stranger slipped into a coma and seemed to be dead. So they left him. But in the morning when they came back they found him awake, his strength returning. They realized that the snake was thus not the ultimate threat they had imagined, and the stranger could perhaps be trusted after all.

So they all took a small dose of his blood and found that with it their fear of the snake had ended. Their world now expanded greatly to include the forest: its beauty, usefulness and refreshment now were theirs to share. No one was ever left alone to die because he had become lost. In fact, eventually the villagers formed a snake-fighting band and went into the forest and killed their enemy. So the dark woods became transformed from the lair of the evil one into a paradise for people and other animals.

Shackling the Evil Powers

This inner freedom from fears, façades and defenses is the key to external freedom also. While there are a great variety of evils in the world around us the worst of them are those that enslave us by our own unwitting consent. The biblical writers knew that aggressor nations could tyrannize over their neighbors, and the powerful could make life miserable for the weak; but they stressed that the worst evils were unseen and spiritual, not flesh and blood but "the spiritual hosts of wickedness" (Eph. 6:12). Such powers cannot be opposed by votes or money or guns for their power is exercised in the hearts of men and so liberation can come only by freeing men within. Then men can act to change institutions that enslave others.

The testimony of many is that through Jesus and his community just such inner freedom has become theirs. Though he died a seeming failure it happened that the weakness of his love has been more effective down through the ages in liberating mankind than all the armies of man put together. In particular we will see how the story of Jesus liberates man from the evil powers of violence and prejudice that were described in chapter five.

Conquering Violence

In the analysis of American violence given in chapter five we suggested that in many ways it can helpfully be understood as a disease, an evil spirit permeating our society, rather than simply an accumulation of rational, responsible choices by individuals. Among the causes of this plague we listed: our frontier tradition; the way our nation has successfully waged war against weak and sometimes distant peoples; the belief that the American way is God's way and so is to be imposed on all who live on earth. Within individuals, adherence to this violent way of life stems from blindness, self-righteousness, selfishness, anxiety and insecurity, all of which breed hostility toward outsiders—that is, anyone who does not identify himself with us.

In Jesus we find that all these problems are potentially dealt with so that anyone who identifies himself with Jesus and his people will find that the springs of violence within him are capped and a new life of love becomes possible. This change in individuals does not of course end the violence of those who refuse to become Jesus' disciples, but it does end the power that violence has to duplicate itself, to spread itself, by means of *our* violent responses. From a Christian perspective the worst thing about violence is how easily we can become infected by our enemies' attacks: if the Germans bomb our cities we will obliterate theirs; if students dare to throw stones at police we will shoot to kill; if some police sometimes treat blacks roughly the Black Panthers plot to kill policemen and so the police escalate back. While most citizens do not personally participate in this violence, their acquiescence in it, or verbal support of it, makes them accessories and thus participants in it. But through Jesus' death and resurrection the possibility arises of our not being infected by this plague, of staying free from possession by this demon and so of working to end its hold on others.

First, we have very clearly in Jesus' teaching and actions an understanding of the self-defeating nature of violence that can open our eyes to what we are doing. That "all who take the sword will perish by the sword" (Matt. 26:52) is clearly symbolized in the destructions of Jerusalem and Rome, the executors of Jesus. The way Jesus lived was to absorb violence instead of returning it, not fighting back but accepting enemies in love. He died because he refused to try to use violence in return, his death being the acceptance in his own body of the worst his enemies could do to him. His example is not a command telling us we must do likewise; rather his teaching and action reveal to us the ultimate truth about life, which we can accept if we are open to it.

Second, we can see how the internal causes of violence in individuals can be overcome by the Cross. Hostility is not so much a matter of temperament as it is a problem of spiritual health. If I feel guilty about my past, and anxious about my future I will react selfishly in most situations, becoming hostile against anyone who seems to cross me. But when I hear in the story of Jesus that my guilt is absorbed in God's costly forgiveness and my anxiety made meaningless by God's care, then my selfishness and hostility can begin to dissipate. I get angry at others because I am angry at myself, seeing my evil. But when God says to me in Christ "I love you," then I no longer need to worry about my failure, thus ending my self-hatred and hostility.

Jesus' victory over the demon violence was emulated in the action of Alyosha, the youngest of *The Brothers Karamazov* when he came upon a rock fight among young boys. One boy was by himself angrily throwing rocks at a group of four or five others. When the group decided to fire back Alyosha stood between them, begging them all to stop, as Christ stood between man and the oppressing evil powers. For his compassion Alyosha was hit in the back by the lone boy, and in the face by the group. But by his presence and mediation he ended the violence and eventually brought about a reconciliation. By absorbing their violence he ended it. The same has been made possible in us by Jesus' life and death and resurrection, once we identify ourselves with him by faith.

Overcoming Prejudice

A second form that demonic powers take in society—whether ancient or modern—is prejudice. We have suggested above that this too goes far beyond the rational, responsible choices of individuals but is a social disease, a cancer that spreads insidiously throughout the living cells of society. It depends on our need to feel better than other people, our limitations that lead to pigeonholing people according to their groups and, most demonically, it grows out of religious faith—the conviction that we possess the truth.

One of the causes of Jesus' death was his lack of prejudice. He died in order to overcome the systematic prejudices of his nation. He praised the hated Samaritan; he allowed the Quisling tax collector to be his disciple; he healed Gentiles and denied that God would bring vengeance upon them just because they were not Jews; he associated with women, making them his friends; he lived with sinners, seeing his whole life as service to the outcasts; worst of all he directly denied the eternal validity of many of the religious practices of his people, saying that Jews were often worse off than others because their ritual obedience made them self-satisfied. His countrymen simply could not stand such a free spirit in their midst for if too many people abandoned traditional prejudices the system would be threatened. So they killed him. But instead of his death ending his power over prejudice it spread it far and wide, for his wholehearted followers were inoculated by his spirit and the cancer of prejudice was beaten in them.

From the beginning the watchword of the Church has been: "There is neither Jew nor Greek, . . . neither slave nor free, . . . neither male nor female; for you are all one in Christ Jesus" (Gal. 3:28). It was not simply Jesus' example that produced this new view of life, but in addition his death put all together as forgiven sinners, and his resurrection loosed a new power of love in the community of his followers. As long as Christians' minds are centered on Jesus' story then they can continue to see themselves as sinners and non-Christians as others for whom Christ died.

Our natural tendency is to see ourselves as righteous and those outside our community as sinners. As long as that is our attitude we are still in the prideful position of the Pharisee, boasting that ours is the right way and theirs is demonic. More than anything else we within the Church need to remember the story of Jesus' death: it was the good people, the religious people, the churchgoers, God's own people, who killed him. Their religion had become institutionalized and the natural demonic tendencies of human institutions had led inevitably to Jesus' elimination. Dostoevsky was absolutely right when the Grand Inquisitor in *The Brothers Karamazov* had Jesus eliminated a second time because he was too much of a challenge to the Inquisitorial Church.

Throughout the history of the Church almost all branches have absolutized their own theology and practice, acting prejudicially and often violently against those who disagreed, both Christians and non-Christians. The death of Christ proclaims that we are all sinners, so that self-aggrandizement is a constant menace. If we are able to believe that we are always sinners—reconciled sinners—then it is possible for us to see that our institutions, including their theology and practices, are all somewhat distorted by blindness and self-righteousness. Christ is The Way and The Truth, but our way and our truth are only dim reflections of him. We cannot claim perfection for our tradition because perfection lies only in him. But the experience of the early Christians was precisely that they did not need to be perfect, that in fact a denial of any such claims for ourselves was the way to find forgiveness and new life.

Prejudice goes on its cancerous way in our society, as in all societies. Our conditioning has infected us all. But if we identify ourselves fully with Jesus and his story a cure is possible. We will identify ourselves with his non-prejudiced way of life; we will remember that we are sinners who not only are not perfect but crucify the best the more perfect we think we are; we can stand being sinners because we know through Jesus' death that we are forgiven sinners and so do not need to exalt ourselves at others' expense; finally we find that Jesus' spirit of love may be ours today once we join that community in which his love for all is the unifying power.

Conclusion

The whole of Jesus' experience on earth was God's path to victory over the evils that corrupt his good creation. Not just Jesus' death but the whole of his life also was personal involvement in the suffering of God's creatures, suffering that was ultimately victorious. If the Christian understanding of Jesus as the ultimate symbol of God is correct, then we see in him that God is not an aloof ruler, a manipulator of knobs on a control panel, but is instead our suffering Father. The Cross sums up in one event the whole of Jesus' lifetime of suffering love and makes present to us his Father's eternity of entering into our painful slavery in order to win for us his glorious freedom. Only by entering our prison can he free us because the bars are largely in our minds and hearts. Thus it happens, as Bonhoeffer said, "Only a suffering God can help."

"One Old Indian"

Once upon a time, on the Colorado plains that lie at the foot of the Rockies, two communities struggled for possession of the lush land in the valley of the Rio Grande. Cattlemen wanted the valley left open for their herds to graze. Farmers had begun cutting out choice pieces and fencing them off. Eventually fences began to be cut, cattle shot and war seemed imminent. So the two groups met down by the river to decide on how to settle the conflict. Neither would give an inch, insisting that the others had to leave. Suddenly one of the cattlemen came forward and said: "Let's settle it by a duel. I challenge one of you farmers to go into the mountains with no food, only a gun, and whichever one of us returns alive owns all the land." A young farmer accepted the challenge.

So up to 8,000 feet they went for a fight to the death. After five days they had seen and shot at each other but neither man had been able to kill the other. Both were exhausted from having no sleep or food for so long while sneaking around the mountain rocks.

Meanwhile, on the edge of the mountains lived an old Indian in a small shack. He knew and liked both ranchers and farmers and was sorrowful over their conflict. He had heard of the duel and watched the men climb to their date with death. After five days he feared both would die and war would break out on the plains. So he climbed the mountain, taking some flat bread and mountain berry wine to revive the duelers and try to bring them together in peace. When he climbed out into the open, high on a rock, he hallooed to find where the men were. They saw him at once, and with their drowsy eyes mistook him for their enemy. So both aimed quickly and shot him.

When the Indian fell, the two fighters staggered over slowly to the rock, arriving at the same moment, stunned at seeing the other alive. They saw in a moment what had happened and were struck with remorse for their part in killing their would-be savior. Together they sat down and ate the bread and wine their victim had brought them at the cost of his life.

They fought no more but went back down together to their communities and told the story of their Indian friend. The result was that the two communities came to a reconciliation. They eventually agreed on how the land and water could be shared between them.

And every year thereafter, on the anniversary of their friend's death, the communities gather together for a simple meal of flat bread and mountain berry wine. They tell the story and in the telling and the eating any conflicts between the communities that have begun to fester are lanced and healing once more becomes possible.

Suggested Reading

Aulen, G. *Christus Victor*. London: SPCK, 1961.
Barry, F. R. *The Atonement*. New York: J. P. Lippincott, 1968.
Denney, James. *The Christian Doctrine of Reconciliation*. London: Clarke, 1959.
Dillistine, F. W. *The Christian Understanding of Atonement*. Philadelphia: Westminster, 1968.
Kesey, K. *One Flew Over the Cuckoo's Nest*. New York: New American Library, 1962.
Heim, D. K. *Jesus—The World's Perfecter: The Atonement and the Renewal of the World*. London: Oliver and Boyd, 1959.
Hodges, H. A. *The Pattern of Atonement*. London: SCM.
Renault, Mary. *The King Must Die*. London: Four Square, 1958.
Whale, J. S. *Victor and Victim: The Christian Doctrine of Redemption*. Cambridge: Cambridge University Press, 1960.
Wolf, W. J. *No Cross, No Crown*. Garden City, New York: Doubleday, 1957.

Chapter Eight: Inspired Stagehands

Introduction

Love's Army: "The King Is Dead. Long Live the King"

The Army's Mission
Army Life—and Death
The Ultimate Weapon
Soldiers and Civilians

Healing Family

Mother and Brothers
The Heart of the Matter
Beyond a Family
Therapeutic Community
Small Groups
The Church and Therapy Groups
Limitations
Conclusion

Theater Party

"Mr. Roberts"
Worship as Theater
Conclusion

CHAPTER EIGHT

Inspired Stagehands

Introduction

The Author of the drama we call history has come into his play in the paradoxical role of a suffering conqueror of evil. The paradox lies not only in suffering as the way, but also in the fact that the conquest was not completed all at once in the life, death and resurrection of the leading man. Instead the Author has chosen to hand on the task of conquest to those who are left behind, showing further that his way is persuasive love rather than coercive power. The central theme of the drama has become clear: suffering love has broken the stranglehold of the powers of evil and now is moving out to reconcile or overcome the powers completely.

That moving out has now been left in the hands of those who know the theme, who are committed to the Author's vision, and are willing to receive the Spirit of suffering, conquering love that became visible in the leading man's appearance on the stage. His inspired followers are a motley crew doing a bit of everything and so can be called stagehands. They are rarely the leading actors in the play, but they accept all the small, insignificant parts that are too small for the natural ego but are vital to the continuation of the story. Most of all, they work behind the scenes doing everything necessary to keep the play going in the direction the Author intends.

They mend and change sets, help actors dress, find drinks for the thirsty, comfort any who are depressed over their acting, make sure that those who try to sabotage the production are kept at bay and work constantly to overcome the defects that are keeping the production from becoming the masterpiece envisioned by the author.

The band of stagehands known as the Church is depicted in a multitude of symbols in the New Testament. In this chapter we will suggest three central symbols that may help to express for us today what the Church is called to be. It is "love's army": an "army" because it is given the task of battling the powers of evil; "love's" army because its weapons are not physical, coercive, killing ones, but the inner, spiritual power of love, the power found in Jesus that alone can conquer the forces of evil in the universe. This band armed with love must have a distinctive life as its training and support; it must also be seen as a "healing family," one in which all that is necessary for molding, directing and motivating the army is supplied. One central aspect of this family life is its centering on the Father and his task for them. Inspired worship can be understood as a "theater party" in which insight, celebration, uplift, communal unification and many other things take place.

Love's Army: "The King is dead. Long live the King."

A million years ago the acknowledged king of the earth was the tyrannosaurus rex, the most ferocious of all animals. Beside this forty-foot high carnivorous dragon, man was a mouse whose only hope was to hide in caves until the king went away. Tears, pain, destruction and death were man's lot when his small band became the object in this ancient monster's eye.

One day several families were gathered around a fire outside their cave when suddenly the earth shook and trees crashed as the king lumbered down upon them. Everyone ran for his life, but one young man stumbled over a long pole that was stuck in the fire. As he looked up he saw that it was too late to run so he picked up the only weapon at hand, the long pole that was burning at one end. As the tyrannosaurus's mouth came down to maul him he thrust the flaming branch into its mouth and burned it. The beast's response was to jerk its head away and turn and lumber off—the first time it had ever been defeated in battle.

When the families returned and heard what had happened some realized at once that a new day had dawned, for now the king's absolute power was broken and before long a new king—man—would take over. This conquest of their ancient fearsome enemy was so astounding that they knew they had to spread the good news. A few members of the band were sent out to other bands to tell what had happened, to show how the end of this great force of evil could be near if all men believed in and practiced the power of the burning pole. Some believed and were thereafter saved from the dragon's marauding; many refused to believe and so gradually they were destroyed by the still dangerous enemy. Over the years the believers lived in freedom and so began to drive the tyrannosauri away from human populations, even from those who did not believe. Eventually the ancient dragon was eradicated and man was completely sovereign; the kingdom of man had drawn near in that first defeat but it was completed with the destruction of the last of the dragons.

The Army's Mission

The mission given to the Church, the reason for its existence, is the carrying out of God's plan to eradicate evil from his good creation. The great battle fought in Jesus' life, death and resurrection broke the stranglehold of the powers of evil, but the war goes on even though Christians are firmly convinced that final victory is sure.

In our own day the forces of evil are at work all around us. Violence is an evil spirit that permeates our society, fostered largely by the way nation-states use violence to settle international disputes and act violently toward their own people in times of crisis. This is not to say the state is wholly evil but just that it remains a servant-enemy. The Church has the same ambivalent status, for it too is under the powers of evil even though it serves God. The Church has promoted the unChristian values of our society and in doing so carries on the work of the powers of evil, for within the Church there is no adequate challenge to this common American creed: "You get only what you earn; status and possessions are the evidence of human value; competition, beating my neighbor, is the way to enjoy life; religion—any religion—is a good thing." These elements of the American creed foster strife, prejudice, despair and self-righteousness, but the powers of evil have so deeply engrained them in our culture that few of us can escape their insidious chains.

In addition we need to see that the powers of evil are at work in the psychological bonds that strangle so many individuals. Guilt, anxiety, hostility, fear, loneliness and despair are not solely the lot of the "mentally ill." They pervade every strata of society, every organization, every family, and to some extent every individual. They keep us from becoming truly human, from being free to be ourselves, so here too it is a part of the enemy's army that needs to be fought and conquered.

Much more could be said as a description of the evil powers pervading the world but these brief points have been made to suggest the great variety of places and forms and behaviors which the biblical writers saw as the presence of the enemy. For the Church the gospel message of Christ's conquest of this enemy is the impetus to her mission: we are called to *tell* the world that the tyrannosaurus has been dethroned and to *show* in our own society and lives how to live free from his depredation. We are not called to win the battle ourselves, for God is the conqueror of evil who has broken the hold of the enemy by the life, death and resurrection of Jesus. But we are called to be the instrument in God's hands as he spreads his victory from Calvary to the whole cosmos. The Church's reason for being is to serve God as the weapon in his hands. We are his army.

Army Life—and Death

If we imagine the Church as love's army we may be reminded that if she really enters the battles to be fought she will have to bear real pain and suffering. Jesus strongly emphasized the realistic view that if the Church enters the battle against the powers of evil she will have to bear a cross, and her only crown here on earth will be a crown of thorns. Jesus' own experience should make the reality of suffering for any who serve as God's army absolutely clear.

Jesus suffered because he stood in opposition to the forces enslaving mankind in his own day. The Jewish law, with its social and religious structures, put the vast majority of the people in the wrong religiously and so made them live with guilt feelings and social ostracism that prevented them from becoming themselves. Jesus spent his time with the publicans, sinners, prostitutes, drunkards and lepers, treating them all as prodigals in need of a home to come back to. Naturally he aroused the wrath of the religious, political, social and economic powers-that-be of his society and suffered the consequences.

If the Church is to carry on his mission there is no way to escape the pain and suffering every battle entails. In our day there will be cries of "unpatriotic" or even "traitor" if Christians call their nation to love their enemies instead of bombing them. There will undoubtedly be a backlash against any group in the modern world that sees wealth as a stumbling block, as a false god, the way Jesus did. However quietly we may seek out the outcasts—prisoners, homosexuals, migrant workers, welfare families—if we stand firmly on their side in their struggle for dignity as Jesus did we will find that the "good" people, who are essentially the powerful value-setters of our culture, will do their best to discredit us.

Not only must this army be prepared for suffering but also for fighting—thus it must be mobilized, trained, inspired and guided. It cannot have any effect in the struggle God is carrying on if it does not know what the real enemy is, how best to oppose it and how to follow its own general. The "general" of course is Christ, and like almost all great generals he spent time in the trenches learning of the pain and blood and fear and boredom of men at war. When Jesus sends us out as "sheep among wolves," warning of the persecution to come, he speaks from firsthand experience. When he said we do not need to be anxious for money to secure tomorrow he spoke from self-chosen poverty and the security of his Father's presence. We can be sure he knows the trouble we see if we look to him for the army's supplies, mission and directives.

A summary of his instructions is found in his direction given to his first messengers. He told them to proclaim that God is King, to heal the sick, and to conquer the powers of evil oppressing people. In all three points the enemy is seen not as people but as a power of evil lying behind and within society. Paul summarized Jesus' perception well when he said "we are not contending against flesh and blood, but against the . . . world rulers of this present darkness" (Eph. 6:12).

The absolutely central conclusion we must draw from this is therefore that the army God has mobilized is not intended to fight human beings. Unlike all of man's armies which seek to overwhelm other human armies, the army of Christ carries a cross upon which it will hang, for this is apparently the only way that the real enemy can be conquered. This army's weapon is love not gun powder.

The Ultimate Weapon

An army running on love is a paradox, but hopefully it is a stimulating paradox, for it is intended to suggest that we must battle with no holds barred against the forces of evil while at the same time acting in love toward all those people who are the enslaved instruments of the powers. However much it may seem that a person, an organization, a class or a nation is totally at one with the demonic powers, we must hear the New Testament distinction: people are the slaves (often willing) of the powers and so need to be freed, not killed.

Unfortunately, the Church, whenever it finds itself in a conflict with other institutions in society, tends to respond with the weapons and motivations of institutions. It tends to see its own continuation as the primary goal and so uses as its weapons the money, votes, social pressure, and other power that are available. The most common tactic has always been an alliance with the government, the terms essentially being these: the Church will make patriotism—obedience to the government—a cardinal virtue if the government will give the Church a stable place within the social structure. The result in all of the Western world has been that the Church has been an advocate of the political and social status quo, giving up her mission to conquer evil in the structures of society in order to have the security of self-preservation. Instead of love being her ultimate weapon political power has been.

But if the Church is to be the body in which Christ's Spirit conquers evil, the branches by which Christ grows grapes to feed the hungry, the light that dares to shine in satanic corners and so overcome the darkness, then she must abandon political power and seek a new way. Since the powers of evil use the state, Christ's army must not be permanently allied to the state. Since religion can easily be Satan's preeminent weapon the Church cannot aim above all to preserve her present form, traditions and power but must always be open to reformation. If love becomes her chief weapon then people in need will become her chief concern and thus she will be on the front line of the battle against evil.

Soldiers and Civilians

The followers of Jesus are God's suffering servants, his army at work in the world to oppose the demonic powers and to serve as the instruments of God's victory over them. This raises the question of how the army is to be related to those outside her, those who do not join the Church. Is the Church to be a conventional army set off clearly from the world by uniforms and its own meeting places and practices? Or is it to be a guerrilla army, melting into the civilian population and fighting from unseen hiding places in order to surprise the enemy? Or is it a third form, a combination of the other two?

In one way this army is a guerrilla force, for it constantly joins hands with anyone in society who is fighting the same enemy. When rich industrialists exploit workers the Church needs to join the workers in their fight for freedom and dignity. But the Church will not have the selfish motivations of the workers, nor use their sometimes dehumanizing weapons. Instead she will join them—for example, the migrant workers today—until they have enough power to be free from oppression, and then she will leave that battle knowing the workers too may become exploiters if given enough power. In the battles against apartheid and racism in South Africa, against poverty in Appalachia and the Sahara, against political oppression in Latin America and Eastern Europe the Church will join the side of the oppressed, but only for the time being, for as long as they are oppressed.

Thus in many battles in society the Church should be one community among many ranged against oppression; but in addition she always needs to stand apart as a conventional army does, for she never can identify fully with the self-enhancement motives of the oppressed. Even as she joins workers, minorities and citizens in totalitarian lands, she needs to be herself, the one who marches to the beat of a different drummer, made clear in her speech and her life.

While joining the oppressed is her calling, she proclaims that true freedom can come only when God's rule is recognized and accepted. She proclaims Jesus' story as the ultimate symbol of God's rule on earth and calls all people to believe that in Jesus the powers of evil have been broken—if we will just believe this and act on that belief. In this proclamation the Church is completely distinctive, for no other community in the world knows that the ultimate truth about reality is found in Jesus' story. Therefore, even while joining in with others to battle the forces of evil the Church must do so in her own distinctive way, with her own motivation in Jesus' love and her own method seen in Jesus' suffering. Thus it seems both anonymous guerrillas and also publicly visible soldiers offer parables of the way the Church is called to live.

Within the Church in this century there has been an enduring split between conservative and liberal wings, the former stressing evangelism and the latter social action. From what has just been suggested it should be clear that the New Testament was centrally interested in both and that Jesus in particular saw them as completely intertwined. Why have they become detached from each other so much today?

First, it seems that the conservative forces have one-sidedly stressed evangelism because they were well satisfied with the social status quo and saw any Church social action as a challenge to their power, violence, prejudice and wealth. Second, the liberal forces often neglected the proclamation of the gospel because it was an intellectual scandal in many circles, so liberal Christians tried to play it down in order to avoid being called old-fashioned. Naturally both sides were able to point to the errors of the other side and so justify their own one-sidedness.

Jesus' own standpoint seems to lie between the two. He accepted anyone fighting the same battles he was—even when they did not follow him, even a Pharisee (Mark 9:38 f.). But he stood apart in his message, his motivation, his way of life. The Church must do no less if it is to be love's army: it must join anyone willing to battle the powers of evil; but it must always make its own distinctive contribution by love.

Healing Family

The Church envisioned as love's army is intended to suggest that God's people are called to do battle against real evil in the world but must do it in the way their commander-in-chief did, by suffering love. One major limitation of this symbol (and all symbols have limitations as we have noted many times above) is that it does not really suggest the way the Church is called to be a healing community for those within. In order to suggest this aspect we can use the symbol *family*. In particular we might speak of a healing family that is headed and inspired by Jesus, such as the one that once sprang to life along the river Kwai.

Ernest Gordon was a prisoner during World War II in the dehumanizing, debilitating, death-dealing Japanese POW camp next to the famous bridge over the River Kwai in Malaya. In his autobiography *Through the Valley of the Kwai,* Gordon described how "as conditions steadily worsened, as starvation, exhaustion, and disease took an ever-growing toll, the atmosphere in which we lived was increasingly poisoned by selfishness, hatred and fear . . . The weak were trampled under foot, the sick ignored or resented, the dead forgotten."

Then one day very quietly there began the "miracle by the River Kwai." Gordon was suffering from malaria, dysentery, beriberi and ugly ulcers all over his legs. He could not take care of himself and was slowly dying when two strangers, Dusty Miller and Dinty Moore, came to him and offered to nurse him back to health. For no apparent reason, they were willing to spend all their leisure hours in performing the unpleasant tasks that had to be done just to keep the patient clean. They gave him their food, stayed with him, read to him and turned death away from his door empty-handed.

The unapparent reason for their action was that they were both followers of Jesus, members of his healing family. Around the camp other Christians were giving themselves to save their comrades, several at the cost of their own lives. The result was that Ernest Gordon not only regained physical health but found something even more amazing: "What I had experienced—namely, the turning to life away from death—was happening to the camp in general. We were coming through the valley. There was a movement, a stirring in our midst, a presence." The self-giving love which is God's presence had broken into the death-camp in the actions of a few men who brought Jesus' healing family into action.

Mother and Brothers

The symbol of Jesus' followers as his family comes explicitly from him. Once when his physical mother and brothers sought to draw him away from his mission he looked around at those who sat about him and said, "Here are my mother and my brothers! Whoever does the will of God is my brother, and sister, and mother" (Mark 3:34 f.). Those who trusted him, followed him and allowed him to serve them were united to him and so to each other with a bond that can be well symbolized as a family tie. Some of the characteristics of a family that make this a significant symbol of the Church are as follows.

The Heart of the Matter

First, a family provides identity. We take our names from our families and identify ourselves by them because without such an identity we seem to be lost. Jesus' family provides us with an even more basic identity, for it unites us to the basic reality of the universe, to the Father of all fathers, to the Spirit that holds everything in its hand. Once we know that this is our family we have others to stand with, an understanding of how we live in our family, and a solid foundation for our whole lives.

Second, a good family (and in this section we are pointing to a family as God intends it to be, not just to the average family in our society today) provides the essential personal involvement without which we cannot live a truly human life. More and more in this century we are discovering that a family may be one of the very few redeeming communities left. The evil forces in the body politic, the dehumanizing demands of the economic world, the competitive pressures of social life all can be defused by a healing family life. At the present time the growing incidence of mental disability and the growing rates of crime and suicide are very much related to the breakdown in family life as measured by the high divorce rate, the enormous number of children brutally beaten by their parents and the great increase in runaways. A family in which there is deep, close personal sharing and caring will suffer much less from these diseases of the urban technological age. And whenever the Church is this kind of family it can often take the place of failing natural families.

A third aspect of a natural family that offers insight into the family of God is the fact that entrance into it is free. A child is taken in with no questions asked when he is born. He has done nothing to deserve his parents' acceptance and love, and will never be able to repay them directly. Good parents give without counting the cost in sleepless nights, tears shed, pleasures given up, hurts absorbed. Their reward comes in seeing their child grow to true human maturity as he learns to give himself to others in just the way his parents have poured themselves out in self-giving love to him. This is quite like the life given in the family of Jesus—a gift which enables us to grow into people who can give the same gift to others.

Finally, we need to note that in a good family growth comes through discipline that is related to clear and accepted guidelines for behavior. The extremist child psychologists who warned that any discipline would create repressions have been discredited along with the total permissiveness they engendered. Self-giving love accepts a child no matter what he has done, but it also helps by example, discussion, personal involvement and chastening to lead the loved child in a healthy direction. A child without guidelines is like a tightrope walker without a balancing pole: a fourteen year old heroin addict ended her despairing story by saying, "I used to go and tell my mother, kind of hoping that she'd say to me 'Stop and that's final.' But she never did." In Jesus' family the guidelines are open for all to see in the way Jesus lived with people.

Beyond a Family

Naturally the symbol *family* has its limitations as a way of pointing to the Church's way of life. Most important of all is the fact that families today are usually small and impermanent whereas Jesus' family is worldwide and eternal. Families today are usually just two generations of parents and several young children, and when the children grow up that family disappears and others grow up. The Church as Jesus' family must be thought of as an extended family, one like the Kennedys that covers several generations, many people, and has an identity that is carried on even when its central figures are dead. There is an inner spirit in the Church that does not die, that provides a unique identity stretching over time just as

Joseph and Rose Kennedy seem to have provided a long-lasting unity and identity in their family.

A second point at which the symbol *family* may mislead us is in the self-centeredness that is usual in our small families today. There is a sharing of resources within the family but everyone else is outside, strangers with whom we share little. Especially in crowded neighborhoods, families separate themselves from their neighbors by fences and walls so that each can hold firmly to their own possessions. The Church is called to be just the opposite: it is a family that seeks to become universal, to include all mankind within it and so in this respect contradicts our usual thought of what a family is. The early Church's sharing of all resources, as a commune, indicates how seriously the family-sharing style of life was taken, but in ages since we have returned to separate natural families within the Church each firmly grasping its own resources.

Finally, of course, we must recognize that many families in our urban, technological societies are not essentially the personal haven they could be but are just another context for conflict. There are millions of tense, divided or broken families in the United States today, so for their members the symbol *family* may well suggest something to escape rather than to seek. For people from that kind of family this symbol should perhaps be ignored because it will provide the wrong kind of emotional and intellectual impact. But while "family of Jesus" may not help people from conflict-ridden homes to understand the Church, the reverse can happen: once they come to experience a community of sharing within the Church the symbol *family* may then lead them on to see what God intends our natural families to be. If we come to see that in God's family we are freely given identity, personal involvement and all we need for life with others, this could have a significant effect in shaping our ideas and practices at home.

"Jesus' family" is thus a valuable symbol to place beside "love's army" as a way to express more fully what God has called the Church to be. While *army* expressed the mission to the world, *family* speaks significantly of the life within the Church, the way the training, unifying and motivating can be thought to take place. But the "healing" part of our symbol *healing family* has not been touched on yet. How is it to be understood?

Therapeutic Community

In modern society our families are mainly the context for growing up rather than the all-encompassing atmosphere that was known in past centuries, especially in agricultural communities. When the family was a large group including grandparents and uncles and cousins then almost all personal problems could be solved within the family. Today when a family is only four or five people, help must often be sought outside. When we need to be healed we usually have to seek out a healing community and today millions of people have found personal and psychological therapy (healing) in small groups. These may be called therapy groups or encounter groups when conducted by psychologists, while covenant groups or personal development groups are common names within the Church. In this section we will look briefly at how these healing groups operate because the Church is called to provide a quite similar kind of healing.

The "healing" that is available within the Church is a spiritual and personal therapy, something needed by all who come into it. We are simply mistaken if we think that being brought up in the Church, or being dramatically converted to Christ, completely solves our problems of relating to God, to our neighbors and to ourselves. Paul, for example, stressed that he himself had not achieved the goal of conformity to the image of Christ but had to press on toward it (Phil. 3:12 f.).

We too need to know that we remain sinners even though accepted by God. We all have habits, attitudes and relationships that are quite harmful to ourselves and others. We have blindspots to our sinfulness but eyes wide open to find fault with others. We see clearly the partial truth that has opened to us but then exaggerate it so that we believe others to be blind. Even though we are freely accepted we still try to earn our way by hiding our faults. Even though we know true life is in Jesus' suffering way we still often strive for success, prestige, and victory over others to boost our self-image. These wounds are almost universal within the Church but in addition of course there are many individual problems that cut to the depths and need healing. The Church is called and equipped to provide this healing.

Small Groups

A therapy group is usually a small, intimate, free community in which any subject of personal significance can be raised and dealt with. The object of the group is to create an atmosphere in which loving acceptance is offered to all so that openness and honesty in our deepest thoughts, wishes and problems become common. Usually this atmosphere of acceptance must be initiated by at least one member, often the organizer or facilitator of the group, but if the other members do not catch this spirit then the group will never get moving. The amazing experience reported by many is that often when one person begins to listen to, to respond to, to care for, to accept whatever others in the group present, then before long this same way of treating each other begins to spread throughout the group. It is partly the attractiveness of the example. Even more, however, it is probably the effect of *my* being treated this way that somehow enables me to begin acting in the same way toward others. Then gradually a group spirit of acceptance begins to develop and those who found this way difficult begin to be caught up in the group experience and so to be accepting also.

It is absolutely essential that the group convey acceptance no matter what is revealed, for rejection will block up the channels of confession. Without confession we cannot begin to bring out into the open the experiences, habits, thoughts, relationships and doubts that we need to examine with the help of others. But the group's constant acceptance of the person, and constant support of him as an open, growing individual does not mean there is no disagreement or criticism. It is just that in an accepting atmosphere criticism seems much more constructive and thus much easier to hear and accept.

The gradual result in a supportive, effective therapy group is that something has been experienced together that cements the bonds between members more and more. The stories each member tells, the tears and laughter all have joined in, the moments of depression and exhilaration, all provide a common experience that leads each member to feel a common bond with the others and so to enter into the group more closely. Very often the necessary ending of such a group—when members leave college, for example—can be felt as deeply as the breaking up of a family because the bonds may become very close.

A unified group such as this does not simply make a person dependent upon it but works to make each individual more self-aware, more self-controlled, more self-determining—in short, more himself. By encouraging us to bring out our defenses and façades and to deal with them, a therapy group can help us to become more of the potential person God intends us to become. We can gradually be released from the power of habits we thought unbreakable. We can learn to be concerned first of all with the needs of others where previously we had acted primarily in self-centered and defensive ways. The acceptance and support of the group can enable us to become accepting and supportive of others outside the group. The strength we are given by other members of the group can enable us to stand up to the destructive powers of our society, even when we know standing up may mean suffering. At its best, therefore, a therapy group can enable us to become more human—that is, if the standard of what is human is found in Jesus.

The Church and Therapy Groups

In many ways such a therapy group provides the kind of results that the Church aims at but often does not produce. In particular there are three aspects of a good therapy group experience that are central to the Church's life—acceptance, openness and oneness.

As we have noted several times in the preceding chapters, the heart of the gospel is that God accepts us as we are in just the way Jesus accepted publicans, prostitutes, drunkards and other sinners—the way the father in Jesus' parable accepted his prodigal son. The Church preaches this acceptance, but unfortunately preaching is not enough. We only believe that God accepts us when we find the amazing experience of others accepting us even when we begin to reveal to them the dark depths within us. Thus if the Church is to carry God's loving forgiveness into the lives of people who have not experienced it, it must happen in personal contacts and for that a small group, meeting regularly, is ideal.

Second, confession of our failings is central to living the Christian life, for only when we begin to recognize, discuss and repudiate our failings can we begin to live differently. Unfortunately the Church often fails here also. Protestants are encouraged to confess to God but it is very easy to be superficial in such confession, and very easy to continue doing the same harmful things over and over again, unless we are able to grapple in depth with the problem, as we can do in a small group. The immediate support offered by accepting friends as we begin to open up gives us strength to go on. And the insight given by others who experience the give and take of such an intimate group can help us see much in ourselves that we could not see alone.

Finally, a small group in which openness, acceptance, confession and support are central provides a oneness that the New Testament Church knew but is so often lacking in the larger, more impersonal churches many belong to today. Paul's image of the Church as a physical, living, breathing body emphasized this oneness, for the parts of our bodies are bound together inextricably, laughing and crying, rejoicing and suffering together. Such an experience of oneness with a few other people can be so exhilarating, renewing, deepening and unifying that we will wonder how we ever continued on in the pedestrian way of keeping our social distance that so often passes for Christian fellowship within the Church.

Limitations

Naturally the image of a "therapy group" a reality taken from the profession of psychotherapy, cannot simply be equated with what the Church ought to be. This is one image or symbol, and as such must be corrected by other symbols that express other aspects of the Church. All that is needed here is a word or two on some of the limitations of this image as an expression of something central in the Church.

Most significant of all is the fact that therapy groups differ greatly from each other so that some forms are closer to what the Church is called to be than others are. For example, some groups have a dominant leader who is the focus of the life of the group whereas Christians are called to be priests to each other with the unseen God as their focus. In some groups raging criticism is the norm, with members tearing into each other to break down their defenses (saying as they do, "Of course this is only because we accept you and want to help you"!). Among Christians it should be clear that the warm sun of demonstrated acceptance is much more effective in getting others to open their defensive cloaks than is the bitter wind of criticism.

A third characteristic of some group therapies is that they express the psychological theories of their leaders. If the leader thinks sex or authority or religion or whatever else is the source of man's troubles, then the group may become a propaganda vehicle for a concern that is quite contrary to the Christian understanding. For example, some groups so stress the need for overcoming physical inhibitions that they tend to promote sexual promiscuity as a cure for all evils. This is totally divorced from the Christian understanding of how we are to relate to each other.

Finally, therapy groups often share with families one of the weaknesses of religion—prejudice. When a small group has been a fulfilling experience the members may feel sorry for those outside who have not been able to share it. It is a very short step from there to feeling that we on the inside are better than those on the outside, that our group is the best there is. When we feel that way it is a sign that we are still somewhat insecure, still need to be able to play the game "Mine is better than yours" in order to overcome our feelings of insecurity. The only cure is for us to know that in Christ there is no superior and inferior, for all are one in him.

Conclusion

In this section on the healing family I have attempted to suggest what the inner life of love's army is, how it is trained for its task of battling against the powers of evil in the world. In order to enter that battle we must have experienced the support and acceptance that will see us through anything, for only then will we be willing to oppose the demonic powers even at the cost of suffering. But equally important we must have learned to love other people rather than competing with them, or undermining them, or using them, or injuring them. Our natural tendencies are the opposite—we conform to the powers over us, and thus like them try to use or hurt others. Therefore, only a whole new identity, a new family, a healing of our wounds, can lead us to follow in Christ's footsteps in this way. The healing family is not an end in itself but is the continuing training necessary for love's army to proceed on its mission.

Theater Party

Each of the central symbols used so far in this chapter has been an attempt to point to one aspect of the Church in order to bring out something of the reality we find symbolized in the New Testament by a great array of images. One aspect of the Church that has so far been left to the side is the Church's direct relationship to God. The symbol *love's army* suggested something of the Church's relationship to the world as a whole, its calling to do battle with satanic powers in society. The symbol of a healing family suggests something of the inner life of the Church, the way Christians are called to relate to each other. Now we need to present a third side to fill in the picture a little more fully by suggesting how the Church is directly involved with God in worship. In order to suggest *some* of the significant characteristics of worship let us imagine it as a theater party.

"Mr. Roberts"

One evening a group of friends organized a party to go to the theater to see the play *Mr. Roberts.* Most of them had seen the great Henry Fonda–Jack Lemmon movie of this play but it is the kind of story that expresses the human condition in story form so well that every time we see it it opens up new understanding of our own lives. And a stage production, by providing real flesh and blood people before our eyes, seems to involve us in the events even more intimately than a film does. By this empathetic involvement with the characters in the parable we experience something of their agony, frustration, hope and final victory and so have broadened our own realm of experience.

In *Mr. Roberts,* a classic tale of slavery and liberation is told in comic form. The action takes place on a supply ship during World War II, a small ship which sees no action but just sails back and forth "from tedium to apathy." The captain is a small, insecure, ambitious martinet who acts only for his own power and glory, keeping his crew on a short leash as he does. He is the "god of their world," the Satan figure of that floating prison. The executive officer of the ship is Mr. Roberts, a man who cares deeply for the crew and does everything he can for them. At the same time he wants to get away to a warship, to get into the war instead of sitting it out.

The central action of the play is the story of a liberty for the crew. At a liberty port the captain maliciously announces that no one is to have liberty and Mr. Roberts bursts into his cabin to challenge that order as inhuman. As his price for changing the order the captain demands that Mr. Roberts cease sending in his weekly application for transfer; it is an end to his hopes but he pays the price in order to give the crew liberty. Eventually the crew finds out about the agreement and so forges the captain's signature to get Mr. Roberts transferred. On his day of departure the crew's last words to him are, "Thanks for the liberty, Mr. Roberts, thanks for everything."

The final event in the play is stimulated by a letter from Mr. Roberts to his replacement as executive officer, Ensign Pulver. Pulver has been unable to stand up to the captain and demand that the crew's rights be respected and Mr. Roberts's letter is a pep talk on the subject. Then in the same mail another letter arrives saying Mr. Roberts has been killed in action. That final sacrifice transforms Pulver. After a moment of thought his face becomes determined and he charges up to the captain's cabin, plants his foot on the captain's chair and demands, "What's all this crud about no movies tonight?"

As the theater-goers watch the play it suggests to them the prisons that they are caught in and the Satan-captains who rule over them. Even more, in the character of Mr. Roberts we begin to see that if we are willing to pay the price, we can stand and oppose the demonic powers, we can help bring liberty to the oppressed. Ultimately even our death in the cause of liberty may be precisely the thing that can transform others, can lead them to follow in our footsteps, to take up the battle where we left off. In all of this *Mr.*

Roberts expresses the Christian vision of life—slavery, liberty, sacrifice, death, transformation. The viewers, whether they know it or not, have been hearing a modern parable proclaiming the gospel and if they have become involved in it their whole way of life may have been challenged.

After the performance is over the group goes to one of their homes for a continuation of the party. There the discussion is on the meaning of the play, the similarities between our situation and a ship at sea in wartime, and the numerous hilarious moments that make this parable a classic visual comedy. By sharing their thoughts each person's experience is multiplied many times because together they saw and experienced much more than any individual could. By retelling the funniest parts they relive them and rejoice in them and laugh even harder than they did at the play. Then later on in eating and drinking and singing together the mood of a shared celebration of the deepest realities of life comes to the fore. They realize that the whole evening may be for them one in which the inspiration of Mr. Roberts who paid the price to give liberty to others may change their lives also.

Worship as Theater

In many ways worship resembles a theater party. The fact that down through the ages, plays, especially passion and morality plays, have been used so often in worship settings shows that the Church has not always been blind to this aspect of her life. In fact the theater was originally almost completely religious, a vehicle for proclaiming and embodying the faith of the people, and only since the Renaissance has a purely secular theater grown up. Protestantism, with its emphasis on doctrine, right teaching, largely rejected drama as a vehicle for proclamation and worship, while Catholicism and Eastern Orthodoxy carried on the dramatic tradition in their liturgies. Unfortunately they too have largely ignored the possibilities of drama in the sense of plays acted out before the congregation, believing that that was a "worldly" form that might stain the purity of the Church's worship. Possibly a return to this ancient tradition of theater as a form of worship may go a long way toward reviving the Church's worship.

The central parallel between a play and Christian worship is that both tell a story that the audience can enter into and so be renewed or even transformed in their relationships to all around them. A play does this by providing actors who create an atmosphere and a series of events that strike the listener as a real world into which he

CHAPTER NINE

Going Home

Introduction: "The Beginning and the End"

The great day coming when good will triumph and evil will be destroyed was foreshadowed in the crisis that transformed the life of the Alpha Kai Omega fraternity. This fraternity was an anomaly. It had been started years before as an alternative to typical fraternities because its goal was inclusiveness, encouraging students of every race, religion and ethnic group on campus to join. Its national leaders saw it as a symbol of real brotherhood which would put pressure on other fraternities to become more representative of American pluralism. However, on the Lincoln College campus, the local branch had gradually drifted back into conformity with the waspish exclusiveness of its local competitors, its mission essentially forgotten.

A freshman pledge named Josh Malcolm became intrigued with the history of the fraternity and discovered the contradiction between the intentions of its founders and its present behavior. He decided to bring in a Jewish friend to see if he would be accepted or rejected. At the meeting where the decision was to be made Josh found that prejudice against Jews and other minorities was loud and long. So as a vote neared he rose dramatically and read, from the founding constitution of the fraternity, the call for leadership on campus in including all minority groups. After an embarrassed silence the answer came back to him: "That was long ago. Today *we* are the fraternity and we say we like it as it is."

Josh refused to give in. He took his case to the campus community by writing a letter to the newspaper pointing out the hypocrisy of having an inclusive charter while practicing prejudice. Naturally this angered the fraternity's leaders, indeed prompted them to devise a scheme to get rid of Josh. They planted some illegal drugs in Josh's car and then secretly called the college police to denounce him as a dealer in drugs. Despite his pleas of innocence he was convicted on the strength of the planted evidence and dismissed from the college in disgrace. When Josh went back to the fraternity to get his belongings he hunted out the president and swore, "I'll get you for this! You'll be sorry you ever tried to cover up your own mess by destroying me."

A few of Josh's friends in the fraternity had joined him in his crusade to bring the fraternity back to its original mission, but when he was ground under by the leaders they retreated back into their previous silence. But Josh refused to give up. He went to the national headquarters and sparked a secret investigation which led to the conclusion that he was right in his charges against the local leaders. Instead of coming in and overthrowing them immediately Josh urged that his followers be given time to try to convert enough of the brothers to change the local policies.

After a year had passed no changes had taken place, so when the time for the election of new leaders arose Josh suddenly appeared at the meeting accompanied by a lawyer from the national headquarters. The lawyer read a proclamation of the national fraternity policy and denounced the local leaders for subverting the charter. Josh was then given the authority to bring the local back to its true self. The old leaders were solemnly read out of the fraternity, their names erased from its books, not only for their subversion of the charter but even more for their attempted destruction of Josh.

The majority of fraternity members had followed but had not all been actively prejudiced themselves. So they were all given another chance. They would all be suspended from the fraternity immediately, but any who wished to become active again could appeal for clemency and be readmitted if they swore allegiance to the charter's universal brotherhood.

That night the rejoicing went on for all hours at Alpha Kai Omega. At last it had been returned to its mission—to be a light in the conformist darkness of fraternity row. The minorities who were excluded all along the row now had a place to call home. Now at last the long battle was over and the brothers gathered around Josh celebrating the victory of the truth.

Believing in the Future

The biblical story is a drama that points forward to a final act, a great day that has yet to dawn. The Author has suggested some of the major elements in a story like Josh's but the characters do not know in any detail what is to happen. What they do know, however, is the Author's way with them, the central element of the play that will be worked out to a satisfactory consummation.

The major points that will have to be included in any vision of the end are these: God himself is the beginning and end, the one who has planned and written the story, the one whose goals shall ultimately be accomplished; as he is the ultimate Mystery so his goal is shrouded in mystery, but with hints and suggestions and parables given to whet our imagination; the story is his story, expressing his values, his person, his way of relating and so the end will summarize and clarify and reveal him as much as he can be known to us.

Part of his story is the creation of man as a unity of body and spirit, his feet firmly lodged in nature, his head swirling in the heavenly clouds, and both aspects of man will be fulfilled at the end. The central tension of the story is the conflict between God's good creation and the corrupting powers of evil let loose by man's sinfulness. The powers have had their universal sway broken, but only in the end will they disappear when all oppressive forces in the world will be annihilated and man will be freed from inner slavery to blindness, guilt and habit. Since the beginning of the end for evil was found in Jesus' life, death and resurrection he will be a central part of the goal toward which the whole story is heading. His life is the perfection toward which his followers are heading. His serving and suffering are the road along which they must walk. His resurrection is the promise to them that gives them hope, drawing them on to the fulfilling of life—even though it must go by way of the valley of the shadow of death.

Framework of Life

If we are to be human we must hope. As persons, self-transcendence is our most characteristic attribute. We can go back into the past, through memory. We can go outside ourselves and look somewhat objectively at our present situation. But we also can go into the future, seeing ourselves as we will be, as we can be, as we hope to be. Bobby Kennedy was such a man of hope, for he used to say: "Some men see things as they are and ask 'Why?' I dream of things that never were and ask 'Why not?' " He hoped for a nation filled with peace, justice and equality, and his hope made him the great hero to the downtrodden that he was.

It is impossible to live without hope, either as a dream of what is not yet, or as the goal, the end toward which we are heading. A home cannot be built without a picture of the desired result. The builder would not know what materials to buy unless he had been shown the architect's plans for the finished product. Only when those plans have been made is it possible for him to proceed in an orderly fashion, with the reasonable hope that the end result will be something close to the original intention.

In a very similar way we cannot live our lives unless we have a goal. We do not know what steps to take along the way unless we know where the way is heading. We still may make mistakes over the steps, but we will have a chance to be right if we have an idea where we are going. If we have no ideals toward which we are aiming, then we will not know how to change and grow, but will remain stagnant, molded by our past and our environment.

Even more important than ideals in molding our lives is our understanding of what lies at the end of life. Many people believe that in the end all will return to dust, that the human realities are ephemeral. Saul Bellow, in *Herzog*, expresses this "faith" with great power: "But what is the philosophy of this generation? Not God is dead, that period has passed long ago. Perhaps it should be stated death is God. This generation thinks—and this is its thought of thoughts—that nothing faithful, vulnerable, fragile can be durable or have any true power. Death waits for these things as a cement floor waits for a dropping light bulb."

If that is the faith this generation lives by, then it will act accordingly. The vulnerable human things like love, faith and hope, will be seen as only secondary. The chief end in life will be self-preservation, putting off the cement floor as long as possible. The end toward which we see ourselves heading thus is one of the central influences upon our present life—in fact it could be called the framework, the outer boundary within which we must live.

False Hopes

Not all people think "death is God," in fact there are a great many schemes people put their faith and hope in, believing that they provide the keys to the future. Marxists hope for a classless society, one free from economic oppression, but they often work for it by inhuman means that destroy the goal. Believers in evolutionary is drawn for the moment. By drawing us into the story the author is able to provide us with an experience that goes beneath the surface of life, focusing on the deeper realities that we so often miss. Great plays do not simply entertain, they also enhance our experience of life, suggest to us the way things really are, help us to identify where our own experience parallels that of the play, and so lead us to see ourselves and our world in a new way.

Christian worship intends to do that same kind of thing. At its heart is the story of God's involvement in human history, centering in the life, death and resurrection of Jesus. Our trouble in the Church, of course, is that usually this most dramatic of all stories is often made to appear as dull as last year's news. Most preaching does not help us see through the great stories of the Bible to the author and actor who is revealed through them. Instead, sermons are usually theoretical expressions of doctrine, or discussions of practical ethics. Both of these are important, but they are secondary. The primary business of worship is drama: we need to hear the story, to see beneath the surface to the deep meanings it reveals, and then to see how it illumines our own daily experience. If we do not become involved in that way then we have not experienced the presence of the author of that story and our own stories—which is the basic aim of worship in the first place.

The solution to these problems is not easy, but it is available. First, we need to go back to using many more plays in worship services. But even more important is that the leaders of worship become storytellers themselves. Instead of always reading from the Bible sometimes the story should be told dramatically as the preacher remembers it. Even more important is the necessity for preachers to learn to tell stories from today as central elements of their sermons. Instead of seeing an abstract theological or ethical point as central, the preacher needs to tell a story as the main point and then go on to suggest what he sees in the story as a way to encourage the congregation to dig into the story for themselves. If every worshiper could carry away a vivid story that has depths to be opened up to the seeker then worship would once again begin to have the transforming effect it had for ancient Israelites and early and medieval Christians.

Conclusion

The Bible offers a vast array of symbols expressing what God's people are called to be. This chapter has presented three symbols that will be understandable to many people today, each intended to suggest a little of the biblical understanding. None of the three is to be taken literally, to be pressed beyond the limits suggested by the other two. But each may be helpful in letting us imagine what we need to do in order to tune in to God's continuing battle with evil which he carries on today through his people.

Suggested Reading

Berton, Pierre. *The Comfortable Pew.* Philadelphia: J. P. Lippincott, 1965.

Bonhoeffer, Dietrich. *Life Together.* New York: Harper & Row, 1954.

Flew, R. N. *Jesus and His Church.* London: Epworth, 1938.

Gibbs, M., and Morton, T. R. *God's Frozen People.* Philadelphia: Westminster, 1964.

Gordon, Ernest. *Through the Valley of the Kwai.* New York: Harper & Row.

Newbigin, Lesslie. *The Household of God.* New York: Friendship Press, 1954.

Rogers, Carl. *Carl Rogers on Encounter Groups.* New York: Harper & Row, 1972.

Schnackenburg, R. *The Church in the New Testament.* New York: Herder, 1965.

Williams, C. W. *The Church.* Vol. IV. *New Directions in Theology Today.* Philadelphia: Westminster, 1968.

Chapter Nine: Going Home

Introduction: "The Beginning and the End"

Believing in the Future

FRAMEWORK OF LIFE

FALSE HOPES

SOLID HOPE

Death and Life

THE BENEVOLENT ENEMY

UNIMAGINABLE LIFE

The Judge of All the Earth Shall Do Right

INHERIT THE WIND

It Really Matters

"The Last Straw"

No Waiting

Candid Camera

NO EXIT

"Gourmet's Dream"

God's Failure

Man's Freedom

New Heavens and New Earth

UTOPIA UNLIMITED

VISIONARIES WANTED

THE FAMILY GATHERS

Celebration

Open-minded Anticipation

Chapter Nine

Going Home

Introduction: "The Beginning and the End"

The great day coming when good will triumph and evil will be destroyed was foreshadowed in the crisis that transformed the life of the Alpha Kai Omega fraternity. This fraternity was an anomaly. It had been started years before as an alternative to typical fraternities because its goal was inclusiveness, encouraging students of every race, religion and ethnic group on campus to join. Its national leaders saw it as a symbol of real brotherhood which would put pressure on other fraternities to become more representative of American pluralism. However, on the Lincoln College campus, the local branch had gradually drifted back into conformity with the waspish exclusiveness of its local competitors, its mission essentially forgotten.

A freshman pledge named Josh Malcolm became intrigued with the history of the fraternity and discovered the contradiction between the intentions of its founders and its present behavior. He decided to bring in a Jewish friend to see if he would be accepted or rejected. At the meeting where the decision was to be made Josh found that prejudice against Jews and other minorities was loud and long. So as a vote neared he rose dramatically and read, from the founding constitution of the fraternity, the call for leadership on campus in including all minority groups. After an embarrassed silence the answer came back to him: "That was long ago. Today *we* are the fraternity and we say we like it as it is."

Josh refused to give in. He took his case to the campus community by writing a letter to the newspaper pointing out the hypocrisy of having an inclusive charter while practicing prejudice. Naturally this angered the fraternity's leaders, indeed prompted them to devise a scheme to get rid of Josh. They planted some illegal drugs in Josh's car and then secretly called the college police to denounce him as a dealer in drugs. Despite his pleas of innocence he was convicted on the strength of the planted evidence and dismissed from the college in disgrace. When Josh went back to the fraternity to get his belongings he hunted out the president and swore, "I'll get you for this! You'll be sorry you ever tried to cover up your own mess by destroying me."

A few of Josh's friends in the fraternity had joined him in his crusade to bring the fraternity back to its original mission, but when he was ground under by the leaders they retreated back into their previous silence. But Josh refused to give up. He went to the national headquarters and sparked a secret investigation which led to the conclusion that he was right in his charges against the local leaders. Instead of coming in and overthrowing them immediately Josh urged that his followers be given time to try to convert enough of the brothers to change the local policies.

After a year had passed no changes had taken place, so when the time for the election of new leaders arose Josh suddenly appeared at the meeting accompanied by a lawyer from the national headquarters. The lawyer read a proclamation of the national fraternity policy and denounced the local leaders for subverting the charter. Josh was then given the authority to bring the local back to its true self. The old leaders were solemnly read out of the fraternity, their names erased from its books, not only for their subversion of the charter but even more for their attempted destruction of Josh.

The majority of fraternity members had followed but had not all been actively prejudiced themselves. So they were all given another chance. They would all be suspended from the fraternity immediately, but any who wished to become active again could appeal for clemency and be readmitted if they swore allegiance to the charter's universal brotherhood.

That night the rejoicing went on for all hours at Alpha Kai Omega. At last it had been returned to its mission—to be a light in the conformist darkness of fraternity row. The minorities who were excluded all along the row now had a place to call home. Now at last the long battle was over and the brothers gathered around Josh celebrating the victory of the truth.

progress proclaim that advance is inevitable because it is in the nature of things. In many countries the new god is technology, its obvious benefits on a physical level being taken to mean it can solve human, personal, spiritual problems also. At a more sophisticated level we find existentialism which divides man into two parts, objective (physical) and subjective (personal), and hopes that by cultivating the inner life we can ignore the outer one. Perhaps most pervasive of all is religious escapism, the view that there are two worlds, earth and heaven, and that if we join the right club we will get a one-way ticket out of this mess before it all disintegrates.

In all these forms of hope there is a common structure of thought, the same one found in the biblical emphasis on hope. The major points of the common structures are these: (a) the world is evil at the moment, corrupted by forces that seem to be overwhelming; but (b) the future is open, possibilities for reversing the present situation are given to us; (c) the ground for hope is found in hints in the present situation, the small whispers of good in the din of evil, the blades of green life that have burst through the dead rock; so (d) we are called to act, to be agents of the future, to work out our hope in our own world because (e) we are convinced that the good as we see it will ultimately triumph.

All the false hopes (false from the biblical perspective) live on because they have this deep structure of truth that is attractive and convincing to many. But in their narrow and distorted versions of evil, good, and how change comes they all perpetuate evil. One can imagine Amos taking aim and searing them with his passion:

> Woe to you fanatic apostles of Marx!
> Though you hope for an end to oppression,
> New oppression looms as your shadow.
> How can freedom be born from tyranny?
> Your swords shall fall on your own heads,
> For the history you put your faith in
> Shall crush you for your suppression of hope.
>
> Woe to you disciples of Darwin!
> Your hope for natural progress is a false hope.
> You count on the success of the strong
> But the strong and evil often are one.
> How can ultimate good grow from present evil?
> The struggle you put your hope in
> Is the avalanche racing toward you.

Woe to you hard-headed lovers of technology!
Your machines may lift men's burdens
But often at the price of enslaving their spirits.
You see technique as the end of all problems
And so make man a cog in your machine.
Your end will find you wired to a computer:
Marvelous deeds, no person.

Woe to you followers of Kierkegaard!
Though you existentialists rejoice in being personal
You annihilate man by rejecting his home in the world.
You escape into inner freedom
But the price is abandoning outward liberty for all.
You turn inward to yourself
So your self shall shrivel to nothing.

Woe to you pious promoters of religion!
You know there is something beyond
But you divorce it from our real world
And offer only the hope of escape.
Your longing for heaven denies the goodness of earth.
Your care for "souls" hardens you to the pain of bodies.
Your end shall be the bodiless no-life you expect.

Solid Hope

While all people have some hope, founded on whatever they have faith in as the ultimate reality, the Christian view is that the only solid foundation for hope is Jesus himself. Dr. Colin expressed this understanding in Graham Greene's novel *A Burnt-Out Case:* "We have become cynical about progress because of the terrible things we have seen men do during the last forty years. All the same, through trial and error the amoeba did become the ape. There were blind starts and wrong turnings even then, I suppose. Evolution today can produce Hitlers as well as St. John of the Cross. I have a small hope, that's all, a very small hope, that someone they call Christ was the fertile element, looking for a crack in the wall to plant its seed. I think of Christ as an amoeba who took the right turning. I want to be on the side of the progress which survives." So he was working as a doctor in a jungle leper colony, living by the hope Christ had given him.

Clearly hope and faith are two sides of the same coin. If we believe that Christ is "the right turning" then we will have faith in him as the right way and so hope for the fulfillment revealed in him. He had nowhere to lay his head, was not anxious about tomorrow, stored up no treasure on earth, reached out to the helpless, opposed the powerful, battled the forces of evil, came to serve rather than rule. He ignored success in the world's eyes, but suffered for others, thereby living a truly successful life in God's eyes. That is the truth about life according to Jesus and if we trust him we will take that as the truth about real life for ourselves too. We will live by the hope that even though this is failure to the world, it is the path to eternal victory as God has designed the universe.

The resurrection of Jesus is central to this hope. The message proclaimed by the witnesses as they told of the amazing events that had engulfed them was that God had vindicated Jesus' way of life (and death), affirming that Jesus was truly the expression of God's character and will. The story tells us that no evil can befall us that will be of ultimate harm if we trust in Christ by following in his footsteps. Our hope will then be that God will ultimately raise us to his side because we stood with him when there was no apparent victory, only the promise given to us in Jesus.

The picture presented in some New Testament books of Christ returning to earth triumphant is a very effective way to symbolize the fulfillment of the Christian hope. The picture affirms that he is alive, that the evil of the world could not overcome him. He descended into the Minotaur's lair and came back triumphant. It proclaims that he is the one in whom God's promises have begun to come true so that following him is tuning in to the deepest message of the universe. Most of all it pictures a public reign of Christ, the ultimate victory of love over hate, God's annihilation of the forces of oppression, destruction, violence, dehumanization and pollution. By holding this picture before our eyes we will be able to stand firmly on the solid rock of hope that God gave to us in Jesus' life, death and resurrection.

Death and Life

No "apparent" victory is the reality when we face the inevitability of death. We are part of a universe that lives by death, for only if the old dies can there be space and resources for the new to be born. Jesus spoke of this paradoxical connection between death and life: "Whoever would save his life will lose it; and whoever loses his life for my sake and the gospel's will save it" (Mark 8:35); "Unless a grain of wheat falls into the earth and dies, it remains alone; but if it dies, it bears much fruit" (John 12:24).

The Benevolent Enemy

On the tiny planet Calacan in the solar system of the sun Melusina, a pair of rational, spiritual beings came into existence and discovered their world was open before them. They found that babies were born to them and grew up to be quite like them, needing as much space and food and air as their parents did. Quickly the children began to have children and those children to have their own offspring, by which time the grandparents began to get uneasy at the rapid growth of the population. They began longing for the early days when they had not felt they were about to be chased off their own planet. By the time the two founders were a thousand years old there were ten billion people on the tiny planet and everyone felt disaster was approaching.

So at a gathering of the leaders of all the tribes the solution everyone had thought of but no one had dared speak was brought up: "Since no one on Calacan ever leaves once born we will have to prevent any more births; everyone will have to be sterilized." So it was done. No more babies. Only people getting older and older and more set in their ways. No new ideas. No new visions. No creations born in the imagination of children. Stagnation. Sterility. Degeneration. Until salvation came one day in the angel of death who said, "If you are willing to become mortal I will give you new life, continually; but only if you are all willing to die." The people refused the offer, not wishing to give up their own lives just so others could live, so their family and race could continue to develop.

The angel was not insistent. Instead he found a man and a woman from opposite sides of the planet who had escaped sterilization, and dared to take up the angel's offer. Together they were taken to a new planet and told their wish would come true: they would die so that their children could live and creation could go on. So Adam and Eve began their journey blessed by life and death.

Unfortunately for mankind it never remained simple, because death and sin became intertwined. When men recognize their sinfulness they know they have failed to live up to their potential and then death is a threat. It threatens to leave their lives only half-done, so death is the enemy for the individual however much it may be a benefit to mankind. So man has always fought against death.

Tolstoy, in *The Death of Ivan Ilych,* spoke for mankind: "Ivan Ilych saw that he was dying, and he was in continual despair. In the depths of his heart he knew he was dying, but not only was he not accustomed to the thought, he simply did not and could not grasp it. He knew the syllogism: 'Caius is a man, men are mortal, therefore Caius is mortal' but that was different. Caius really was mortal and it was right for him to die; but for me, little Vanya, Ivan Ilych, with all my thoughts and emotions, it is altogether a different matter. It cannot be that I ought to die. That would be too terrible."

Death is thus a problem for us, and not just as we grow old. From the day we appear the sword hangs over us: as soon as we have been born we are old enough to die, and many do. Death, if it is the *absolute* end, not only destroys the future but also the present. If a black high school student concludes that even if he graduates from college he will probably not be able to get the kind of job that he aspires to, then he finds it impossible to work hard enough to get into college. Likewise if we are just going to be dust, then we will act as those for whom dust is the ultimate reality. Pleasure now, if it can be found, will be our only goal. We will be like the tuberculosis patient who wept at the prospect of giving up his pleasurable life in order to be cured. A friend urged him, "Go and get well. Nothing else matters." "But if nothing else matters," he replied, "what good is there in getting cured?"

But he went. We would go too, if we saw death as the end. If nothing follows, then the driving force in our lives, our overriding goal in every circumstance, will be self-preservation. Raskolnikov, the murderer in Dostoevsky's *Crime and Punishment,* felt that drive when he said: "Where is it I've read that someone condemned to death says or thinks, an hour before his death, that if he had to live on some high rock, on such a narrow ledge that he's only room to stand, and the ocean, everlasting darkness, everlasting solitude, everlasting tempest around him, if he had to remain standing on a square yard of space all his life, a thousand years, eternity, it were better so than die at once! Only to live, to live and live! Life whatever it may be!"

That cry for life would find a ready echo in many people the world over and nothing causes more of the evils of civilization than our fear of, and flight from, death. Why do we react violently when we are attacked? Because we feel we must save our lives. Why do we strive to gain all the wealth we can, not caring much who is ground down under our feet? Because we feel we have to live life to the fullest. Why do we allow neighbors to be attacked in the streets and fellow-citizens to suffer in ghettos? Because I cannot risk losing my life since it is all I have. Why do Church members find it difficult to tread the way of the Cross, seeking out those who suffer and bearing their burdens? Because many Church people deep down in their hearts are afraid of death, not believing God's promise of eternal life.

Thus death is not only a personal problem, it is a social problem also; fear of death makes our social ills worse and prevents human solutions from arising. Science has not solved the problem of death. Modern man has not learned how to live with death, except in anguish.

Unimaginable Life

The ultimate gift of God to man is life, a different level of life, one quite beyond our imaginations, called "eternal life" by the early Christians. The hope for this life is an essential motivating power in Christians today, a hope based on the resurrection of Jesus from the dead. Though there is no logical, necessary connection between Jesus' new life and ours there is a personal connection: the same Father who raised him from the dead has promised to be our raising Father also. If his promises proved trustworthy in Jesus' life, he is worthy of trust by us also.

The effect of this trust is a firm grip on our Father's hand and vision and a much looser grip on our lives here and now. If we firmly believe his promise, then we do not need to be anxious about tomorrow, to lay up treasures on earth to preserve ourselves in time of need. Instead we can see the constant, present needs of others around us and give our resources to them as Jesus did.

The hope of life held out before us is of a relationship to God and so to others that fulfills all the deep longings we have so far had to leave unanswered. The reward God gives is not something other than himself, it is himself that he gives. This means there is no essential conflict between Paul's accent on God's grace and Jesus' emphasis on God's reward. In a peculiar way rewards may be gracious and grace may be a reward.

First, consider rewards: the offer of a reward can change our behavior, but what the reward is and what it is offered for makes a great deal of difference. If a gangster offers ten thousand dollars for the murder of a competitor, that is a demonic reward, for it may lead someone to sinful behavior. However, if a father offers to play with his son when he finishes his homework this could be called a gracious reward: the reward itself is good for the child and the behavior promoted is also good for him. The grace enters in when the one offering the reward cares enough to encourage behavior that is good for the one doing it and offers a reward that is personal and beneficial. Jesus did just that, calling people to follow him and offering them eternal fellowship with himself and his Father as the reward.

Along these lines we can see how Paul's emphasis on God's

gracious gift of life in Christ can be seen as a reward. It is not that we deserve it, and if we find "deserve" to be part of our understanding of "reward" then this argument will fail. But I am using "reward" in the general sense of "positive, pleasurable, beneficial results following an action." Our action is trust in God; the rewarding result is a relationship with God now and forever. Though we do not deserve anything, God has offered us everything. All we have to do is open ourselves to receive it.

The life we receive is simply God himself. In the ancient story of the division of Palestine among the tribes of Israel, Levi was given no inheritance for the Lord had said to them "I am . . . your inheritance" (Num. 18:20). The Levites were the priests, and the New Testament speaks of all Christians as being God's priests (1 Peter 2:5), so for them God himself is their inheritance. God does not say to them, "Bear a thousand pains for me on earth and I will repay you with ten thousand pleasures later." Instead he says, "You may have life now and forever if you will allow me to be the center of your desire." If we desire him above all things we may have him. And in having him we have all the important things also, including the promise of new heavens and a new earth.

The Judge of All the Earth Shall Do Right

How we are going to move from this decaying world into the recreated earth is not particularly important. All the biblical imagery of the return of Christ, the raising of the dead, the angelic legions and all the rest is meant to underline one essential hope: in the end God's will shall be done, for the Author will bring his drama to a conclusion satisfying to himself and fulfilling for his creation. Two elements of the story of the end do stand out and need to be imagined by us, however, the day of judgment and the reality of hell.

Inherit the Wind

Judgment day is an image burned deeply into the Bible's skin. Daniel, Matthew and Revelation each have visions of the day that have lived in the imaginations of artists, poets and ordinary believers through the centuries. The visions differ greatly, however, showing that artists are at work expressing their deepest understanding of reality in pictorial or parabolic form. These are not specially revealed forecasts but deeply true extensions of the artist's experience and knowledge of the Creator of time and eternity.

It Really Matters

Above everything else the image of the last assize, the great courtroom where God (or Christ) is the judge, is an expression of the faith that this is a moral universe. Right will triumph in the end, evil will be defeated, exposed and punished.

In preexilic Israel it had been believed that on earth goodness would be rewarded with material blessings and personal happiness while evil would always be punished by deprivation of them. But the tragedy of life became more obvious with time—the baby born dead with no moral fault, the tyrant living in luxury; Job suffering degradation, Solomon living at ease with his harem. This world clearly does not provide a material and obvious equation between what a man deserves and what he gets. But God is just, he cannot allow such a state of affairs to exist forever. So very quickly the image of a day of judgment arose, a day when everything would be set right.

From this perspective the image of the day is a vital symbol of an essential aspect of the Christian view of reality. On the basis of God's dealings with Israel, especially his personal presence in Jesus, we believe that this is a moral universe: it does matter in the long run whether we take the high road or the low road. Our faith is in God who is the unseen moral backbone of the universe; we do not base our lives on the surface flow of events in which justice and injustice are mixed.

"The Last Straw"

Joseph Malone was pleased with the start of his project. He was the owner of a small ghetto market that had been the target of some shoplifters during the winter. Three hungry boys had been caught stealing fruit and Joseph had gone to court with them. He had asked the judge to put them on probation and release them to him, so that he could try to help them. He found an old garage, with asphalt in front and had helped them make it into a clubhouse with a basketball court. It seemed to be working.

During the next few months, however, he began to have doubts. First, he heard that the boys in the club had refused to let a classmate into the club because he was an Indian. Joseph decided to let that pass, not to press them, hoping that they would eventually let the Indian boy in. Then word came to him that one cold evening the boys had cut down several small trees that had recently been planted along the ghetto streets. They had tried to burn them in the garage furnace for heat but had produced nothing but smoke. Joseph had sent his clerk over to find out what had happened and to warn the boys that if the police arrested them again they were jail-bound.

For a while all seemed calm; Joseph saw the boys now and then and thought they had responded to his interest. But then late one night he was awakened by someone yelling that there was a gang fight over near the clubhouse. So he rushed over there and walked out into the street, yelling at both sides to stop. As he grabbed one of his boys the youth stabbed him with his knife, badly wounding him. That adult blood flowing abruptly stopped the fight and the boys all fled. But there was no escape.

The next day Joseph sadly told the police that his attempt at reclamation had failed. The clubhouse was closed down. The boys were taken away to reform school. And Joseph went out into the streets to find a few new boys with whom to try again.

No Waiting

Many ancient Israelites were at a disadvantage in understanding judgment for they saw rewards and punishments largely in material terms. In those terms the wicked seem to do better than the good, because no moral obstacles stand in their way. Stalin gets his way because he cares nothing about morality, while six million Jews are destroyed because they do not fight. A complete reversal seems needed for justice to prevail.

The New Testament expands the definition of rewards and punishments greatly, however, pointing to the personal, psychological and social experiences of individuals as the realm in which retribution is primarily found. Just as eternal life is a gift given *now* to those who follow Christ, so also eternal death is already at work in those who oppose him. Judgment takes place now, no waiting is required. He who troubles his household does not have to wait until his death to inherit the wind, for the emptiness of family enmity comes immediately.

The alcoholic knows that his day in court has passed, his sentence imposed and his prison carried around with him in his need to drink. The adulterer has found already the meaning of loss in the destruction of the lifelong relationship he could have had. The man who lives for himself alone finds that he is all he has and so is poverty-stricken.

Literature is filled with portraits of such men, outwardly beautiful, inwardly a mass of worms. Graham Greene pictured one on whom judgment had already come in the *Burnt-Out Case,* his story of Querry, a famous architect: "His heart . . . was calloused with pride and success." When asked one evening if he wanted anything he answered " 'Nothing. I want nothing. I no longer know what suffering is. I have come to an end of all that too.' " When he thought of his previous faith in God, "there were moments when he wondered if his unbelief were not after all a final and conclusive proof of the King's existence. This total vacancy might be his punishment for the rules he had willfully broken." Even the most basic human evil—rebellion against God—carries its own retribution immediately with it—life without God, without love, without community, without meaning.

Candid Camera

While our evil recoils on us as soon as we contemplate it, still the final word is not said in our life on earth. None of us recognize the fullness of our bondage to ourselves. We all think that we have been largely successful in avoiding present judgment. Just as we have escaped speeding tickets by knowing where the radar traps are located, so we think we have escaped the tickets of life by sinning judiciously rather than blatantly.

Judgment day for us is then to be imagined as the moment when a sign flashes before us: "You have been on candid camera all your life." Then we will see the truth about ourselves, and our punishment will be the despair of realizing that we are self-made men and women. We will be confronted by the life of Christ and the joy of truly living that was his own and his gift to those who have lived for him. Then we will see the extent to which we have failed ourselves, wasted our talents, debased our humanity, and corrupted the lives of others. We will be like a student who received back an essay he wrote and found every page filled with red marks marking his failures. No arbitrary grade at the end can really matter, he knows what he has done by the comments along the way.

There will be no arbitrary marks at the end of our lives either. God will not judge us on whether we are religious, or pious, or say the right words, or happen to have been born in the true tradition. Appearances will be forgotten because His x-ray vision will go down to the deepest secrets of our lives—what we really are. The judge's question at the end will be simple: "How have you responded to my love that was offered you?" Those who have rejoiced in his love and forgiveness will cry, "Father, I am not worthy to be called your son." Those who have refused his love will refuse him too saying, "You never offered me any, and I don't want any now." And that is the final step on the road to hell.

No Exit

"Hell" is a popular word but an unpopular subject. If we believe that there is justice at the foundation of the universe, then the vision of a place of punishment seems to be a necessary symbol of the future righting of the wrongs that are so prevalent on earth. What we imagine it to be will be molded by our experience of life.

Gourmet's Dream

On the outdoor terrace of a gourmet restaurant one diner leaned back in his chair and loosened his belt to let the full pleasure of his meal permeate him. As he basked in the warmth he was rudely brought back to earth by a skinny beggar boy standing across the fence and asking, "Mister, can I have a quarter to get some beans for my family?" Incensed at this intrusion the man called for the waiter to chase the nuisance away.

That night the man dreamed he was one of a flock of sheep. He and a number of other sheep were bigger and stronger than the rest and used their advantage to get most of the food and the good water. They were fat and grew more powerful because they ate so well. The weaker majority of the flock were largely skin and bones, their lambs usually dying quickly because of lack of milk in their mothers.

Suddenly the owner of the flock appeared and took action against the fat sheep. He crowded them together into a small soundproof room with one-way mirrors for walls so that no one could see them but they could see out. They saw the abundant food and clean water the rest of the flock were now fed, but could get none of it themselves. Slowly they began to weaken, to lose the fat off their bones, to find their skin shriveling until they looked as bad as the rest of the flock had looked under their bullying. They hoped that their ordeal would stop there, but it did not. They kept on looking out, arguing among themselves who was to blame, fighting for dominance, until finally they starved to death, their bodies decayed and nothing was left but bones and dust.

At this point the dreamer woke up and thought: "What a weird dream! I wonder what it meant. Probably nothing." So he promptly forgot it, rolled over and went back to sleep.

This imagery found in the Hebrew tradition (in Ezek. 34 and 37) echoes that in many other traditions (Egyptian, Persian, Buddhist, etc.) when the future life was looked upon as a time when people would get what they deserve—either good or bad. When religion judges people essentially by their acts, what they deserve, then this scheme works fairly simply. However, in the Christian understanding everyone deserves punishment but God graciously reverses this in Christ. How then are we to combine these two emphases, judgment according to deeds done and mercy based on God's love alone? No simple answer is available, and the New Testament offers two opposing pictures as symbols enabling us to hold on to both sides of this paradox: there is a picture of eternal punishment (Matt. 10:28) and there is the hope that "in Christ shall all be made alive" (1 Cor. 15:22). Either side taken literally to the exclusion of the other distorts the Christian vision. We must hang on to them both and see where that leads us.

God's Failure

The great objection to thinking of some people eternally separated from God is that this seems to mean that God has failed in his goal of reconciling all men to himself. If some men are able to evade God's goal, to stand back and not be drawn by his love, then this means that love is not the final word about reality. It means that man's evil is the final word. For a Christian who loves his neighbor and wants him to come to know God's love, there is no prospect more appalling than the nightmare that God's love will in the end prove insufficient. Instead of there being a unity to creation, there will be a final duality, some united to God, some going on forever against God's will and intentions.

If eternity will perpetuate the divisions found in this world, then our view of God and our view of this life are radically affected. Taking hell as an eternal reality is like trying to think of the Civil War as never-ending. Instead of four years of carnage, after which the dreams and intentions of the fathers four score and seven years before come true, we would now have passed our 115th year of war, the Founding Fathers' dreams being in ashes. Hell for eternity is like the division between black and white getting worse and worse until finally hearts are so hardened that no reconciliation is possible, forever. We know that the Civil War ended and unity has gradually been restored; we know that reconciliation between blacks and whites is a growing reality. Can we really believe that God's love will be frustrated, his intention in creation aborted, his gift of Christ to the whole world undelivered?

There can be little doubt what the Christian will wish for: he will wish that by one means or another God will bring all men to himself. Since it seems clear that this does not happen on the earth he will hope that it will happen some other way. His hope will be based upon the God whom he knows and serves. If love is eternal and omnipotent, then evil cannot in the final analysis be equal to it. The promises of universal salvation in various places in the Bible (Isa. 2:2; Rom. 5:18) thus emphasize a central aspect of the biblical vision of God.

Man's Freedom

However, the contrary picture of a hell awaiting sinners must not be ignored. We must not ignore it for two reasons: Jesus spoke of hell as an eternal reality, a symbol of God's destruction of the body and soul of those who decide against him; second, if we are right in thinking that we are free, and that our choices really matter, then we must retain hell as the goal toward which our choices of evil are taking us. If our choices only affect our lives here and now, but have no final and eternal importance, then we are not really free. Instead we are playing around at a game in which the issue has been reached apart from us!

The effect of a firm belief in a universal salvation is paradoxically very similar to the result of naturalistic belief that death is the absolute end. They both agree that the goal is identical for all. If that is the case then there is no *ultimate* importance to anything we do: our choices have only *immediate* consequences, affecting the way we feel, so our choices will then justifiably be those that make us feel good. In such a world there would be no right or wrong, no sacrifice, no real self-giving love; everything would be selfish, for nothing other than the immediate life would matter.

For most people it is clear from experience that we affect our future greatly by the way we act now. Someone who refuses to accept love, turns in upon himself, creating a shell for protection, and finally makes himself into one who cannot accept or give love. The problem of eternity is not that God refuses to forgive us—in Christ he has already reached out and offered forgiveness to all men. We can imagine that on judgment day he will repeat the same offer. As the famous saying goes, "God will forgive us, that's his business." But we are wrong in thinking that we will necessarily be able to accept God's forgiveness. That is the trapdoor into hell—the final refusal to accept God's love by those who have hardened themselves and ceased to be human.

For these reasons it is impossible for a Christian to do away with the symbol of hell. It is not to be thought of as an arbitrary punishment imposed for sinning, as imprisonment, or cutting off the offending hand, or even hanging, were arbitrary punishments for theft. Hell must be understood as the loveless world men are creating for themselves by their rejection of God's presence. It is a world that Sartre sketched in his play *No Exit*—a room without doors in which three people who cannot stand each other have to endure each other forever. It is the grey, lonely world C. S. Lewis pictured in *The Great Divorce*, a world of ghastly nothingness, separation, self-inflicted suffering.

While hell as a real possibility must be retained, this does not mean that a hope of its limitation cannot also be held. The Book of Revelation speaks of an end to hell, for the day will come when both death and hell will be thrown into the lake of fire. If this is to be, it is because a reconciliation between God's eternal, sovereign love and man's choice is possible, even if we cannot really imagine it. God's love and man's freedom are not really contradictory. We know something of the possibility of their joining when we see that the overwhelming love of a man for an independent woman need not contradict her freedom. She can remain entirely free but still respond to his love and join her freedom to his. Likewise it is conceivable that even those men who have completely rejected love will in the end be warmed by it, drawn to it, transformed by it, becoming able to find the exit from their closed room by being enabled to accept God's outstretched hand. This hope is founded on faith in the creator of all who made everything and can remake everything. In fact that is what he promises, new heavens and new earth.

New Heavens and New Earth

Throughout the history of the Church the common hope of Christians has been that they will leave the earth sometime after death and go to heaven, the home of God, to live there for eternity. It is thus striking to hear a New Testament scholar say that he knows of "no passage in the New Testament which promises that we shall go to heaven when we die" (G. B. Caird). We hear of "paradise" (Luke 23:43) or "my Father's house" (John 14:2) as the goal of those who have died, but never of "going to heaven." The truth seems to be that the New Testament writers did not believe God was going to abandon the earth to the powers of evil by taking his followers elsewhere. Rather the biblical hope was for a transformed universe, a re-creation of the heavens and the earth.

The reasons for biblical hope focusing on the redemption of the earth rather than escape from it are manifold. First, God called his created universe good and so the abandonment of it to evil would be ultimate defeat. We are not to imagine that man was the only part of creation God was interested in; quite the contrary man is the steward of creation, called to care for it and help it develop. Paul very specifically looks forward to the redemption of the whole creation, not just man, for he proclaims "the creation itself will be set free from its bondage to decay and obtain the glorious liberty of the children of God" (Rom. 8:21).

Second, God's promise for the renewal of the world is based on man's psychosomatic unity, the complete intertwining of matter and spirit in himself. The biblical writers did not look upon man as a separable partnership of body and soul, with the soul going off elsewhere after death as Plato thought. Instead the Hebrew view was that man's spirit or person exists only in an embodied form. No body, no person. That is why the Christian hopes for the resurrection of the body, for that means bringing the person to new life, to a new physical life of some sort, in a physical environment.

The third aspect of God's way with the world that implies a new creation not an escape is the picture of him as the Author of History. This story is his story, the stage is his stage, the goal is his goal and if it has been worthwhile he is not going to destroy it all at the end. Instead he is going to bring it to the perfection that he intended for it in the beginning. A summary of this hope is in the vision of a New Jerusalem which stands for the fulfillment of all God's dealings with man. Can you imagine this? "Then I saw a new heaven and a new earth; for the first heaven and the first earth had passed away, and the sea was no more. And I saw the holy city, new Jerusalem, coming down out of heaven from God, prepared as a bride adorned for her husband" (Rev. 21:1 f.).

Utopia Unlimited

Nothing could be more utopian, more idealistic, more fantastic, than trying to imagine that the earth will have the attributes of a bride: beauty will be everywhere, instead of just where men have not yet lived; purity will permeate all relationships; gaiety will be the daily portion of all; love will be the most obvious and vigorous motivation everywhere. All the demonic powers in society will be eradicated, and all the human failures reversed.

Beauty will be everywhere. Instead of grey-brown polluted water flowing in our rivers, there will be clean fresh naturally beautiful water, clear as the sea over the coral reefs in Bermuda where you can see down to forty or fifty feet. The decay of the world's cities will be reversed, so that instead of the blight caused by human selfishness there will be openness, safety and pleasure in living there. The ugliness of suffering from disease, famine and war will become past history. Never more will there be seen pictures of the empty, staring eyes of African children, their bones visible through their skin, their bellies distended by starvation, their lives torn by war. In their place the pictures will show the beauty of young boys and girls who have the opportunity to fulfill their potential, growing in wisdom and stature and in favor with God and man.

The beauty of the bride depends largely on the purity that is symbolized in the whiteness of her dress, especially the purity of her single-minded devotion to one man. The world's beauty will depend on its purity also, for an end to war, to famine, to urban decay, to pollution will only come with a change of heart. When the world's heart comes to be centered on its Creator, and on the neighbor who is his presence, then purity will permeate every nook and cranny. When the neighbor is seen as one in whom God dwells, one for whom he suffered, one he loves, then it will be impossible to sneer "nigger," "honkie," "wop," "Jap." Prejudice will be ended one day, that is a sure hope. As our racism is burned out of us, so also will be our violence. How can I fight my brother when in him I meet the One who died for me? The evil demons of racism and violence are doomed. Their backs are broken at Calvary and on Easter: we shall overcome someday.

With the end of the demonic powers that plague the world and a return to the beauty of creation, both God's and the best of man's, the gaiety of a wedding day will fill the air from coast to coast, from continent to continent, from pole to pole. No longer will the dehumanization of a machine-bound technology and a paper-bound bureaucracy choke the humanity out of us. Lives will be freed to be human; fully, joyfully human for the first time. The pain and suffering of broken lives, caused by an endless chain of bad relationships from generation to generation, will be ended; new relationships, healing bonds of love, will be available for all. The commonest sounds in the air will be singing and laughter; the symbol of this new world will be dancing and embracing, for joy will be everywhere.

Behind the visible scenes of the utopia of Christian hope will be the strongest motivation of the bride on her day—self-giving love. God himself will be in everyone, reversing the age-old chief motivations of self-preservation and self-enhancement. No longer will business operate first of all for profit, but first of all for people. No longer will the world's goals be material, but everyone will see fulfillment in terms of personal relationships, living for others. Every day will be like a wedding day, a day in which the beloved is more important than anything, a day in which a whole new life is beginning, a day in which nothing at all seems impossible.

Visionaries Wanted

If that is a small portrait of the earth as God has dreamed of it and promised it, how is it going to come to pass? There have been many in the history of the Church who have said that since the new world is God's gift man must not and cannot do anything about bringing it into being. But it should be clear by now that such a dichotomy between what God gives and what man works for completely misunderstands God's relationship to man. God will bring this new world, but he will bring it through man. God is not outside of man manipulating history. He has chosen the weakness of the Cross, his presence as self-giving love, as his way of renewing the world. Therefore the question is not whether God or man is the architect of the New Jerusalem, but how man can climb on God's bandwagon that is already rolling.

The bandwagon started millennia ago in God's promises and fulfillments in history. In Christ's resurrection God gave not only the vision, but also the great push that will bring in the new world by its own momentum. We can delay his parade by standing in the road, sabotaging the wagons, opposing his people and his vision. Or we can climb on, becoming cheerleaders, calliope players and clowns, hastening the day when the end of the road will be reached, when the whole world will have become a circus. Either way, the goal will be reached. With us or without us the world will be changed, but we can share in the greatest show on earth if we are willing.

"If we are willing," that is the supreme issue we must face. At the moment we cannot see that this is the final victory parade, but we must choose now anyway. The decision for Christ means an acceptance of the biblical vision of what the whole world is to become—conformed to Christ, fulfilling all that God intended for his creation. If we accept that vision as our own then we cannot help but join in the quiet revolution God has been carrying on for thousands of years. We will then turn our work and our play toward the bringing in of the utopia sketched above. We will work for the beauty of the earth and an end to starvation and pollution. We will fight for purity with the weapon of the cross's suffering love aiming to end all oppression in society. Our attitude at all times will be thanksgiving for the good already present, joy in the reality of love experienced, a vigorous hope in the transformation unfolding. If we are committed to the Author's way we will join the parade now, abandoning our spectator attitude, our hoarding of our resources. If we refuse to join in, standing instead for the political, social, economic and personal status quo, we have refused God's call and do not follow him. We hesitate because we *may* have to give up things we have found our meaning in heretofore: our status, our treasure, our pleasures, perhaps even our lives.

The only way to overcome that natural human hesitancy is by overcoming our fear of death, and that has become possible in God's promise of eternal life. No man in this generation exemplified this Christian commitment to God's vision of a new world more than Martin Luther King, whose motivation came from God's promise and vision.

On the night before he died, Brother Martin spoke these words of hope and vision:

"Well, I don't know what will happen now. We've got some difficult days ahead. But it really doesn't matter with me now. Because I've been to the mountaintop. I won't mind.

"Like anybody, I would like to live a long life. Longevity has its place. But I'm not concerned about that now. I just want to do God's will.

"And he's allowed me to go up to the mountain. And I've looked over, and I've seen the promised land.

"I may not get there with you, but I want you to know tonight that we as a people will get to the promised land.

"So I'm happy tonight. I'm not fearing any man. Mine eyes have seen the glory of the coming of the Lord."

The Family Gathers

That coming glory is the Father's renewing love already offered to his rebellious child. The world is God's child in the process of growing up. She has gone from the innocent days of infancy, when she did not know right from wrong, to the rebellious days of adolescence when wrong is deliberately and defiantly chosen in order to assert independence. The hope that the Bible holds out is that there will come a day when mankind will have grown to maturity, coming back to a friendship with God that rebellion has destroyed. In that day the world will be a bride united to Christ her groom in the family of God.

Celebration

No image of eternal life is more appealing to people of all ages than the vision of the great marriage feast of God's Son. Israelites knew the joy of the family gathering at feast-time, and Jesus entered into the festivities of wedding feasts with great gusto. He enjoyed them so much that he especially used a wedding as an image of what the gathering of resurrected mankind will be.

No time of celebration is greater than the day when a bride comes to full life by placing her hand in her husband's. It is a day of immense anticipation, overflowing joy and celebration going on until all hours. It is a time to rejoice in and experience the gift of love, the pleasures of friendship, the wonderful "happening" of a symbolic and meaningful event. Everything good that we remember from the day of our own wedding, or our child's wedding, or a good friend's, is the foundation emotion and memory for beginning to think about eternal life.

A similar experience in the depths of its meaning is the quiet yet happy gathering of good friends around a dinner table. For some reason, a table seems to join people together, and food shared provides a common experience of rejoicing in the good things of creation. But most of all good friends find the opportunity to share themselves, their deepest thoughts, their hopes, fears and troubles and so to be bound more closely in love than before. A meal like that is Communion, it is the Lord's Supper, for God himself is present as the love which binds friends together as members of his family. That too is a foretaste of what God has in store for those who love Him. The gathering of friends now is the beginning of the eternal life that will be experienced when God's whole family gathers.

Open-minded Anticipation

No one knows what exactly awaits us as eternal life. All that a Christian can say is that God is generous so that the life awaiting us will be the best of this life expanded and elevated beyond our wildest imaginations. There life will be truly human, the potentialities of each person will be allowed to expand to their fullest, the ability and opportunity to love will be constant.

There is no need for us to be able to say for certain what the details of the goal will be like for we are drawn on by a vision only dimly perceived. I remember climbing in the Presidential mountains in New Hampshire one spring, heading up the side of Mt. Adams. I had been told by a companion that there was a cabin near the top, and when the way got steep and the snow on the branches chilled our bones just the thought of a cabin—no other detail—pulled me on. Part of the fun of something new is not knowing, but imagining, and so striving forward to reach it. There has to be something basic desired—a cabin for shelter and rest, a new life in which the best of this will seem insignificant—but an agnostic anticipation of the details in no way slows us down.

As I thought about the cabin I guessed that it would be more like a lean-to, something to keep the rain and snow off and allow for a little shelter. Since the cabin was three thousand feet up from the nearest road it seemed impossible for much to have been carried up the mountain on the trail we were taking, cutting back and forth across a rushing stream. But the thought of any shelter, any place to stop, was enough to pour adrenaline into us as the loads on our backs and the weight of our boots seemed to get greater and greater.

You can imagine my surprise when we arrived at the cabin and found not only a shelter, but warmth from a blazing wood stove, other people there already to gather us in, bunks to sleep on, blankets to cover us, and a porch with a stunning, awesome, glorious view looking down the valley. It was as if I were expecting a tent and found a palace, or expecting a rocky uphill road and found a smooth path through a garden, or anticipating the coldness of a motel and walked into the warmth of a loving home. My expectations had drawn me on, but the reality far outshone my expectations, as far as the lovely earth is from the rocky, barren moon, as far as Pope John is from Hitler, as far as love is from indifference.

All we know of that cabin at the top of our mountain is that God our Father, who has made himself known to us as Jesus of Nazareth, awaits us. His cabin will be filled with the warmth of outgoing love, so that everyone who walks in the door drained and weary, cold and hungry, will find himself anew. Life will be the keynote of the celebration in that cabin: death will be gone, decay and debilitating diseases will be forgotten, shame and guilt and fear and hostility will be wiped away by the all-embracing welcome of our reunion with our Father.

All those who were integral parts of our lives here will be there for us to celebrate with. All those whom we have ignored or hurt will be there for us to begin again with. All the possibilities that we missed the first time round will come back to us anew. But above everything else, we will be filled by Him who is self-giving love, knowing we are completely loved and so being able to live for those around us.

Suggested Reading

Alves, R. A. *A Theology of Human Hope.* Washington, D.C.: Corpus Books, 1969.

Braaten, C. E. *The Future of God: The Revolutionary Dynamics of Hope.* New York: Harper & Row, 1970.

Caird, G. B., et al. *The Christian Hope, Theological Collection No. 13.* London: SPCK, 1970.

Capps, W. H. *Time Invades the Cathedral.* Philadelphia: Fortress, 1972.

Fackre, Gabriel. *The Rainbow Sign: Christian Futurity.* Grand Rapids: Eerdmans, 1969.

Heim, D. K. *Jesus the World's Perfector.* Translated by D. H. van Daalen. Edinburgh: Oliver and Boyd, 1959.

Lewis, C. S. *The Great Divorce.* New York: Macmillan, 1946.

Lynch, W. F. *Images of Hope: Imagination as Healer of the Hopeless.* Notre Dame: University of Notre Dame Press, 1965.

Marty, Martin E., and Peerman, D. G. *New Theology No. 5.* New York; Macmillan, 1968.

Moltmann, Jürgen. *Theology of Hope.* Translated by J. W. Leitch. New York: Harper and Row, 1967.

Pittenger, N. *"The Last Things" in a Process Perspective.* London: Epworth Press, 1970.

Robinson, John A. T. *In the End God.* New York: Harper & Row, 1968.

Discussion Questions

INTRODUCTION

(1) What do you think of the story of the Snowman?
(2) What do you think of the idea that all the biblical talk about God is parabolic, that is, symbolic?
(3) Do you agree with the suggestion that symbols are intended to appeal to our emotions and imagination as well as to our minds?
(4) How do you respond to the basic assertion that those biblical symbols which are no longer common in our culture need to be transculturated into symbols that are our own?

Chapter One: IMAGING GOD

(1) What meanings and feelings arise in you when you envision God as "our Sun"?
(2) What do you take this statement to mean: "Jesus was the ultimate symbol of God"? Do you agree or disagree with the statement?
(3) How do you respond to the modern expression of Jesus' parable of "The Lost Sheep" as "The Lost Schoolboy"? What is gained and lost by such re-writing?
(4) How have you usually understood the statement "God is love"? Does the book agree or disagree with your view?
(5) What feelings does the story of David and Andy arouse in you?

Chapter Two: CREATED IMAGE

(1) Do you agree that "man in some way reflects God, symbolizes him, represents him and mediates him"?
(2) Do you think that the various forms of human dominion provide a good foundation for thinking about God's rule over creation? Why or why not?
(3) What do you think of "The Farmer's Three Sons" as a modern version of "The Talents"?
(4) What does the symbol of God as Husband mean to you?
(5) How do you understand the word "spirit"? How does that compare with the understanding expressed here?
(6) Do you think it is wise to point to the mystery within ourselves as a way to suggest something of God as the mysterious center of his people?

Chapter Three: The Author of History

(1) What is said here on the differences among Liberty, Freedom and Choice? Are these useful distinctions?
(2) How do you answer the question at the end of the story of "The American and the Greek"?
(3) Do you think Imagination is as important a human attribute as this chapter suggests?
(4) Which of the four symbols—Puppeteer, Repairman, Person, Wisdom—comes closest to the picture you hold of God?
(5) What do you think of the suggestion that "God as Author" is a valuable symbol for us to use?

Chapter Four: Rebellion and Reprisal

(1) Was the parable of the Tightrope helpful to you in understanding the varieties of human sinfulness? Why or why not?
(2) What do you think of the suggestion that the human situation is always one of Pressure, Inferiority and Insecurity?
(3) How do you respond to the parable entitled "Coming of Age"?
(4) Which of the three types of Rebellion described seems to you to be the most common one? Which of them is most a temptation for you?
(5) What kinds of "façades" and "defenses" have you seen spring up?
(6) What do you make of "The King's Statue"?

Chapter Five: God's Servant—Enemy

(1) What was the message you found in the parable "The Children of Light"?
(2) How have you usually interpreted the evil spiritual powers mentioned throughout the Bible?
(3) Is it helpful to you to think of Violence as an evil spirit, "an infectious disease"? Why or why not?
(4) What do you think of the analysis of Prejudice given here? Do you agree that Religion is one of its chief sources?
(5) Do you think there are forces at work around you that lead *you* to think or act in ways that are not truly Christian? Does recognizing such forces absolve you of all blame?

Chapter Six: Conqueror of Evil

(1) What thoughts and feeling were stirred up in you by "The Gang"?

(2) Is the symbol "God the Conqueror of Evil" valuable to you?
(3) Does it help you to imagine that in Israel and in Christ God has created "an expanding island of freedom in love surrounded still by a hostile sea of tyranny and hate"?
(4) Do the memories of Washington, Lincoln and King help you in any way to get inside the stories of Moses, David, and Jeremiah?
(5) What do you make of the story of Josh Knight? Does it help you at all in understanding what Jesus meant by "binding the strong man"?
(6) Do you agree that in Jesus we see that God serves rather than dominating?

Chapter Seven: ONLY A SUFFERING GOD CAN HELP

(1) How have you heretofore thought the variety of symbols used to point to the victory of God in Christ are related? Do you agree with the suggestion made in this chapter?
(2) Does the Cross make you see that Infinite Power is an idol constructed by man in his sinful image?
(3) Do you agree that Jesus was crucified *because* he brought forgiveness not simply *in order to* bring forgiveness?
(4) Do you agree that forgiveness and reconciliation can only come when the innocent person bears the pain? Does God bear such pain?
(5) What do you make of the claim that Jesus' death in some way was able to shackle the evil powers of Violence and Prejudice?
(6) What do you think of the parable "One Old Indian"?

Chapter Eight: INSPIRED STAGEHANDS

(1) How do you respond to the parable on conquering the King?
(2) Does the symbol "Love's Army" offer anything helpful to you in understanding the Church? What?
(3) In what way is the Church like a family to you?
(4) Do you think worship should be in any way like the theatre? What ways?
(5) What is your favorite image of the Church? Why?

Chapter Nine: GOING HOME

(1) What do you make of the parable on the Alpha Kai Omega fraternity?
(2) Is hope central in your life? Why or why not?
(3) What false hopes are most tempting to you?

(4) Is death a "Benevolent Enemy" to you?
(5) Do you agree that we should hold onto both the biblical images of the future—Universal reconciliation *and* eternal Hell?
(6) What vision of eternity do you hold?